SOCIAL ISSUES, JUSTICE AND STATUS

MIGRANT WORKERS

SOCIAL IDENTITY, OCCUPATIONAL CHALLENGES AND HEALTH PRACTICES

Social Issues, Justice and Status

Additional books in this series can be found on Nova's website under the Series tab.

Additional e-books in this series can be found on Nova's website under the eBooks tab.

SOCIAL ISSUES, JUSTICE AND STATUS

MIGRANT WORKERS

SOCIAL IDENTITY, OCCUPATIONAL CHALLENGES AND HEALTH PRACTICES

QINGWEN XU
AND
LUCY P. JORDAN
EDITORS

nova publishers
New York

Library of Congress Cataloging-in-Publication Data

ISBN: 978-1-63485-272-2

Published by Nova Science Publishers, Inc. † New York

CONTENTS

PREFACE

Worldwide labor migration has transformed and reshaped various fields of government policy and professional practice. Despite its economic feature, labor migration is associated with non-economic social phenomena that scholars have increasingly paid attentions to in both sending and receiving destinations. For practitioners in the field of education, medicine, nursing, social work, mental health, public health, and other professional practices, the human face of labor migration — migrant workers' and their families' daily challenges — often reveals the human cost of migration behind the image of economic gain and benefits. Migrant workers and their families are facing vexing challenges ranging from basic needs to psychosocial wellbeing, despite who they are and where they come from. Traditional ways of thinking and knowing cannot address these challenges adequately; rather, established divisions of professions, systems, disciplines, and/or areas of practice might just be the factor that constrains the ability to clearly articulate compelling problems and adds an additional layer of complexity to problem solving.

This book focuses on country policies and practices, and draws on theoretical ideas that provide the intellectual basis. In addition, it offers vivid examples of how migrant workers manage to work, pursue economic security, strive and adjust in new communities, define and negotiate self and identity, and seek health and wellbeing. While the book illuminates shared challenges and experiences for each groups of migrant workers, i.e., low-skilled workers, internal migrants and other types of migrating laborers, the book also synthesizes the intersectionality across all migrant workers, as they remain committed to bettering the lives of their families and communities, in origin countries and new host countries and communities. This volume reflects the efforts of interdisciplinary research and collaboration. Based on empirical studies and policy analysis, the researchers draw broader implications for evidence-based practice and policy in migration studies, and offer practical suggestions for policy and service delivery design, including formal and informal mechanisms of support which can inform the professional reader.

When we worked on this collection, more than a million migrants and refugees started and continue to cross into Europe, a crisis as countries have struggled to cope with the influx and deal with resettling people, a regional crisis which is also creating division within the European Union. Such a crisis stresses the increasing concerns about the intractability of massive social problems linked to migration, economic inequality, and social intolerance. It is our hope that this book will stimulate further debate and discussion to improve the lives of diverse groups of migrants, and promote more inclusive strategies and policies at the local, national and supranational levels, policies that will recognize the multifaceted experience of migrants, their families, and the communities they inhabit both near and far.

With all the appreciation, we thank our contributors for their dedications to working with migrant workers and their families and communities, guiding policy and practice through rigorous research, and promoting a just global society.

Qingwen Xu from New Orleans

Lucy P. Jordan from Hong Kong

LIST OF CONTRIBUTORS

Iris L. Acejo, Ph.D., is a research associate at Seafarers International Research Centre of the School of Social Sciences at Cardiff University, United Kingdom. Dr. Acejo received a Ph.D. in Social Sciences from Cardiff University. Her research focuses on transnational migration of seafarers and the role of seafarers' wives. She is also interested in the communication practices and remittance behavior between migrants and their families.

Jemel P. Aguilar, MPH, MSW, Ph.D., is on faculty at the University of Saint Joseph in Hartford Connecticut, the United States. Dr. Aguilar studies the social and psychological aspects of accessing HIV-related treatment and the experiences of populations of color living with HIV. Dr. Aguilar's research projects resulted in peer-reviewed articles in prominent social sciences journals including the Journal of Human Behavior in the Social Environment, Journal of HIV/AIDS in Social Services, Journal of Community Practice, Qualitative Social Work, and Social Work Research.

Anjali Borhade, MSW, MPH, has been working with migrant populations in India for fourteen years. She has an MS in social work and public health from Tulane University, the United States, and a Ph.D. research fellow at the University of Oxford, the United Kingdom. Her research is focused on developing plausible solutions for urban migrants for primary health care in India. She is currently working with the Indian Institute of Public Health as an associate professor, and she is a founding director of the pioneering Disha Foundation, an NGO that supports migrant rights, including health. In the last fourteen years she has been actively engaged in various interventions, research, and high-level advocacy initiatives with state and national government to ensure the rights of migrants in India.

Young Do, LMSW, CASAC, is the Assistant Clinical Director of Hospitality House, TC, Inc. in Albany, New York, the United States, and has worked in the field of substance abuse for over ten years. He currently teaches as an adjunct instructor at Cazenovia College and the University at Albany, State University of New York. He is also a doctoral candidate at the School of Social Welfare at the University at Albany.

Aimee Hilado, Ph.D., LCSW, is an assistant professor of social work at Northeastern Illinois University in the United States and the Founding Manager of the Refugee One Wellness Program, a mental health program serving immigrants and refugee children and adults in the largest resettlement agencies in Chicago. Her teaching, research, and practice interests are informed by her clinical work with trauma-exposed new immigrants. Dr. Hilado has been recognized at national conferences including the Zero to Three National Training Institute and the Council on Social Work Education for her practice and research efforts around immigrant mental health and has served as an expert witness and consultant in the area of mental health on state criminal cases.

Philip Hong, Ph.D., MSW, is a professor in the School of Social Work at Loyola University Chicago and a Faculty Associate of the Center for Social Development (CSD) at Washington University in St. Louis, the United States. Dr. Hong's main academic interest is in poverty and workforce development with a focus on developing bottom-up strategies for empowering low-income individuals and families in their quest to achieve self-sufficiency.

David Jaffee, Ph.D., is professor of Sociology at the University of North Florida, the United States. His current area of research focuses on the political economic dynamics associated with globalization, urban development, neoliberalism, and the port logistics industry.

Lucy P. Jordan, Ph.D., MSW, is assistant professor in Social Work and Social Administration at the University of Hong Kong. Her research focuses on how national and transnational social policies impact on the intimate lives of families and children, with a particular focus on migration, social reproduction and market employment.
E-mail: jordanlp@hku.hk.

Narine N. Kerelian is a MPH, MSW and Ph.D. candidate in the Social Work and Social Administration Department at The University of Hong Kong. Her research interests are in highly skilled migration (young transmigrant professionals), social policy, diversity/multiculturalism, and sense of place.

Trang Mai Le, MSW, is a lecturer of social work at the Vietnam Trade Union University in Hanoi, Vietnam. Her research interests focus on gender-based violence, sexual orientation discrimination, migrant workers, sexual and reproductive health and rights. She is a gender activist who believes in advocacy through an evidence-based research.

Yong Li, MPH, MSW, LCSW, Ph.D., is an assistant professor of the Department of Social Work at Plattsburgh State University of New York. Dr. Li received his doctoral degree and M.S.W. degree in social work from the University at Albany, State University of New York. Dr. Li's research has focused on mental health and psychological well-being among Asian and Latino immigrants and their families in the United States.

Marta Lundy, MPH, MSW, Ph.D. and LCSW, is professor in the School of Social Work, Loyola University Chicago, the United States. She teaches in the MSW and PhD Programs, and is an Associate faculty member of the Women's Studies/Gender Studies Program at Loyola and a member of the Graduate School. Her research focuses on aspects of family life, and most recently, on the immigrant family.

Gaoming Ma is a MPH, MSW and Ph.D. candidate at the Department of Social Work, The Chinese University of Hong Kong. His research interest centers on the migrant regulation in China, the education of migrant children, social citizenship and social capital theories.

Lenore E. Matthew is a doctoral student in the School of Social Work at the University of Illinois at Urbana-Champaign. Her practice and research focus on social policy, the care economy, and gender inequities in global labor markets. She has conducted research with the ILO and the UN Volunteer Program, and has received various awards in the areas of social justice, women's rights, and international development. She holds a MSW from the University of Illinois at Urbana-Champaign and a Master of International Relations from Dublin City University in Ireland.

Huong Nguyen, MPH, MSW, Ph.D., MA, is an assistant professor of social work at the University of South Carolina, the United States. Her research focuses on international social work and Buddhism-inspired approach to mental health services, with special attention to Vietnam.

Tuan-Anh Nguyen, Ph.D., is an associate professor in the Faculty of Sociology, University of Social Sciences and Humanities, Vietnam National University, Hanoi. His research focuses on kinship relations and social and economic change in villages in Northern Vietnam, although he has recently extended his research to livelihood adaptations in the context of climate change.

Blanca M. Ramos, Ph.D., is an associate professor at the School of Social Welfare, the University at Albany, State University of New York, where she teaches social work with immigrants, Latinos in the U.S., multiculturalism in a global society, social welfare practice theory, and social work practice. She has published in the areas of health disparities and mental health with a focus on Latinas and Puerto Rican women.

Helen Sampson, Ph.D., joined the Seafarers International Research Centre at Cardiff University School of Social Sciences in the United Kingdom in 1999 and became the Director in 2003. Her first degree is in Sociology and she holds a Postgraduate Certificate of Education (Economics and Social Studies – FE/Secondary) and a Ph.D. Dr. Sampson's research interests include multinational crewing, training, women seafarers, the impact of changing technology on seafarers' work, issues of regulation, family life, globalization, and seafarer health and safety. Her book *International Seafarers and Transnationalism in the 21st Century (2014)* won the prestigious British Sociological Association/BBC Radio Four award for 'Ethnography'.

Uma A. Segal, Ph.D., is professor at the University of Missouri – St. Louis and holds a Research Fellow appointment with the University's International Studies and Programs. She is a visiting professor at the University of Tskuba (Japan) and has an affiliate appointment at Universidade de Fernando Pessoa (Portugal). Dr. Segal's research interest is immigrant and refugee integration. She has served as Editor-in-Chief of the *Journal of Immigrant and Refugee Studies* (2004 – 2012), Fulbright Fellow (2013 – 2014) and in 2013 also received the

Council on Social Work Education's Partners in the Promotion of International Education (PIE) award.

Soma Sen, Ph.D., teaches in the Master Program of the School of Social Work, San Jose State University in California.. Dr. Sen's overall research interest lies in the area of minority health and related issues, particularly among Asian Americans and Asian Indians, with a focus on HIV/AIDS. Her scholarly activities include: role of gender, culture and poverty on health seeking behavior and access to health care services among underserved population; sex work and sex trafficking and HIV/AID; immigration and human trafficking; social networks, social capital and their health impacts among migrant populations.

Noreen M. Sugrue, Ph.D., is at the University of Illinois at Urbana-Champaign (UIUC) in the United States where she is an assistant professor and research associate in the Women and Gender in Global Perspectives Program. She also is a faculty affiliate in the Center for Global Studies and the Center for African Studies at UIUC. Her research is concerned with broad questions related to inequality and poverty and distributive justice both domestically and internationally, in the areas of health, healthcare labor, gender, and social policy.

Maria Vidal de Haymes, Ph.D., is a professor in the School of Social Work of Loyola University in Chicago, the United States, where she teaches courses in areas of social welfare policy and migration studies. Her research focuses on the themes of migration, child welfare practice with immigrant and indigenous groups in the United States, and poverty. Dr. Vidal de Haymes is the Co-editor of the Journal of Poverty.

Suzie S. Weng, MPH, MSW, Ph.D., is an assistant professor of Social Work at the University of North Florida in the United States. Her area of research focuses on access and utilization of social services through a cultural lens including both barriers and interventions.

Qiaobing Wu, Ph.D., is assistant professor at the Department of Social Work, The Chinese University of Hong Kong. Her research focuses on education and health outcomes of children and youth, social capital, health disparities and welfare policy in the context of internal and international migration.

Qingwen Xu, Ph.D., is on faculty at Tulane School of Social Work, the United States. Over the years, she has been deeply engaged in community oriented research and emphasized on community mechanisms and dynamics to address local concerns. Dr. Xu's work is situated at the interaction of globalization, community development, and social welfare. With a better understanding of the community perception and behavior among vulnerable groups of people, including ethnic minorities and/or migrant groups of people in the U.S. and abroad, she has been searching innovative community practices and initiatives to improve the health and mental health of vulnerable groups of people.
E-mail: qxu2@tulane.edu.

Mengxi Zhang is a MPH, MSW and Ph.D. candidate at the Tulane University School of Public Health and Tropical Medicine in Global Health Systems and Development, the United States. Her research centers on migration population and medical evaluation methodology. She completed her MPH in epidemiology from Tulane University. Prior to Tulane, Mengxi received her bachelor in preventive medicine from Capital Medical University School in China.

INTRODUCTION

In: Migrant Workers
Editors: Qingwen Xu and Lucy P. Jordan
ISBN: 978-1-63485-272-2

Chapter 1

MIGRATION, LABOR MARKET AND WELLBEING: THEORIES, POLICIES AND PRACTICE

Qingwen Xu[1,*] and Lucy Jordan[2,†]
[1]School of Social Work, Tulane University, New Orleans, LA, US
[2]Department of Social Work and Social Administration, University of Hong Kong, Hong Kong

INTRODUCTION

High rates of migration are part of the much-discussed phenomenon of globalization: the increased movement of goods, currency, skills, ideas and people. The total number of international migrants worldwide was 243.7 million in 2015, accounting for 3.3% of the world's population, an increase of 41% since 2000 (UN Department of Economic and Social Affairs, 2015). Significantly, the vast majority of migrants move in search of better employment opportunities elsewhere; the increasing size and diversity of transnational movements of people echoes the growing trend of labor mobility — most migrants worldwide (72%) are of working age (from 20-64) (see Figure 1 and 2, UN Department of Economic and Social Affairs, 2015; International Labour Organization [ILO], 2015a and 2015b). In developed countries, including both traditional countries of immigration such as Australia, Canada, and the United States, and previous emigration countries such as Southern European countries, jobs are particularly available at the high and low ends of the labor market (Cholewinski, 2005; Münz, 2008). The global competition for the talent has intensified and countries are creating new ways to encourage and attract skilled workers' migration (Hawthorne, 2014). Meanwhile, due to population aging and the absence of willing domestic workers, rich countries are increasingly looking outside their borders for low-skilled workers in agriculture, food-processing, construction, manufacturing, and low-wage services such as

* Qingwen Xu: Editor of the Book. School of Social Work, Tulane University, 127 Elk Place, New Orleans, LA 70112, US. Email: qxu2@tulane.edu.
† Lucy P. Jordan: Editor of the Book. Department of Social Work and Social Administration, University of Hong Kong, Pokfulam Road, Hong Kong. Email: jordanlp@hku.hk.

domestic work and home health care (Münz, 2008). Thus, migrant workers from poorer countries are recruited to fill the demand. Among developing countries, blossoming markets and emerging economies are pulling low-skilled workers from their own rural areas, as well as attracting skilled workers from both high-income and other middle-income countries. While traditional streams of internal migration, i.e., moving from rural areas to urban cities for jobs and opportunities, are persisting for example as well known in countries like China, these fast-developing countries are also becoming immigration destinations slowly (Skeldon, 2011). Countries worldwide are changing their roles, developing immigration policies, and participating in the global labor market.

Labor migration is a phenomenon that concerns all regions of the world and has had a profound effect in both developed and developing countries (ILO, 2015); equally migrant workers and their families face myriad challenges in their home villages as well as receiving communities. Both sending and receiving countries, or any country falling in the middle of the spectrum, have been twisting their positions between either regulating the flow of migration or protecting migrant workers and their families' rights and wellbeing. The regulation of migration and the rights of migrant workers are among the most controversial policy issues around the world. In public debates, migrants have been viewed as development "heroes" for both receiving and sending communities (e.g., Rodriguez, 2002), "free riders" who threaten the job and welfare security in host communities (e.g., Costa, Cooper and Shierholz, 2014), and/or "victims" of exploitation by employers and by migration policies as well (e.g., Sung, Delgado, Peña and Paladino, 2013). Theoretical arguments that favor incoming migration and equal protection policies emphasize the responsibility liberal democracies have to promote global and/or distributive justice; proponents for migration restriction argue that equal rights protection for migrants runs against the interests of states and might even not benefit migrant workers themselves. Consequently, countries have adopted various practices of protecting (or regulating) migrant workers and promoting migrant friendly communities. Migration in today's global era is by and large linked to work and labor market and the quest for decent work opportunities, either within countries or across international borders.

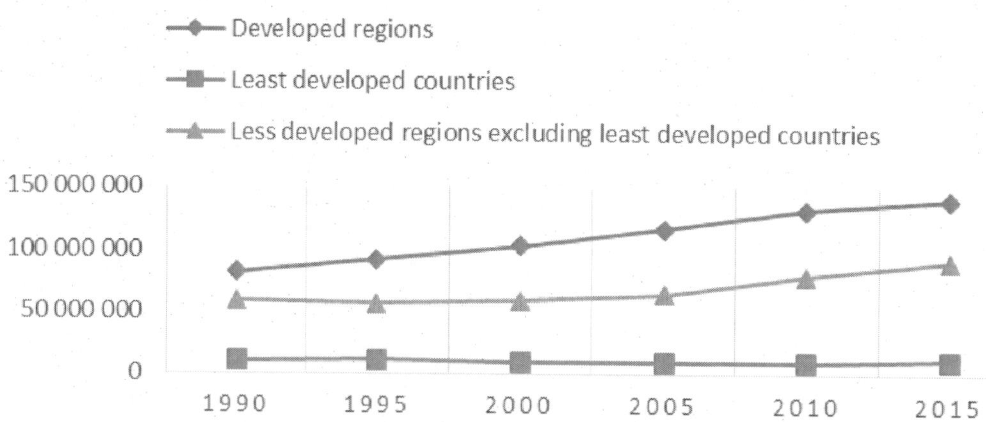

Figure 1. International migrant strock by country of destination 1990-2015.

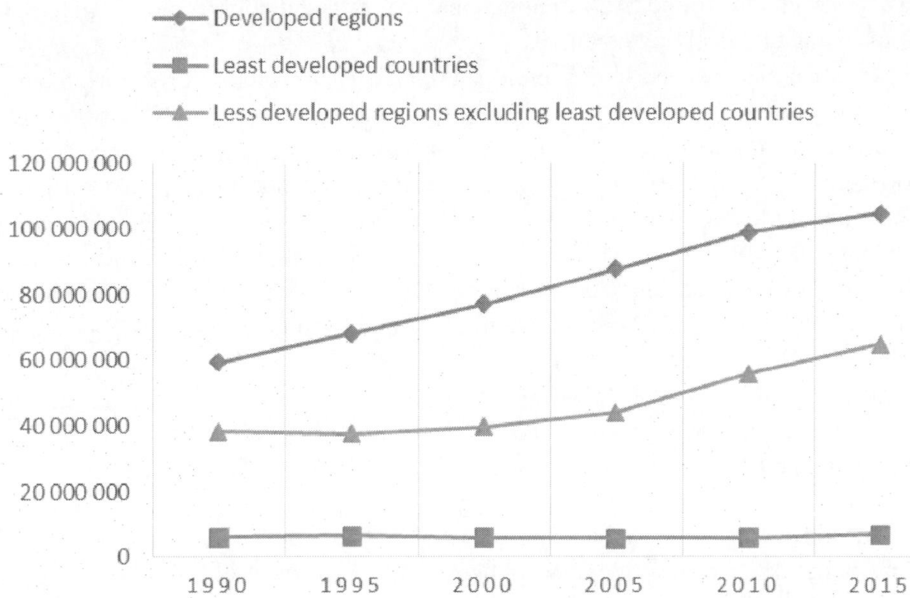

Figure 2. International working age (20-64) migrant stock by country of destination 1990-2015.

Policy Framework: Protection vs. Regulation

In general, there is a lack of international institutions to set standards and ensure the conformity with international legal norms. The most recent international effort to protect migrant workers is the United Nation's International Convention on the Protection of the Rights of All Migrant Workers and Their Families (the Convention hereafter). The Convention received the 20 ratifications necessary for entry into force in 2003; however, among the 27 current signatories, major immigrant receiving countries are notably absent. The Convention established a highly comprehensive framework that covers sets of civil, political, economic, and social rights for migrants and their families, even including those living and/or working abroad illegally, temporarily and/or sporadically (Lönnroth, 1991). This human rights-based framework is significant particularly due to its comprehensive rights protection extended to undocumented and temporary migrant workers. Despite the seemingly universal principles, early assessment of the Convention has indicated the unsolvable issues that the Convention has suffered from and thus prevent the Convention from being widely ratified, for instance, the lack of dynamics to reflect the changing global migration trends, and the lack of attention to political and economic reality as well as various vested interests of the states (Lönnroth, 1991). Recent literature offers evidence and arguments concerning various reasons behind states' reluctance towards its ratification (Cholewinski, de Guchteneire and Pecoud, 2010); by all means, such low popularity reflects states,' particularly traditional immigration countries' unwillingness to give up their discretion and ability to outline (often restrict) the rights of migrants living and working in their territories (Ruhs, 2013). For the most part, over decades, there has been little progress of the Convention's ability to protect and thus substantially improve the human rights situation of irregular migrants, i.e., both undocumented and/or temporary migrant workers (Bosniak, 1991); the Convention has faced significant barriers due to the overriding national interests and commitment to the norms and structures of migrant receiving countries.

The International Labour Organization (ILO) has played a vital role of protecting migrant workers' rights in workplace and in fact built the foundation for the UN Convention. Eight ILO core conventions cover subjects that are considered as fundamental principles and rights at work including against forced labor and child labor and for freedom of association and non-discrimination (Cholewinski, 2013). The ILO position is that all labor standards should apply to migrant workers in the workplace regardless of their status. Other international organizations, for instance, the World Bank emphasizes remittances, informal economy, and the role of migration in the development of migrant-sending underdeveloped countries (World Bank, 2015); the International Organization for Migration (IOM) considers international migration management as a core element in the technical design and implementation of migration policies (IOM, 2005). To varying degrees, efforts by both the World Bank and IOM illustrate how the movement of people can be managed as an object of technical expertise and intervention within programs, with arrangements of international authorities, and disregard of human and labor rights as central and intrinsic elements of coherent migration and development policies; their efforts lack the human face that international migrants have a high risk of suffering economic exploitation, social exclusion, human insecurity, and criminalization (Andrijasevic and Walters, 2010; Delgado Wise, Márquez Covarrubias and Puentes, 2013). The variety of criticisms of the World Bank and IOM reflects liberal academics' and human rights organizations' resentment on the neoliberal globalization. Contemporary migration is embedded in inequality; the IOM's attempt to managerialize migration policies in countries as different as the United States and African countries, and the World Bank's overoptimistic assessment of the impact of remittances are not helpful to either regulate migration or protect migrant workers, especially given the unequal power distribution between migrant sending and receiving countries, subtle social economic mechanisms that characterize migrant populations, and the fundamental contributions made by migrants to the destination countries.

It is noted, in recent years, multiple international organizations, including the ILO, World Bank, UNICEF, and UNHCR, have started a joint effort to develop a human rights indicator in order to document and quantify the condition and welling of migrants and their families, and thus facilitate and monitor state progress and compliance with legal obligations (Cernadas, LeVoy and Keith, 2015). The indicators are conceptualized and assess human rights for migrant workers and their families from four broad areas: non-discrimination and equality of treatment, right to education, right to health, and right to decent work, with detailed breakdowns of indicators for process and outcomes (see Table 1). At the same time, there have been attempts to move towards global governance mechanisms in migration, and collaboration between migrant associations and international human rights organizations. For instance, the Global Forum on Migration and Development, established in 2006, adopts an intergovernmental consultation process, a unique participative working method, involving governments and policy makers from a varied background, UN and other international agencies as well as academia and civil society organizations, in order to increase the understanding and cooperation on issues of migration and development (Castles, 2011).

Table 1. Human Rights Indicators Under Development

Areas	Sub-Areas	Examples
Non-discrimination and equality of treatment	• Equality before the law • Discrimination against migrants by public or private actors nullifying or impairing equality of social rights • Combating racism and xenophobia	• Human development rate and gap • Number of complaints of discrimination
Right to education	• Access to education (compulsory and non-compulsory) • Equitable education conditions • Cultural acceptability • Curricula and education resources	• Percentage of migrant children who attend and finish compulsory and non-compulsory education • Number of child migrants that attend language training programs
Right to the enjoyment of the highest attainable standard of physical and mental health	• Accessibility of health facilities, goods and services • Cultural acceptability of health services • Natural and occupational environment • Sexual and reproductive health • Child health care	• Rate of mortality, morbidity, life expectancy and prevalence of disease; • Number of access to health services in their native language
Right to decent work	• Access to decent and productive work • Just and safe working conditions • Equal treatment and prohibition of discrimination • Access to social security and social protection • Protection against forced labor • Protection against migrant child labor • Healthy workplace environment • Trade union rights, collective bargaining and social dialogue	• Migrant workers' access to unemployment, old-age benefits • Wage gap • Rate of informal workers

Cernadas, LeVoy and Keith, 2015.

Despite international efforts, the migration policies in each country vary widely from regulating migration to protecting migrant workers. In the book *Price of Rights* (2013), Ruhs offers empirical evidence concerning the relationships between a country's openness to labor migration and the social economic political rights granted to migrant workers (see Figure 3 for selected country's average openness indicators), and argues that generally, there is a trade-off between certain rights (often rights to access government welfare programs for workers and their family members) and openness, and there are fewer restrictions imposed on higher-skilled migrant workers than lower-skilled workers. That is, a country's openness to migration is associated with limitations on rights; on the contrary, a country's openness to wanted groups of migrants (i.e., skilled workers) is associated with more generous protection of migrants' rights (Ruhs, 2012 and 2013). While these observations look like a common sense, it reveals that national policies towards migrant workers' regulation and rights are not ideology-oriented and value-based; rather they are national interests oriented and economic and political pragmatism dominated. When facing economic migration, no country is a moral superpower; countries, despite their differences in immigration history, geographic location, culture and tradition, welfare state mechanism, as well as market dynamics, lack a full commitment to the protection of migrant workers' and their families' rights and wellbeing, as pronounced in the Convention.

It should be noted that the mechanisms of regulating migrants' admission and protecting migrant workers' rights are more complex than what Ruhs' openness indicator can illustrate. These indicators need to be understood in the context of country's immigration history. In Figure 3, the US ranks high in terms of its openness that might correctly reflect its immigrant country status; however this result only considers US immigration programs for the desired skilled workers programs and does not account for the reality that millions of undocumented migrants live and work in the country. And undocumented migrant workers and their families are basically deprived any accessibility to labor protection, welfare programs and social services except primary education and health care for medical emergency (Gleeson, 2010; Kullgren, 2003). The openness indicators should also be understood in the context of country's legal and political strategy. In the case of Sweden, its high openness indicator had been associated with tight labor migration control enforced jointly by the government and labor unions, as well as the universal welfare provision to migrant workers and their families; admissions of migrant workers for several decades had been tied to job offers that were verified by labor unions as needed until 2008 (Brochmann and Hagelund, 2012; Boräng and Cerna, 2015). Canada and Australia, two traditional immigration countries, in spite of low ranking in terms of openness indicator, have established points-based immigration systems that prioritize desirable human capital and grant migrant workers with the access to health and social services (Donald, 2014; the Law Library of Congress, 2013). In summary, states retain their sovereign privilege to decide on the criteria for admission and expulsion of non-nationals, and a country's openness to migrant workers is subjected to its dynamic political social and economic systems. Jointly, countries are selecting and attracting certain groups of wanted migrant workers and consequently protecting their and their families' social economic rights. The rule derived from the 1951 UN Refugee Convention that there is "no economic refugee" implies that the right to move across national borders to improve economic prospects has never been warranted. Nonetheless it should be noted that in today's economic and social climate, states' privilege to regulation is subject to their obligations and commitment to international human rights; protecting migrant workers, both those lawfully permitted workers and those in an irregular situation but moving for work anyway, is paramount.

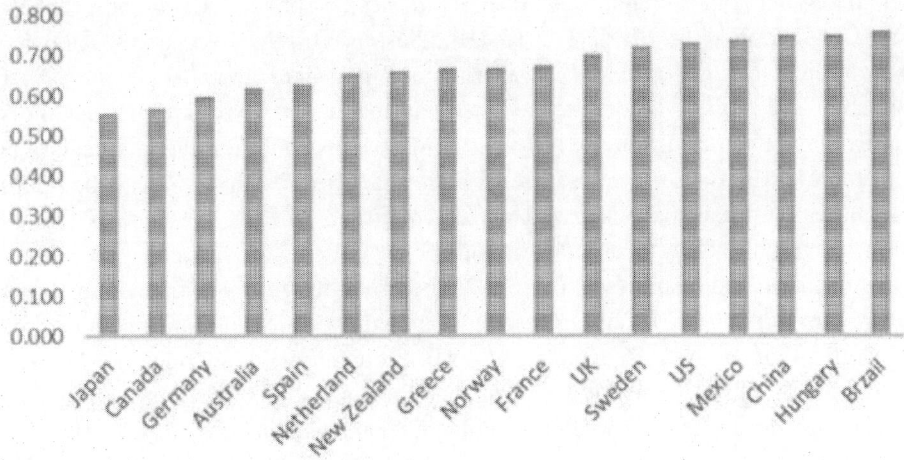

Data is from Ruhs (2013) Table E.A.3, pp. 203-205.

Figure 3. Country openness indicator (average).

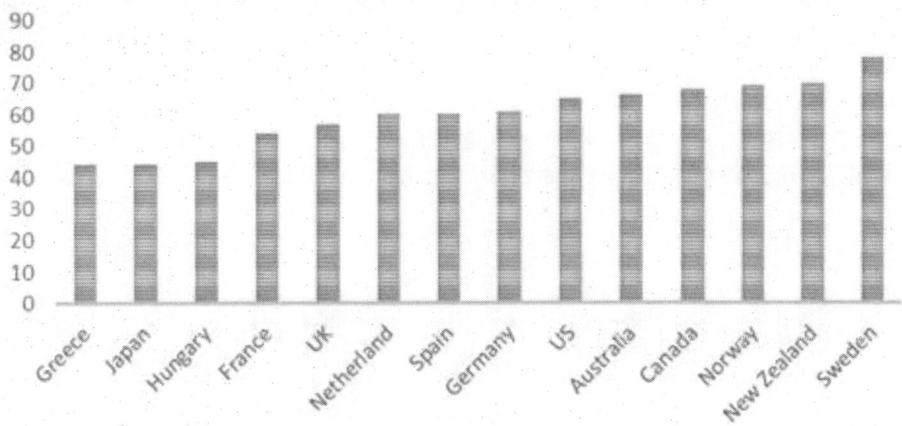

Data is from Huddleston, Bilgili, Joki and Vankova (2015).

Figure 4. Country migrant indicator 2015.

Table 2. Correlations of MIPEX Sub-Areas

	1	2	3	4
1. Labor Mobility	--	.641*	.324	.136
2. Access to Education	--	--	.561**	.491*
3. Access to Health	--	--	--	.287
4. Anti-discrimination	--	--	--	--

Data from Huddleston, Bilgili, Joki, and Vankova, 2015.

* Correlations is significant at the 0.05 level.

** Correlations is significant at the 0.01 level.

Trends in protecting migrant workers and integrating them in the receiving communities have emerged across countries' policy reforms and practice. The Migrant Integration Policy Index (MIPEX), a comparative assessment of migrant integration policies in all European member states and other major developed countries, is one relatively new approach to analysis. Data reported in MIPEX 2015 (Huddleston, Bilgili, Joki, and Vankova, 2015) suggests different country rankings comparing openness indicators (see Figure 4), further demonstrating the policy inconsistence between receiving workers (i.e., openness) and integrating migrants (i.e., granting full access to social economic and political rights). In addition, the MIPEX data indicates certain policy preferences that seem to be adopted by these countries. A brief analysis based on 22 countries' MIPEX data shows that positive education integration policy is associated with better policies for labor market mobility and access to education and health (see Table 2). When roughly grouping the countries based on their history and system of receiving migrants, including major migrant receiving countries (i.e., Australia, Canada, New Zealand and the US), migrant arriving countries (i.e., Belgium, France, Germany, Italy, Netherland, Portugal, Spain, and the UK), non-migrant receiving countries (i.e., Greece, Hungary, Japan, Poland, Romania, and South Korea), and social democratic welfare states (i.e., Denmark, Finland, Norway and Sweden), results from ANOVA and post hoc tests (see Table 3) indicate that there is a lack of significant difference in anti-discrimination policies across all four country groups, as well as labor market mobility policies across three country groups (difference between non-migrant receiving countries and social democratic welfare states is an exception). In addition, the significant differences concentrate on education and health integration policies between non-migrant receiving countries and all other groups of countries. Such trends and patterns suggest that major policy differences concerning migrant workers and their families concerns their social protection and welfare rights, this is one point this edited volume seeks to address.

Table 3. Differences of MIPEX Sub-Areas by Country Groups

Mean difference/SE	Major Migrant Receiving Countries vs. Migrant Arriving Countries	Major Migrant Receiving Countries vs. Non-Migrant Receiving Countries	Major Migrant Receiving Countries vs. Social Democratic Welfare States	Migrant Arriving Countries vs. Non-Migrant Receiving Countries	Migrant Arriving Countries vs. Social Democratic Welfare States	Non-Migrant Receiving Countries vs. Social Democratic Welfare States
Labor Market Mobility	-2.00/7.36	13.92/7.76	-18.50/8.50	15.92/6.49	-16.50/7.36	-32.42/7.76**
Access to Education	18.75/7.50	38.58/7.91**	4.00/8.66	19.83/6.62*	-14.75/7.50	-34.58/7.91**
Access to Health	11.75/5.57	27.50/5.87**	6.25/6.43	15.75/4.91*	-5.50/5.57	-21.25/5.87*
Anti-discrimination	15.63/10.15	25.92/10.70	16.00/11.72	10.29/8.95	0.38/10.15	-9.92/10.70

Data from Huddleston, Bilgili, Joki, and Vankova, 2015.

* Significant at the 0.05 level.

** Significant at the 0.01 level.

DISPARITIES IN EMPLOYMENT, HEALTH AND WELLBEING

Variation in policy regimes and practices influence migrant workers' rights and wellbeing across diverse domains. Human rights violations and disparities in employment, health, mental health, and family wellbeing associated with migration and migrant status are widely reported and documented across countries. In many countries, migrant workers have higher unemployment rates and, when in employment, tend to be exposed to higher risks of over-qualification, and experience considerable job insecurity (Ambrosini and Barone, 2007). In workplaces, migrant workers face multiple forms of exploitation such as working for less pay or no pay or late payment (ILO, 2015b); this reality is further compounded by the gap between the wages promised to migrants by private recruiting agents and real wages (IOL, 2015b), and between migrants' wages and national workers' wages (ILO, 2014). Further, a systematic review of literature in 2007 (Ahonen, Benavides and Benach, 2007) indicates that migrant workers across various countries including both agricultural workers, day laborers, and other types of urban non-agricultural workers, and even skilled workers have experienced increased risks of occupational injuries, associated with negative health consequences. Such disparities in wage, occupational safety, and job security have been consistently observed in both developed and developing countries (e.g., Arcury and Quandt, 2003; Gajigo and Verdier-Chouchane, 2014; Landsbergis, Grzywacz, and LaMontagne, 2014; Sichlar, Ximing, Gustafsson and Shi, 2007).

Most studies of migrant health focus on differences with the non-migrant population in the respective host countries/urban communities providing insights into differences in environmental exposures and access to health care services. Migrants are often (at least initially) more healthy and have better mortality outcomes than non-migrant populations in their receiving countries and remaining populations in their countries of origin (the so-called healthy migrant effect or selection effect) (e.g., Agyemang, de-Graft Aikins, and Bhopal, 2012; Singh, Rodriguez-Lainz, and Kogan, 2013; Spallek, Zeeb and Razum, 2011), by and large because the act of moving for employment and financial improvement usually requires those involved to be in good health. However, such health advantages have been consistently challenged when looking at detailed health outcomes. For instance, Modesti and colleagues in 2014 summarized a huge body of work (Modesti, Agostoni, Agyemang, Basu, et al., 2014) and stated that age-standardized and sex-specific stroke mortality rates in Great Britain in certain historical time periods were higher for migrant groups compared with natives; hypertension was three-fold to four-fold more prevalent among African migrants than the native European population; and prevalence of diabetes mellitus were much higher among migrants than among native peers with few exceptions. Additional examples such as, Latino farm migrant workers in the US suffered significant poorer oral health (Dodd, Schenck, Chaney and Padhya, 2015); middle and old age migrants from low- and middle-income countries demonstrated higher levels of frailty in northern and western Europe (Brothers, Theou and Rockwood, 2014). While biomedical explanations might count for a large part of health disparities, there is a consensus that migrants' lack of equal access to health care, including both preventive care and treatment, and access to culturally appropriate quality health care are the primary concerns that contribute to such health disparities.

Although the evidence for mental health problems among migrants in general is mixed, it has been discussed that negative environmental factors associated with migrant status and often ethnic minority status in the receiving countries — structural inequalities, various types of discrimination experience, and/or pressure of adjustment and acculturation — contribute to increased risk of mental illness (Bhugra and Minas, 2007). In addition, migration associated factors, such as family separation, experience of crossing border particularly illegally, loss of social status due to skill and education non-transferability, are common stressors in migrants' lives (Bhugra, 2004). Thus, it is understandable to observe higher prevalence of common mental disorders and distress and persistent symptoms among migrant populations, as documented by a collection of studies published in 2009 (Fassaert, de Wit, Tuinebreijer, Verhoeff, et al., 2009; Gater, Tomenson, Percival, Chaudhry, et al., 2009; Levecque, Lodewyckx, and Bracke, 2009; Mirsky, 2009). For many low skilled migrant workers, mental health problems might be directly related to their undocumented status (Sullivan and Rehm, 2005), precarious living conditions (Teunissen, Sherally, van den Muijsenbergh, Dowrick, et al., 2014) as well as financial and employment-related difficulties (Wong, He, Leung, Lau and Chang, 2008); increased depression, anxiety, uneasiness, and feeling of powerlessness clearly associate with their limited resources and financial insecurity. In addition, factors such as fragmentation and confusion of identity, the loss associated with moving away from familiar contexts and support networks, the difficulties of adjustment and settlement, and the pressures on changed family structures and relationships, all can erode the migrants' resilience and thus increase vulnerability to mental illness. The migration and settlement process could be especially stressful for migrants who do not have access to a community of people with similar backgrounds. For migrants with mental health needs, high distrust of professionals (e.g., Musa, Schulz, Harris, Silverman, et al., 2009), cultural beliefs against seeking mental health services (e.g., Jimenze, Bartels, Cardenas, Daliwal, et al., 2012), and lack of health literacy and English capacity (e.g., Kim, Worley, Allen, Vinson, et al., 2011), have led to under-utilization of mental health services; such situation not only reflects the failure of most societies to offer services effectively responding to the reality of ethnic, cultural, and linguistic diversity, but also further jeopardize migrants' health and mental health status (e.g., Blignault, Ponzio, Ye and Eisenbruch, 2008; Koopmans, Uiters, Devillé, and Foets, 2013; Lindert, Schouler-Ocak, Heinz and Priebe, 2008).

Migrant families' wellbeing has been the topic of scholarship across diverse disciplines. There is a long history of research to understand migrant families, including their decision making of moving, family arrangements for migration, stress and coping associated with migration, and changing family role and relationships (e.g., Glick, 2010; Harbison, 1981; Root and de Jong, 1991; Sluzki, 1979). Migrant families experience a diversity of family forms, including indefinite separation when the family remains in the country of origin while the migrant takes up a fixed term employment contract overseas, temporary separation while a migrant travels to new destination and family waits for reunification in the destination, and family migration when the whole family moves to a new destination together (e.g., Antman, 2013; Baldassar and Merla, 2014; Graham and Jordan, 2011; Pratt, 2012; Ryan and Sales, 2013; Zentgraf and Chinchilla, 2012). The family form is significantly influenced by the policy regimes of the receiving countries; right to a family life appears to be part of international debates only in recent years as the realization of rights for migrant workers to decent work (Kontos, 2013; Tryfonidou, 2009).

The evidence about the impact of different family structures remains somewhat inclusive, although generally family migration or family unification after a temporary separation, which results in serial migration, has been considered the more desirable outcome because it helps promote migrants' effective integration (Wickramasekara, 2015). Perhaps this assessment reflects the historical prevalence of this type of migration from and to the traditional sending and receiving countries such as the United States, European Union countries, Australia and Canada as well as from the historical colonial states to the European core countries (e.g., Africa, South Asia to UK; Africa to France; Latin America to South European countries), a migration pattern that has a long history associated with indefinite family separation with migrant living abroad long-term and family remaining in the countries of origin. Ironically, the recent trend of familialization of work, which has been primarily observed in domestic and care work and result in the increasing feminized migration, is associated with the defamilialization of workers; migrant women and their family members are forced into a situation to negotiate family arrangements, gender identities and transnational parenthood (Fresnoza-Flot, 2009; Graham, Jordan, Yeoh, Lam and Sukamdi, 2012; Lutz and Palenga-Möllenbeck, 2012). The increasing feminized migration has further endangered the family relationships and particularly fueled the concern about the negative impacts on children's well-being among those who are 'the left-behind' as a mother's absence has a stronger detrimental effect than a father's (Antman, 2013; Cortes, 2015; Jordan and Graham, 2012; McGuire and Martin, 2007; Yanovich, 2015). This scholarship is echoed amongst researchers of internal migration in countries such as China as left-behind children fare worse in terms of education, behaviors and health outcomes (e.g., Gao, Li, Kim, Congdon, et al., 2010; Wu, Palinkas, and He 2011; Wu, Tsang, and Ming, 2014).

Transition to new culture, residential and occupational environments add to stress for individuals and interpersonal family relationships; migrant families experience a wide variety of stressors, including diminished social support network, conflicts in intergenerational relationships, conflicts and changes in marital relationships, poor housing, separation and reunification, and discrimination, while the salience and impact on family well-being might depend on the families' ethnicities, cultures, reasons for migration and other social and contextual factors (Bush, Abrams-Muruthi, Bohon and Kim, 2016; Jordan and Liang, 2014). For instance, sequential and simultaneous family migration offers disparate views on family well-being. Chain, serial and delayed family migration are reflected in the sequential flow of family members when family members and kinship networks can provide important supports to one another during the period of transition. Sequential migration may help to alleviate some of the stress that may accompany simultaneous family migration; however, readjustment to living together following an extended period of absence may result in irreconcilable family relationship disruptions (e.g., Smith, Lalonde and Johnson, 2004; Suårez-Orozco, Todorova and Louie, 2002). When family supports were not available and tangible, abundant evidences have showed the critical resources embedded in the migrant community (e.g., Ayón and Naddy, 2013; Chou, 2012; Chua and Wellman, 2015; Ryan, Sales, Tilki and Siara, 2008; Wu, Tsang and Ming, 2014). There is good reason to conclude that contextual factors including host cultural context and policy environment, migrant social support networks in destination, characteristics of occupation and residential environments may either alleviate or exacerbate elements of individual and interpersonal stress associated with family migration.

Disparities and concerns in employment, health and mental health outcomes and family wellbeing have been discussed with layers of factors associated with receiving country's structure and condition (e.g., whether migrant workers have formal entitlement to legal protection and whether migration status affect their ability and willingness to enforce their rights), and individual worker's characteristics (e.g., less educated and low-skilled workers have limited power to maximize their income and control over their work, and educated and skilled workers cannot transfer their training and skills equivalently) (Sargeant and Tucker, 2009; Underhill and Quinlan, 2011; Underhill and Rimmer, 2015). Of particular importance is whether migrants live and work legally in the receiving country; for instance, as we discuss in the previous section, while different country has granted various degree of right to health, problems in accessing health services seem to be generally greatest for undocumented migrants (Rechel, Mladovsky, Ingleby, Mackenbach, and McKee, 2013). Meanwhile, whether migrants live in a situation of irregularity (e.g., lack of security in job, food, housing, financial resources, etc.) is critical to their wellbeing as well. The situation is further complicated through short-term, circular, seasonal, and return migration. In view of the vast diversity of socioeconomic and living conditions throughout migrants receiving countries, there is a general consensus that the physical and psychological wellbeing of migrant workers and their families does to a large degree depend on the specific country.

SCOPE OF THE BOOK

This book focuses on country policies and practices implemented by agents within the context of global labor migration. Although it has a decidedly practical focus, it draws on theoretical ideas that provide an intellectual basis for the field. Within this volume, there are three cross cutting themes — occupational challenges, health and wellbeing, and social identity — that by all means interconnect to each other.

Occupational Challenges. Low-skilled migrant workers are often employed in occupations with known health and safety concerns, which could be exemplified by migrants' disproportionate share of occupational fatalities and injuries in the US for instance (Quandt, Schulz, Talton, Verma and Arcury, 2012; Schenker, 2011), noting that precarious work, cultural factors and the demands of production may preclude workers from even reporting injuries and incidents (Reid, Lenguerrand, Santos, Read, et al., 2014). For skilled migrant workers, occupational segregation due to gender, race/ethnicity, and/or nativity leaves migrant workers clustered in the certain categories of jobs and contributes to discrepancies in wage gap and occupational attainment (Alonso-Villar and del Río, 2013; Catanzarite, 2000; Meng and Zhang, 2001). Challenges in employment and workplace influence not only migrant workers' health and financial wellbeing, but also contribute to migrants and migrant families' social integration as they seek experience of belongingness and esteem in the new community and society.

Health Practices. Given the health and mental health disparities between migrants and natives, emphases are placed on the barriers to accessing health care and services, possible ways of improving service provision to migrants, and migrant health policies and practices that have been developed. Migrant workers do have unique behavioral patterns of health and mental health service use. Nonetheless, migrant workers' behaviors are responding to structural parameters in the receiving community and society (e.g., Palmer and Xu, 2012; Xu and Brabeck, 2012); the promoting of health and wellbeing of migrant workers is related to the integrity and ethical practices of a larger society. Meanwhile, migrant workers face a various challenges during migration, adjustment and settlement; however they are not merely a group of people who passively wait to be accepted, integrated and cared for in migrant destinations. Migrant workers also bring in strong cultural values and practices that help them cope with the process of integration, and individuals and communities of shared cultural heritage offer strong supports promoting health and wellbeing. Improvement of migrant health and provision of access for migrants to appropriate health and mental health services is not without challenges, but knowledge about what steps need to be taken to achieve these aims is needed.

Social Identity. Social identity is a multi-dimensional classicization as individuals, and as members of collectivities (Jerkins, 2014). After leaving their origins, efforts to maintain migrants' own culture and ethnic identity and struggles to become acculturated in the destination community and society are common experience of identity reconstruction. Migrant workers are constantly negotiating discourses of cultural and ethnic boundaries to understand their migration experiences and at the same time rework discourses of their social identity. It is noted that their identification with such collective units as migrant groups, ethnic organizations, and cultures is socially constructed (Padilla and Perez, 2003). Variables such as power, hierarchy and resource availability would affect migrants' tendency to perceive one group and/or one culture more favorably than the other. In this process, the formation of social identities, as transnational workers, new urban community members, and/or immigrants and returnees, is subjected to local community contexts and located at the interplay of social structure and economic agencies.

Given the three prevailing themes, we divide the book into three parts based on migrant workers' primary characteristics. Part I provides research predominately concerning low-skilled workers in precarious working environments, their health and mental health status and needs, and ways they strive to secure wellbeing for self and their families. Part II focuses on internal migrant workers, whose migration from rural villages to urban cities by and large mimics the experience of international low-skilled immigrant workers but with dissimilar context. Unlike international immigrant workers who often work in advanced economies and settle in developed countries, internal migrant workers is part of the inevitable force of urbanization and essential for the economic and social prosperity of emerging economies. Worryingly, many internal migrants are not able to equally share the benefits of urban residents; and protecting internal migrant workers' social and economic rights to assure their wellbeing is essential. Part III is a collection of studies that turns the focus to the dynamics of circular transnational labor migration including seafarers and returning migrant workers, and explores young professional workers epitomizing the search for "talent" migration increasingly prevalent in global cities.

In Part I, the chapter 2 contributed by Matthew and Sugrue focuses on an ever-growing global group of workers — women and girls who become increasingly participating in the formal economy and meet the need of domestic workers in developed counties. In the context of global gender equality movement, women's status increasingly arises as a result of enhanced education and employment opportunities; at the same time, female migrant workers face the challenge to either serve the traditional role offering the care at home, or commodify the care by joining in the global labor force. The latter one exposes them to the high risk of not being protected from an assortment of abuses ranging from economic to social in the workplace. The authors analyze the global demand and supply of domestic workers, review their precarious working condition, and argue for advocacy and intervention from practitioners. The authors indicate that enforcing employment contracts should be a tangible step to take in order to protect these vulnerable, often invisible, essential workers.

Hilado, Hong, Vidal de Haymes and Lundy in the chapter 3 start with the discussion about interconnections across the pursuit of economic opportunities, migrants' social support, and their adjustment and acculturation. Their research about Mexican economic migrants in the city of Chicago describes a group of migrants who have been known for concentrating on low-skilled job category and experiencing various vulnerabilities ranging from illegal status to poverty in the American history. As successful economic and social integration is essential to their American Dream, this chapter offers empirical evidence showing that greater financial stability and better acculturation results are associated with more resources derived from formal and informal social support networks. The authors thus discuss the value of community-based networks and argue for the role that social institutions play to promote migrant workers' economic and social wellbeing.

The chapter 4 contributed by Sen and Aguilar discuss the growing migration population in Sub-Saharan Africa in the context of global HIV/AIDS epidemics. While migration in Sub-Saharan Africa demonstrates a unique pattern of intraregional movement, labor migrants by all means share similar characteristics as what had been observed in many destination countries during their early years of immigration — male dominated migrant work force, concentrating in precarious jobs (mining industry in particular), frequent moving back and forth between home and workplace, poor working condition and social isolation. Noting that the majority of global HIV infections are in developing, or "resource-poor" countries and Sub-Saharan Africa reports the worst AIDS infection data, this chapter examines how migration acts as a conduit for disease transmission, thus increases migrants' vulnerability to HIV. The chapter pays close attention to the socioeconomic environment, and argues that social disruption and stress associated with migration lead to high-risk behaviors among migrant workers that amplify the likelihood of HIV transmission. In conclusion, the authors propose a social capital oriented framework as well as the leadership mobilization model as an HIV/AIDS prevention strategy, which focuses on education and community collaboration, to supplement current public health model based prevention and intervention programs.

Chapter 5 by Li, Ramos and Do focuses on mental health issues of Puerto Rican women in the US Despite their US citizen status, Puerto Ricans overall are workers concentrated in low-skilled, low-paying jobs as well, and poverty persists among this group of migrants for the long term. Puerto Ricans women experience additional social inequalities associated with sexism and racism; economic oppression, racial and gender discrimination, cultural conflict, and the loss of social support systems often place them at risk for psychosocial stress and psychological stress. Further, the unique circular migration pattern between the island Puerto Rico and the mainland US gives rise to new stressors as this involves facing a 'neither here nor there' situation and thus a sense of loss of cultural identity. This chapter is to address a common challenge in mental health practice with migrant populations: a culturally appropriate and migration applicable measurement of psychosocial stress. Surveying a group of Puerto Rican women in upstate New York, authors validate the Hispanic Women's Social Stressor Scale and further indicate that stressors related to employment, familial strain, and acculturation appear more salient among Puerto Rican women. Their findings underscore the need to consider gender and unique migrant subgroup characteristics in mental health practice and migration research.

Part II of the book has three chapters that deal with internal migration in three Asian countries: Vietnam, India and China. These three Asian countries in the last few decades have all experienced massive multi-directional labor migration, from rural villages to urban cities, from resource-poor regions to economic zones, and from small towns to metropolitan areas, primarily due to their market-oriented economic reforms and development. While moving internally, migrant workers show characteristics as seasonal migrants (moving during certain period of time), floating population (moving without clear destination), and/or circular migrants (moving back and forth). Meanwhile, such migration by all means is internally controlled. Thus, the migrant workers' wellbeing are subject to countries' political systems, social and cultural norms and economic situation.

Chapter 6 examines the impact of living and working environments on physical and mental health of rural-to-urban migrant workers in Hanoi, Vietnam. Le, Nguyen and Nguyen provide narratives directly from migrant workers and indicate that most migrant workers endured very poor living and working conditions without health insurance or benefits, and many developed physical health problems; they were also socially isolated as "outsiders" of the city, leading to the feeling of lonely, anxious, and homesick, and coped with physical and psychological health issues primarily by self-care — remaining very mindful about diet and sleep habits, and minimizing risky behaviors. The authors note a considerable threat to migrant workers' health and mental health, and a general lack of social and government efforts to integrate migrants to cities which has left migrant workers to defend themselves.

Borhade and Zhang in Chapter 7 begin with an introduction of seasonal migrant workers in various Asian countries and then describe the food security concern among seasonal migrants in Nashik India. Noting that the primary barrier of access to government food programs and other services is the welfare programs' low portability, the authors discuss how India's public welfare programs in general and food assistance programs in specific have not responded to the changed economic condition and seasonal migration patterns; local government's inability to implement a new policy, which is designed for the benefit of migrant workers, further worsens the food insecurity. Using the case of Disha Foundation food project, the authors advocate for an increasing role played by nongovernment organizations to facilitate the communication between local governments and migrant communities, educate and empower migrants, and monitor and enhance government administration.

Chapter 8 contributed by Ma and Wu examines the relationship between regulating migration and the social rights in the context of China's internal migration. While China's *Hukou* system (i.e., Household Registration System) has been notorious for creating two classes of citizens where rural-to-urban migrant workers would not have equal access to health care, education and other welfare programs, the authors observe that recent reforms of *Hukou* system have not generated any positive effects on the migrant workers' rights. The authors argue that this is due to the inherent mechanism of social rights. Social rights have a natural characteristic of the spatial inequality so as to distinguish insiders and outsiders. An upward universalism of social rights and a downward distribution of social resources work together and shape the multi-layered welfare boundaries. These invisible boundaries do not necessarily correspond to rural-urban boundary set up by *Hukou* system; equal rights particularly equal social welfare rights have no ground to be realized. Ma and Wu's conceptualization of welfare boundary not only illuminates the future *Hukou* reform in China, but can also help to understand and to improve migration policies in other countries.

Part III of the book focuses on how social identity has been shaped and maintained for three groups of migrant workers. Both the chapter 9 and 10 consider the same transnational labor force seafarers. Sampson and Acejo in Chapter 9 explore an under-explored aspect of migrant social identity — seafarers' social identity — drawing upon ethnographic fieldwork conducted in a town in the Philippines and on board a cargo vessel. As a significant group of migrant workers who regularly return to home (usually annually), seafarers rely on their wives to maintain social relationships and social status in their absence. Standing in for seafarers in a variety of family and community roles, wives protect the absent husbands' social identity in their home communities. Jaffee and Weng in Chapter 10 comprehensively explain how seafarers are part of a global labor market and constituting a migrant transnational labor force whose social identity is formed as a consequence of the nature and location of their work, and the multi-national composition of the seafarer community. The chapter also review the conditions of work and associated occupational health and safety hazards, including the mental health impacts associated with long periods confined to a vessel, piracy, and separation from family, as well as how they have organized to address these terms and conditions of their labor. The authors propose a governmental regulation framework operated by the labor supplying countries to replace current practice to better protect seafarers and improve their quality of work and life.

Chapter 11 contributed by Segal studies a recent migration phenomenon — the return of expatriates. Noting that an increasing pool of working-age migrants return to their countries of origin, and "circular migration" is rising with the ease of transportation and globalization, the chapter discusses unique challenges faced by this group of migrants, such as unmatched job skills and work opportunities in the homeland, difficulties of reintegration and reconfiguration of social identity, and their family and children's struggle with adaptation and acculturation. The author suggests that nations must recognize the returned migrants as a potential asset to help bridge their talent gap due to "brain drain," thus have the responsibilities to develop effective policies, programs, and services to assist this unique group of migrant workers reestablish themselves so that nations can maximize the use of their human capital.

Chapter 12 by Kerelian and Jordan focuses on highly skilled young transmigrant professionals. The authors situate their study in the global city Hong Kong, and review the highly-skilled migrant attracting policies as a trend within the Asia-Pacific, through the examples of Tokyo and Singapore, which are looking to gain a competitive advantage and realize world city aspirations. Narratives from British and American young transmigrant professionals reveal the human dimension of migration — providing both opportunities and challenges to this group of migrant professionals, and explore the meaning of place in shaping their social identify and feeling of belongingness. Unlike other contributors in Part III, critical questions raised by the authors are not so much about the migrant group and community; rather, the chapter addresses the skilled workers' migration, their social identity formation, and evolving diversities in conceptualization of global city. Thus, the authors ask for more holistic policy approaches for a city that is willing to be a place for all the migrants.

NOT AN END

This collection is only a start in the exploration of complex and varied lives of global migrants, and is able to unfold a small part of migrant workers' life — job, family, community, health, emotional wellbeing, and social identity. As migrants will continue to play a significant role in the future workforce worldwide, both within and across national boundaries, strategies to best address vulnerabilities and promote protective factors are essential. Each of the chapters in this volume provides the reader with background and context of diverse aspects of migration from across the globe enabling an assessment of how localized context is a reflection of wider points of commonality, contributing to better understanding theoretical explanations within the interdisciplinary field of migration studies. In addition, all of the authors offer practical suggestions for policy and service delivery design, including formal and informal mechanisms of support which can inform the professional reader. It is our hope that it will stimulate further debate and discussion to improve the lives of diverse groups of migrants, and promote more inclusive strategies at the local, national and supranational levels that recognize the multifaceted experience of migrants, their families, and the communities they inhabit both near and far.

REFERENCES

Agyemang, C., de-Graft Aikins, A., and Bhopal, R. (2012). Ethnicity and cardiovascular health research: pushing the boundaries by including comparison populations in the countries of origin. *Ethnicity and Health*, 17(6), 579-596.

Ahonen, E. Q., Benavides, F. G., and Benach, J. (2007). Immigrant populations, work and health: A systematic literature review. *Scandinavian Journal of Work, Environment and Health*, 33(2), 96-104.

Alonso-Villar, O., and del-Río, C. (2013). Occupational segregation in a country of recent mass immigration: evidence from Spain. *The Annals of Regional Science*, 50(1), 109-134.

Ambrosini, M., and Barone, C. (2007). *Employment and working conditions of migrant workers*. Retrieved from Dubline, Irland: http://www.eurofound.europa.eu/observatories/eurwork/comparative-information/employment-and-working-conditions-of-migrant-workers.

Andrijasevic, R., and Walters, W. (2010). The international organization for migration and the international government of borders. *Environment and Planning D: Society and Space*, 28(6), 977-999.

Antman, F. M. (2013). The impact of migration on family left behind. In: Constant, A. F. and Zimmermann, K. F. (Ed.), *International Handbook on the Economics of Migration* (pp. 293-308): Edward Elgar Publishing.

Arcury, T. A., and Quandt, S. A. (2003). Pesticides at work and at home: exposure of migrant farmworkers. *The Lancet*, 362(9400), 2021.

Ayón, C., and Naddy, M. B. G. (2013). Latino immigrant families' social support networks: Strengths and limitations during a time of stringent immigration legislation and economic insecurity *Journal of Community Psychology*, 41(3), 359-377.

Baldassar, L., and Merla, L. (Ed.) (2014). *Transnational families, migration, and the circulation of care: Understanding mobility and absence in family life*. New York: Routledge.

Bhugra, D. (2004). Migration and mental health. *Acta Psychiatrica Scandinavica*, 109(4), 243-258.

Bhugra, D., and Minas, I. H. (2007). Mental health and global movement of people. *The Lancet*, 370(9593), 1109-1111.

Blignault, I., Ponzio, V., Rong, Y., and Eisenbruch, M. (2008). A qualitative study of barriers to mental health services utilisation among migrants from mainland China in South-East Sydney. *International Journal of Social Psychiatry*, 54(2), 180-190.

Boräng, F., and Cerna, L. (2015). *Swedish labour immigration policy: The role of unions, employers and political parties*. Retrieved from https://www.compas.ox -2015-127-Bor%C3%A4ng-Cerna_Swedish_Labour2.pdf.

Bosniak, L. S. (1991). Human rights, state sovereignty and the protection of undocumented migrants under the International Migrant Workers Convention. *International Migration Review*, 25(4), 737-770.

Brochmann, G., and Hagelund, A. (2012). *Immigration policy and the Scandinavian welfare states 1945-2010*. Palgrave Macmillan.

Brothers, T. D., Theou, O., and Rockwood, K. (2014). Frailty and migration in middle-aged and older Europeans. *Archives of Gerontology and Geriatrics*, 58(1), 63-68.

Bush, K. R., Abrams-Muruthi, B. A., Bohon, S. A., and Kim, H. K. (2016). Adaptation among immigrant families: Resources and barriers. In: Price, C. A., Bush, K. R., and Price, S. J. (Ed.), *Families and Change: Coping With Stressful Events and Transitions* (pp. 179-202). SAGE Publications.

Castles, S. (2011). Bringing human rights into the migration and development debate. *Global Policy*, 2(3), 248-258.

Catanzarite, L. (2000). Brown-collar jobs: Occupational segregation and earnings of recent-immigrant Latinos. *Sociological Perspectives*, 43(1), 45-75.

Cernadas, P. C., LeVoy, M., and Keith, L. (2015). *Human rights indicators for migrants and their families*. KNOMAD Working Paper 5. Retrieved from http://picum.org/picum.org/uploads/publication/KNOMAD%20Working%20Paper%205%20Human%20Rights%20Indicators%20for%20Migrants.pdf.

Cholewinski, R. (2005). *Protecting migrant workers in a globalized world*. Washington, DC: Migration Policy Institute. Retrieved from http://www.migrationpolicy.org/article/protecting-migrant-workers-globalized-world.

Cholewinski, R. (2013). International standards and processes for the protection of migrant rights. *The Encyclopedia of Global Human Migration*. Washington DC: Migrtion Policy Institute.

Cholewinski, R., de Guchteneire, P., and Pecoud, A, (Ed.) (2010). *Migration and human rights: The United Nations Convention on Migrant Workers' Rights*. Cambridge University Press.

Chou, K.-L. (2012). Perceived discrimination and depression among new migrants to Hong Kong: The moderating role of social support and neighborhood collective efficacy. *Journal of Affective Disorders*, 138(1), 63-70.

Chua, V., and Wellman, B. (2015). Social networks in East and Southeast Asia II: Labor migration, opportunity, social media, and well-being. *American Behavioral Scientist*, 59 (9), 1055-1065.

Cortes, P. (2015). The feminization of international migration and its effects on the children left behind: Evidence from the Philippines. *World Development*, 65, 62-78.

Costa, D., Cooper, D., and Shierholz, H. (2014). *Facts about immigration and the US economy*. Economic Policy Institute. Retrieved from http://www.epi.org/publication/immigration-facts/.

Delgado Wise, R., Márquez Covarrubias, H., and Puentes, R. (2013). Reframing the debate on migration, development and human rights. *Population, Space and Place*, 19(4), 430-443.

Dodd, V. J., Schenck, D. P., Chaney, E. H., and Padhya, T. (2015). Assessing oral cancer awareness among rural Latino migrant workers. *Journal of Immigrant and Minority Health*, first online May 28 2015.

Donald, A. (Producer). (2014). *Immigration points-based systems compared*. BBC UK Politics. Retrieved from http://www.bbc.com/news/uk-politics-29594642.

Fassaert, T., Wit, M. A. S., Tuinebreijer, W. C., Verhoeff, A. P., Beekman, A. T. F., and Dekker, J. (2009). Perceived need for mental health care among non-western labour migrants. *Social Psychiatry and Psychiatric Epidemiology*, 44(3), 208-216.

Fresnoza-Flot, A. (2009). Migration status and transnational mothering: the case of Filipino migrants in France. *Global Networks*, 9(2), 252-270.

Gajigo, O., and Verdier-Chouchane, A. (2014). *Immigrants, skills and wages in the Gambian labor market*. Working Paper NO. 203, African Development Bank Group. Retrieved from http://www.afdb.org/fileadmin/uploads/afdb/Documents/Publications/Working_Paper_203_-_Immigrants__Skills_and_Wages_in_the_Gambian_Labor_Market.pdf.

Gao, Y., Li, L. P., Kim, J. H., Congdon, N., Lau, J., and Griffiths, S. (2010). The impact of parental migration on health status and health behaviours among left behind adolescent school children in China. *BMC Public Health*, 10(1), 1-10.

Gater, R., Tomenson, B., Percival, C., Chaudhry, N., Waheed, W., Dunn, G., Creed, F. (2009). Persistent depressive disorders and social stress in people of Pakistani origin and white Europeans in UK. *Social Psychiatry and Psychiatric Epidemiology*, 44(3), 198-207.

Gleeson, S. (2010). Labor rights for all? The role of undocumented immigrant status for worker claims making. *Law and Social Inquiry*, 35(3), 561-602.

Glick, J. E. (2010). Connecting complex processes: A decade of research on immigrant families. *Journal of Marriage and Family*, 72(3), 498-515.

Graham, E., and Jordan, L. P. (2011). Migrant parents and the psychological well-being of children left behind in South-East Asia. *Journal of Marriage and Family*, 73, 763-787.

Graham, E., Jordan, L. P., Yeoh, B.S.A., Lam, T., Asis, M. and Sukamdi (2012). Transnational families and the family nexus: Perspectives of Indonesian and Filipino children left behind by migrant parents. *Environment and Planning A* 44: 793-815.

Harbison, S. F. (1981). Family structure and family strategy in migration decision making. In: De Jong, G. F., and Gardner, R. W. (Ed.), *Migration decision making: multidisciplinary approaches to microlevel studies in developed and developing countries* (pp. 225-251). New York: Pergamon.

Hawthorne, L. (2014). *A comparison of skilled migration policy: Australia, Canada and New Zealand*. Retrieved from http://sites.nationalacademies.org/cs/groups/pgasite/documents/webpage/pga_152512.pdf.

Huddleston, T., Bilgili, Ö., Joki, A.-L. and Vankova, Z. (2015). *Migrant Integration Policy Index 2015*: Barcelona/Brussels: CIDOB and MPG.

International Labour Organization (2014). *Global Wage Report 2014/15*. International Labour Organization, Inclusive Labour Markets Labour Relations and Working Conditions Branch. Retrieved from http://www.ilo.org/global/research/global-reports/global-wage-report/2014/lang--en/index.htm.

International Labour Organization (2015a). *ILO global estimates on migrant workers: Results and methodology Special focus on migrant domestic workers*. International Labour Organization. Retrieved from http://www.ilo.org/wcmsp5/groups/public/---dgreports/---dcomm/documents/publication/wcms_436343.pdf.

International Labour Organization (2015b). *Promoting decent work for migrant workers*. International Labour Organization. Retrieved from http://www.un.org/en/development/desa/population/migration/events/coordination/13/documents/backgrounddocs/GFMD_ILO_Discussion%20Paper_Promoting%20Decent%20Work%20for%20MWs.pdf.

International Organization for Migration (2005). *Bordering on control: Combating irregular migration in North America and Europe*. International Labour Organization.

Jenkins, R. (2014). *Social identity (fourth edition)*. Routledge.

Jimenez, D. E., Bartels, S. J., Cardenas, V., Daliwal, S. S., and Alegría, M. (2012). Cultural beliefs and mental health treatment preferences of ethnically diverse older adult consumers in primary care. *The American Journal of Geriatric Psychiatry*, 20(6), 533-542.

Jordan, L.P. and Graham, E.F. (2012). Resilience and well-being among children of migrant parents in Southeast Asia. *Child Development* 83(5), 1672-1688.

Jordan, L.P. and Liang, Q. (2014). Filling a service gap for divided families: The case of China and Hong Kong. *Journal of Ethnic and Cultural Diversity in Social Work* 23(3/4), 223-238.

Kim, G., Worley, C. B., Allen, R. S., Vinson, L., Crowther, M. R., Parmelee, P., and Chiriboga, D. A. (2011). Vulnerability of older Latino and Asian immigrants with limited English proficiency. *Journal of the American Geriatrics Society*, 59, 1246-1252.

Kontos, M. (2013). Negotiating the social citizenship rights of migrant domestic workers: The right to family reunification and a family life in policies and debates. *Journal of Ethnic and Migration Studies*, 39(3), 409-424.

Koopmans, G., Uiters, E., Devillé, W., and Foets, M. (2013). The use of outpatient mental health care services of migrants vis-à-vis Dutch natives: Equal access? *International Journal of Social Psychiatry*, 59(4), 342-350.

Kullgren, J. T. (2003). Restrictions on undocumented immigrants' access to health services: The public health implications of welfare reform. *American Journal of Public Health*, 93 (10), 1630-1633.

Landsbergis, P. A., Grzywacz, J. G., and LaMontagne, A. D. (2014). Work organization, job insecurity, and occupational health disparities. *American Journal of Industrial Medicine*, 57(5), 495-515.

Levecque, K., Lodewyckx, I., and Bracke, P. (2009). Psychological distress, depression and generalised anxiety in Turkish and Moroccan immigrants in Belgium. *Social Psychiatry and Psychiatric Epidemiology*, 44(3), 188-197.

Lindert, J., Schouler-Ocak, M., Heinz, A., and Priebe, S. (2008). Mental health, health care utilisation of migrants in Europe. *European Psychiatry*, 23, Supplement 1, 14-20.

Lönnroth, J. (1991). The International Convention on the Rights of All Migrant Workers and Members of Their Families in the context of international migration policies: An Analysis of ten years of negotiation. *International Migration Review*, 25(4), 710-736.

Lutz, H., and Palenga-Möllenbeck, E. (2012). Care workers, care drain, and care chains: Reflections on care, migration, and citizenship. *Social Politics: International Studies in Gender, State and Society*, 19(1), 15-37.

McGuire, S., and Martin, K. (2007). Fractured migrant families: Paradoxes of hope and devastation. *Family and Community Health*, 30(3), 178-188.

Meng, X., and Zhang, J. (2001). The two-tier labor market in urban China: Occupational segregation and wage differentials between urban residents and rural migrants in Shanghai. *Journal of Comparative Economics*, 29(3), 485-504.

Migration Policy Institute (2013). *Migration olicy Institute tabulation of data from the United Nations, Department of Economic and Social AffairsTrends in International Migrant Stock: The 2013 revision (United Nations database, POP/DB/MIG/Stock/Rev.2013).* Retrieved from http://esa.un.org/unmigration/migrantstocks2013.htm?mtotals. http://esa.un.org/unmigration/migrantstocks2013.htm?mtotals.

Mirsky, J. (2009). Mental health implications of migration. *Social Psychiatry and Psychiatric Epidemiology*, 44(3), 179-187.

Modesti, P. A., Agostino, P., Agyemang, C., Basu, S., Benetos, A., Cappuccio, F. P., ... for the ESH Working Group on Hypertension and Cardiovascular Risk in Low Resource Settings. (2014). Cardiovascular risk assessment in low-resource settings: a consensus document of the European Society of Hypertension Working Group on Hypertension and Cardiovascular Risk in Low Resource Settings. *Journal of Hypertension*, 32(5), 951-960.

Münz, R. (2008). *Migration, labor markets, and integration of migrants: An overview for Europe*. SP Discussion Paper No. 0807. World Bank Social Protection and Labor.

Musa, D., Schulz, R., Harris, R., Silverman, M., and Thomas, S. B. (2009). Trust in the health care system and the use of preventive health services by older black and white adults. *American Journal of Public Health*, 99(7), 1293-1299.

Padilla, A. M., and Perez, W. (2003). Acculturation, social identity, and social cognition: A new perspective. *Hispanic Journal of Behavioral Sciences*, 25(1), 35-55.

Palmer, N. and Xu, Q. (2012). Social capital, migration, and health in the urban Chinese context. *Journal of Ethnic and Migration Studies*. 39 (1), 1-20.

Pratt, G. (2012). *Families apart: Migrant mothers and the conflicts of labor and love*. Minneapolis, MN: University of Minneasota Press.

Quandt, S. A., Schulz, M. R., Talton, J. W., Verma, A., an Arcury, T. A. (2012). Occupational eye injuries experienced by migrant farmworkers. *Journal of Agromedicine*, 17(1), 63-69.

Rechel, B., Mladovsky, P., Ingleby, D., Mackenbach, J. P., and McKee, M. (2013). Migration and health in an increasingly diverse Europe. *The Lancet*, 381(9873), 1235-1245.

Reid, A., Lenguerrand, E., Santos, I., Read, U., LaMontagne, A. D., Fritschi, L., and Harding, S. (2014). Taking risks and survival jobs: Foreign-born workers and work-related injuries in Australia. *Safety Science*, 70, 378-386.

Rodriguez, R. M. (2002). Migrant heroes: Nationalism, citizenship and the politics of Filipino migrant labor. *Citizenship Studies*, 6(3), 341-356.

Root, B. D., and De Jong, G. F. (1991). Family migration in a developing country. *Population Studies*, 45(2), 221-233.

Ruhs, M. (2012). The human rights of migrant workers: Why do so few countries care? *American Behavioral Scientist*, 56(9), 1277-1293.

Ruhs, M. (2013). *The price of rights: Regulating international labor migration.* Princeton, NJ: Princeton University Press.

Ryan, L., and Sales, R. (2013). Family migration: The role of children and education in family decision-making strategies of Polish migrants in London. *International Migration*, 51(2), 90-103.

Ryan, L., Sales, R., Tilki, M., and Siara, B. (2008). Social networks, social support and social capital: The experiences of recent Polish migrants in London. *Sociology*, 42(4), 672-690.

Sargeant, M., and Tucker, E. (2009). Layers of vulnerability in occupational safety and health for migrant workers: Case studies from Canada and The UK. *Policy and Practice in Health and Safety*, 7(2), 51-73.

Schenker, M. (2011). *Migration and occupational health: Understanding the risks*. Migration Information Source. Retrieved from http://www.migrationpolicy.org/article/migration-and-occupational-health-understanding-risks.

Sicular, T., Ximing, Y., Gustafsson, B., and Shi, L. (2007). The urban-rural income gap and inequality in China. *Review of Income and Wealth*, 53(1), 93-126.

Singh, G. K., Rodriguez-Lainz, A., and Kogan, M. D. (2013). Immigrant health inequalities in the United States: Use of eight major national data systems. *The Scientific World Journal*, 2013, 21.

Skeldon, R. (2011). *China: An emerging destination for economic migration*. Washington, DC: Migration Policy Institute. Retrieved from http://www.migrationpolicy.org/article/china-emerging-destination-economic-migration.

Sluzki, C. E. (1979). Migration and family conflict. *Family Process*, 18(4), 379-390.

Smith, A., Lalonde, R. N., and Johnson, S. (2004). Serial migration and its implications for the parent-child relationship: A retrospective analysis of the experiences of the children of Caribbean immigrants. *Cultural Diversity and Ethnic Minority Psychology*, 10(2), 107-122.

Spallek, J., Zeeb, H., and Razum, O. (2011). What do we have to know from migrants' past exposures to understand their health status? A life course approach. *Emerging Themes in Epidemiology*, 8(1), 1-8.

Suårez-Orozco, C., Todorova, I. L. G., and Louie, J. (2002). Making up for lost time: The experience of separation and reunification among immigrant families. *Family Process*, 41 (4), 625-643.

Sullivan, M. M., and Rehm, R. (2005). Mental health of undocumented Mexican immigrants: A review of the literature. *Advances in Nursing Science*, 28(3), 240-251.

Sung, H.-E., Delgado, S., Peña, D., and Paladino, A. (2013). Tyrannizing strangers for profit: Wage theft, cross-border migrant workers, and the politics of exclusion in an era of global economic integration. In: Brotherton, D. C., Stageman, D. L., and Leyro, S. P.

(Ed.), *Outside justice: Immigration and the criminalizing impact of changing policy and practice* (pp. 247-267). New York: Springer.

Teunissen, E., Sherally, J., van den Muijsenbergh, M., Dowrick, C., van Weel-Baumgarten, E., and van Weel, C. (2014). Mental health problems of undocumented migrants (UMs) in the Netherlands: a qualitative exploration of help-seeking behaviour and experiences with primary care. *BMJ Open*, 4(11).

The Law Library of Congress (2013). *Points-based immigration systems*. The Law Library of Congress Global Legal Research Center. Retrieved from http://www.loc.gov/law/help/points-based-immigration/Points-Based%20Immigration%20Systems.pdf.

Tryfonidou, A. (2009). Family reunification rights of (migrant) union citizens: Towards a more liberal approach. *European Law Journal*, 15(5), 634-653.

UN Department of Economic and Social Affairs (2015). *Trends in international migrant Stock: The 2015 revision (United Nations database, POP/DB/MIG/Stock/Rev.2015)*. Retrieved from http://www.un.org/en/evelopment/desa/population/migration/data/estimates2/estimates15.shtml.

Underhill, E., and Rimmer, M. (2015). Layered vulnerability: Temporary migrants in Australian horticulture. *Journal of Industrial Relations*, first online September 3, 2015.

Underhill, E. Q., Michael. (2011). How precarious employment affects health and safety at work: The case of temporary agency workers. *Relations Industrielles/Industrial Relations*, 66(3), 397-421.

Wickramasekara, P. (2008). Globalisation, international labour migration and the rights of migrant workers. *Third World Quarterly*, 29(7), 1247-1264.

Wickramasekara, P. (2015). Migration regimes and their linkages for family unity, integrity and development. In: Panizzon, M., Zürcher, G., and Fornalé, E. (Ed.), *The Palgrave handbook of internaitonal labour migration: Law and policy perspectives* (pp. 146-180): Palgrave MacMillan.

Wong, D. F. K., He, X., Leung, G., Lau, Y., and Chang, Y. (2008). Mental health of migrant workers in China: prevalence and correlates. *Social Psychiatry and Psychiatric Epidemiology*, 43(6), 483-489.

World Bank (2015). *Migration and remittances factbook 2016 (Third Edition)*. World Bank. Retrieved from http://siteresources.worldbank.org/INTPROSPECTS/Resources/334934-1199807908806/4549025-1450455807487/Factbookpart1.pdf.

Wu, Q., Tsang, B., and Ming, H. (2014). Social capital, family support, resilience and educational outcomes of Chinese migrant children. *British Journal of Social Work*, 44(3), 636-656.

Wu, Q., Palinkas, L. A., and He, X. (2011). Social capital in promoting the psychosocial adjustment of Chinese migrant children: Interaction across contexts. *Journal of Community Psychology*, 39(4), 421-442.

Xu, Q. and Brabeck, K. (2012). Service use among undocumented Latino immigrants and their families. *Social Work Research*. 36 (3), 209-222.

Yanovich, L. (2015). *Children left behind: The impact of labor migration in Moldova and Ukraine*. Migration Policy Institute. Retrieved from http://www.migrationpolicy.org/article/children-left-behind-impact-labor-migration-moldova-and-ukraine.

Zentgraf, K. M., and Chinchilla, N. S. (2012). Transnational family separation: A framework for analysis. *Journal of Ethnic and Migration Studies*, 38(2), 345-366.

PART I: PRECARIOUS JOB, LOW-SKILL WORKERS AND HEALTH AND MENTAL HEALTH

In: Migrant Workers
Editors: Qingwen Xu and Lucy P. Jordan
ISBN: 978-1-63485-272-2

Chapter 2

MIGRANT DOMESTIC WORKERS AND THE PROVISION OF CARE: CURRENT CHALLENGES AND FUTURE DIRECTIONS

***Lenore E. Matthew*[1,*] *and Noreen M. Sugrue*[2]**
[1]School of Social Work, University of Illinois at Urbana-Champaign, US
[2]Women and Gender in Global Perspectives Program, Center for African Studies, and Center for Global Studies, University of Illinois at Urbana-Champaign, US

ABSTRACT

There is an ever-growing global demand that women and girls become more educated as well as be afforded enhanced opportunities to participate in the formal economy. At the same time, the world's population is aging and there are increasing numbers of disabled and chronically ill non-elderly persons. These shifting demographics along with changes in work patterns are producing a global decline of multigenerational households. In addition to the demographic changes, there has been an overall increase in wages and disposable income. Taken together, these conditions are producing both an increasing demand and competition for domestic workers who provide care, and a decreasing supply of local women to perform this work. For many developed, middle-income, and developing countries, the solution for filling the gap between the increasing demand for and shrinking local supply of domestic workers is to increase the number of migrant female workers. This situation necessitates advocacy and intervention from practitioners because without it, most of these migrant domestic workers will not be protected from an assortment of abuses in the work place. In this chapter, we explore some of the consequences produced by this perfect storm for migrant domestic workers. Finally, we suggest specific policy and advocacy activities that practitioners may undertake in order to provide protection to these vulnerable, often invisible, essential workers.

* Corresponding author: Lenore E. Matthew, School of Social Work, University of Illinois at Urbana-Champaign, 1010 W. Nevada Street, Urbana, IL 61801, US. Email: lematth2@illinois.edu.

INTRODUCTION

Over a century ago, Rubinow (1906) argued that gender inequity and inequality, along with employment bias against women and immigrants, as well as the willingness of immigrants to take on any job for very little compensation while also accepting long and arduous work hours, leads many women, *particularly* migrant women, into jobs as domestic workers. He further noted that these women take care of homes, provided childcare, and did whatever was asked of them in order to meet the needs and wants of household members. Migrant women today, especially migrant domestic workers, find themselves in a situation eerily similar to that of migrant women in 1906.

Today, global demographic shifts such as the growing aging population, increasing numbers of the non-elderly disabled living outside of institutions, and rising numbers of females acquiring higher levels of education and also entering the formal labor market, have yielded new care voids that, in turn, have produced migratory pathways that take females away from their families, communities, and countries. That is, changing demographics worldwide have produced a seemingly insatiable global demand for poor migrant females from low- and middle-income countries who will cheaply and often by way of the informal economy, provide care for the young, the disabled, the ill, and the elderly in wealthier homes.

This demand for "cheap care" is at odds with a myriad of national and global development initiatives aiming to educate and create formal labor market options for women and girls in low- and middle-income countries. This tension gives rise to a very complicated situation. In poor communities in low- and middle-income countries, far too many females are left with the following labor option: abandon the idea of securing formal education and training, thereby precluding significant, if any, participation in the formal economy, and become a migrant domestic worker with the hope of earning enough money to meet all of the demands that will be placed on her salary.

Across the globe, the job of a migrant domestic worker is low paying (UN Women, 2013). Yet on these low wages these women are required to pay for their own basic needs, and often expected and even forced to send money home to pay for the care of their own family members. Further complicating this situation, the women migrating and performing domestic and care work are often poor; in addition, their jobs likely to be beyond the regulatory oversight and reaches of host countries. This thereby renders migrant domestic workers easy targets for an array of abuses. Together, these economic, social, and political conditions create a vicious cycle of an increasing number of kin needing care and more women from low-income countries migrating for low paying jobs with few, if any, opportunities to redress abuses.

Underpaid work, whether in one's own country or in a host country, must become a distant memory if global economic and gender equity goals and targets are to be met. This is especially challenging for migrant domestic workers—the left behind workers. Migrant domestic workers are those who will neither earn a living wage nor acquire skills that are transferable to higher paying jobs within the formal economy. The migrant domestic worker confronts unique barriers, in that she is all too often an individual with no advocate, no avenues for the rectification of rights violations, and no voice.

In this chapter, we explore some of the consequences that this perfect storm has for migrant domestic workers. For far too many of these workers, the work is arduous, the pay minimal, and the workplace abuses ever present, while options, regulations, and protections are few and far between. Within this context, there is a clear space for practitioners such as social workers to push for improving the terms of employment as well as the everyday working conditions confronting migrant domestic workers across the globe.

CONTEXT: MIGRANT DOMESTIC WORK AND THE GLOBAL GENDER EQUALITY MOVEMENT

In the name of fairness and gender equity, there is an ever-growing global chorus demanding that women and girls become more educated while also being afforded enhanced opportunities to participate in the formal economy. And while suggesting that females not be educated or encouraged to participate in the formal labor market is not part of any national or international agenda, it also must be recognized that policies aimed at educating and training females do not include them becoming domestic workers, in spite of increasing demand for such workers.

A strident commitment to enhancing the educational and economic opportunities for all females is evidenced in part by the adoption and support of the Millennium Development Goals (MDGs) and the Sustainable Development Goals (SDGs). These goals specifically target enhancing education and employment opportunities for all females, as well as eradicating gender inequities. In addition, there also are a number of nations (e.g., Brazil [cf., Lessa and Rocha, 2012], India, and Morocco) that have adopted incentives for achieving national commitments to gender equity, improving the educational opportunities for girls, and increasing formal employment opportunities for all females. These policies are enacted, in part, because there are ample data supporting the contention that it is the educational and economic conditions of females that best reflect the overall well-being of a nation (e.g., Hill and King, 1995; Klasen, 2002; LeVine, LeVine, and Schnell, 2001). In addition, increasing the likelihood that children will have positive health, social, and educational outcomes is tied to women receiving basic education and being able to economically care for their families, especially their children.

At the same time that these policies are being implemented, countries in all regions of the world are experiencing the aging of their populations as well as a growing number of persons living with chronic diseases and disabilities. In addition, the economies of many migrant-sending regions (e.g., Southeast Asia, Central America) have been unable to create enough local job opportunities, particularly for women (UN Women, 2013). While at the same time in migrant-receiving locales, shifting family structures, including educated female heads-of-household joining the workforce coupled with changes in job and work patterns in the increasingly globalized and technology-driven labor markets, have led to a global decline in the number of multigenerational households. This decline has rendered fewer families able to provide requisite care to dependent kin. Finally, in tandem with these demographic changes, we are witnessing an overall increase in wages, hence disposable income, for large segments of the world's population, with the greatest absolute rate increases registering in developing countries. Taken all together, these conditions have produced a perfect storm of increasing demand for migrant domestic workers to provide care along side a decreasing supply of local women able or willing to perform this work in their home countries.

Shaped by socially embedded views of gender roles and responsibilities, caretaking and domestic work are still seen as the segments of familial responsibilities that belong almost exclusively to females (Hochschild, 1997; Hochschild and Machung, 2012). Even if women in low- and middle-income countries are employed within the formal economy, all too often their wages are insufficient to provide the needed basic income for their families *and* the additional resources required to purchase kin care. Together, this context is likely to mean that women living in developing and middle-income countries who enter the formal labor market will be required to work a second and even third shift to meet the familial needs that are deemed their responsibility, or redistribute their care burden to other kin, most likely other females in the family (Ehrenreich and Hochschild, 2002). However, if familial resources allow, another caregiver—most likely a female—will be hired to take over or share the care responsibility. And in ever increasing numbers within developed, middle-income, *and* low-income countries, the latter is very often taken on by migrant domestic workers (UN Women, 2013).

While terms and conditions of migrant domestic work do vary across countries, this work is all too often characterized by abhorrently low pay, precarious living and working conditions, and the requirement that workers live away from their countries, family, and culture. Given this context, who does this work? And who buys it?

Domestic Work and Migrant Workers

The demographic transformation of a society presents challenges to the ways we think about and define domestic work. When dependent populations become significantly more numerous and represent an ever-growing portion of the total population, what is required is a broader definition of domestic work reflecting increasing and evolving personal care needs. Amidst various definitions of domestic work set forth by scholars, policymakers, and practitioners (e.g., Jenkins and O'Leary, 1995; Parreñas, 2001; Ramirez-Machado, 2003), domestic work is, by international convention, defined as, "…work [that is] performed in or for a household or households…" and includes "…tasks such as cleaning the house, cooking, washing and ironing clothes, taking care of children or elderly or sick members of a family…" and other home-based care tasks for one or multiple households which is or are not the worker's own (International Labor Organization [ILO], 2011). A *migrant* domestic worker, therefore, is a domestic worker, "…who cross[es] borders in search of decent work and sustainable livelihoods" (UN Women, 2013, p. 4). Across the globe, most migrant domestic workers are women seeking jobs in the care economy—particularly in migrant domestic workers' niche market of "cheap" home-based care (UN Women, 2013).

The current definitions of domestic work require an expanded conception. Today, in addition to performing the traditional work of household chores and tasks, domestic work now more than ever is likely to include providing personal care to dependent members of a household. Domestic work has become more than performing tasks such as cooking and cleaning. The domestic worker is now required to take on ever increasing responsibilities for the personal and even medical care needs (e.g., washing, toileting, feeding, medicating) of the dependent members of a household. In other words, the domestic worker has evolved from an assistant charged with the tasks of running a household (e.g., laundry, some child care/babysitting, cooking, cleaning) into a nursing and personal care assistant domestic care worker.

A Demographic Snapshot

In 2013, the International Labor Organization (ILO) estimated that there were approximately 53 million domestic workers across the world, 83 percent, or 44 million, of whom are female (ILO, 2013a). Between 1995 and 2010, there was an approximately 19 percent growth in the number of domestic workers worldwide, rising from 33 million domestic workers in 1995 to 54 million in 2010 (ILO, 2013a). Domestic workers account for about 12.2 percent of all employed girls aged 15-17 (ILO, 2013a). Although limitations in current data render it impossible to estimate the exact share of migrant domestic workers who are female, it is known that females are significantly overrepresented among that group of laborers (ILO, 2013a).

The greatest increase in demand for domestic workers registers in Asia and the Pacific on the one hand, and Latin America and the Caribbean on the other (ILO, 2013a)—two regions that traditionally have been exporters of domestic workers. This shift in demand, and evolving trend, is attributable to two conditions: *i*) within those areas, general regional economic growth and an increase in household incomes have yielded increasing levels of disposable income thus allowing more people to purchase household care; *ii*) there is an increase in demand for domestic workers because of the care void created by increasing numbers and per cents of educated females entering the formal economy (ILO, 2013a).

In many industrialized countries, it is poor migrant women who hold jobs as domestic workers (ILO, 2013a). In Europe, the countries with the largest number of domestic workers are Spain, Italy, and France (ILO, 2013a). In Italy, for example, approximately 28 percent of female migrant workers are domestic workers in private households; in France that percent is about twenty-one (ILO, 2013a). Meanwhile, in spite of problematic economic conditions, Spain has seen a dramatic increase in its number of domestic workers, rising from about 335,000 in 1995 to around 747,000 in 2010 (ILO, 2013a) with data documenting that more than one-third of female migrant workers employed as domestic workers. Sending countries to Spain are most likely to be other Spanish-speaking countries from Latin America (ILO, 2013a). For example, about one-third of migrant domestic workers in Spain are from Ecuador and slightly more than 10 percent are from Colombia (ILO, 2013a).

In sub-Saharan Africa, many nations are exporters of female domestic workers but they also have a fair amount of internal migration of such workers. Internally, domestic workers tend to move from rural to urban areas thus rendering the hiring of domestic workers in many sub-Saharan countries an urban phenomenon (ILO, 2013a). That is, in addition to the out of country migration from sub-Saharan nations, many young girls in countries from that region are sent to live in other parts of their home country in order to serve wealthier family members, or to labor in the homes of people who can afford to feed, house, and minimally pay young girls (ILO, 2013a). South Africa, for example, has the largest number of domestic workers in sub-Saharan Africa, with the majority of them found in and around metropolitan areas of Durban, Johannesburg, and Pretoria (ILO, 2013a). As both urban populations and economic growth continue to expand in this region, the demand for domestic workers providing care in the home will only increase. This demand is exacerbated by increasing life expectancy, particularly among groups such as the urban middle class and people living with once life-threatening diseases (e.g., HIV/AIDS) (African Development Bank, 2011; Mayosi et al., 2009).

With the vast number of poor women laboring in domestic work, the question facing each of us as we go foreword is: will the supply of migrant domestic workers be enough to meet global and local demand?

Supply and Demand

Although exact projections are difficult to calculate because of the informal characteristic of this work, the need for migrant domestic workers will continue well into the mid- and late twenty-first century (e.g., Shutes, 2011). In particular, the demand for domestic care jobs is anticipated to dramatically increase between now and 2050, due to a variety of demographic and economic factors. For example, in 1950 approximately 8 percent of the global population was 65 years of age and older; in 2011 that percent was about 11, and in 2050 that percent is projected to be 16. Another way to think about this is that between 1950 and 2005, overall global life expectancy rose from 47 to 69 years, with females outliving men (Pew Research Center, 2014). And while there is great variation within and among regions of the world (e.g., life expectancy in Middle Africa is 51 years compared to New Zealand and Australia were it is 84), it is projected that for most regions, life expectancy will soon be 70 years for females and 67 for men (Pew Research Center, 2014).

As people age, they are likely to require assistance with activities of daily life. These data illustrate why an expansion of the definition of domestic work must be made to include basic care work. This latter type of work involves personal assistance (e.g., bathing and toileting) as well as assistance with other activities of daily living (e.g., cooking, grooming, dressing, walking). This is work that is less than skilled medical care and more than just assisting in the maintenance of a household.

Changes in life expectancy are not the only factors that are and will continue to be drivers of increasing demand for migrant domestic workers. In developed and developing countries, we have witnessed a growing number of females accessing education and participating in the paid formal economy (Ortiz and Cummins, 2013; World Bank, 2011). Despite societal norms, more females are unwilling or unable to provide unpaid domestic care to family members, contributing to global reductions in the number of multigenerational households (Sweeting, Bhaskar, Benzeval, Popham, and Hunt, 2014) while also causing a familial care crisis (Lunenfeld and Stratton, 2013; Wagner and Brath, 2012). As wages and household incomes increase in many parts of the world, some females are given the option of outsourcing familial and care responsibilities. This trend has yielded the rising demand for "cheap" domestic and household help, especially in the area of childcare and eldercare. It is female migrant domestic workers from poor areas of the world who are most likely to meet at least a significant portion of that increasing demand.

Other factors driving the demand for migrant domestic workers who provide care include a continuing rise in the number of non-elderly people living with chronic conditions and an increase in non-communicable diseases across populations. Diabetes, once a disease of the

"West," is now in every country. Globally, 285 million people have Type II diabetes and by 2030 that number is projected to be 438 million, with two-thirds or 292 million of these people living in low- and middle income- countries (Hu, 2011). Disability is also a factor. Measuring disability and its prevalence can be more difficult than identifying and counting the elderly or the young. But as a 2011 report on the prevalence of disability from the World Health Organization and the World Bank (WHO, 2011) notes, including children, over a billion people (or approximately 15% of the world's population) are estimated to be living with a disability. Of those living with a disability, it is estimated that 110 (2.2%) to 190 (3.8%) million experienced significant difficulties in functioning.

These prevalence estimates are higher than previously found, which indicates an increasing rate of people living with disabilities. While not all persons with disabilities will require assistance with daily activities, many will. People with severe disabilities require significant assistance in order to carry out personal care and hygiene as well as other basic activities of daily life. As such, people living with illnesses and physical disabilities often require both labor-intensive assistance with daily life activities and low-skill, low-tech medical care on a daily basis; the more assistance needed, the more labor necessary to provide it. Therefore, in order to meet the current and emerging global health care needs, what is required is a large workforce that is trained in semi-skilled care provision. What we are beginning to see that the people most likely to provide the required essential care and assistance are domestic workers, or the unskilled. These workers are most often migrant female workers (Ehrenreich and Hochschild, 2002; United Nations Office of the High Commissioner for Human Rights [OHCHR], 2010; Walsh and Shutes, 2013; Shutes, 2011).

At the same time that demand for migrant domestic workers who provide care is increasing, supply will be decreasing. The dwindling supply of migrant domestic workers is, in part, attributed to the declining ratio of people aged 15-64 to people aged 65 and older (Organization for Economic Cooperation and Development [OECD], 2009). This declining ratio, attributable to decreasing birth rates as well as the aging of the population, means there will be fewer familial or employable able-bodied non-elderly persons to care for the elderly and the disabled. Put more succinctly, since 1970, the youth-dependency ratio has been declining worldwide while the over-65 dependency ratio has been rising (Mirkin and Weinberger, 2001). The Republic of Korea, for instance, experienced a rapid fertility decline after 1970, and the total dependency ratio fell to an unusually low level of 39 by 2000 (Mirkin and Weinberger, 2001). The overall ratio will not begin to rise appreciably until after 2015, but then is projected to rapidly increase, due to an aging population. Kenya, on the other hand, shows an extremely high child-dependency ratio, with a total dependency ratio of 115 in 1980 (Mirkin and Weinberger, 2001). Kenya had one of the highest levels of fertility in the world, estimated at 8.1 children per woman during the period 1960 to 1980, before beginning a rapid fertility decline, which is projected to continue. But by 2000, Kenya's under-15 and over-65 ratios were similar to those seen in the Republic of Korea 30 years earlier.

This decreasing supply of domestic workers is also due in part to females' greater participation in the formal economy and the push for all women and girls to be educated and join the formal workforce. At the same time that there are large quantities of global resources allocated into programs aimed at improving the opportunities and lives of females, the dependent members of families, be they the very young, the non-elderly disabled, or the elderly, are increasing in number. One consequence of this is that females within families are facing conflicting choices. If females are to remain in school, enter the formal economy, and be afforded more equity than ever before, the unremunerated familial work traditionally done by females will need to be shared by all in the family—including males. If that does not occur, the family will be required to purchase those services. That is, families will need to hire non-familial females to take on the domestic and care work that was once performed for free by females within the family. Assuming that efforts to educate and formally employ females are successful, the hiring of non-familial females to provide domestic and care work will be occurring at the same time that the pool of available workers will be decreasing. Put more succinctly, as attaining the targets of the SDGs becomes a reality, the shortage of migrant domestic workers will become exacerbated as the supply of such workers dissipates and demand for them increases.

According to traditional economic theory, both the wages for and supply of migrant domestic workers will increase, i.e., there will be more women willing to do those jobs—jobs, which, in theory, *should* pay well and provide secure employment. However, if the lessons from female-dominated occupations within developed countries are at all applicable, then such basic economic theory will not translate as predicted. For example, in the developed world, nursing shortages are endemic, be they nurses on the front-line or those teaching in colleges and universities. Yet wages for clinic nurses and nursing faculty have been stagnant or very slow to rise. Furthermore, developed countries have long faced a labor shortage of paraprofessional healthcare workers, i.e., those who provide personal care and assistance with daily living to the disabled and the elderly (Nelson, 2012). Yet for these jobs, wages remain very low, in spite of high and increasing demand for such workers and static or dwindling supply. What wage and benefit increases have occurred are far from what is predicted by simple demand and supply theories of economics. And the dearth of providers continues to hold steady.

In short, the demand curve is neither triggering an increase in wages nor an increase in the supply of such workers. Far too many native-born females are not interested in paraprofessional jobs—the hours are too long, the wages too low, the work too hard. In an attempt to meet current short-term demand, countries have turned to migrant care workers, often under-employing them while also underpaying them. These migrant workers are neither a trigger nor a cause for the low wages paid to paraprofessionals; rather they are seen as a solution for filling the care gap. These workers are migrants with no voice and few powerful advocates. While many of these underemployed workers are found in hospitals, nursing homes, care centers, and community organizations, most migrant domestic workers secure employment in private homes. It is these migrant domestic care workers that are the lowest paid, least protected, and most vulnerable to economic, social, physical, and psychological abuse.

Working Conditions and Challenges of Migrant Domestic Workers

Although the terms and conditions of migrant domestic work vary widely across and even within countries, various characteristics are common across the globe. After being female, earning poverty level wages is their most common denominator. It is female migrants who are the most likely to be underpaid and work uncompensated hours while at the same time incurring the greatest debts for work-related costs such as uniforms, on-site living quarters, and fees to job placement agencies (Van Hooren, 2012). Across the world, there are dauntingly few examples where domestic workers are not earning below, often well below, national minimum wages. When comparing the wages of local domestic workers to those of migrant domestic workers, the gap is alarming; migrant domestic workers earn significantly less than even the lowest paid local domestic workers. In addition, migrant domestic workers are particularly vulnerable to economic exploitation, due to their limited bargaining power and barriers such as precarious documentation status (OHCHR, 2010).

Time inflictions are another common problem that most migrant domestic workers endure. Specific hours and workdays are often not guaranteed nor are they clearly stipulated. Work schedules are likely to be unpredictable and out of workers' control. Unpredictability runs the gamut and ranges from a regular workweek of 40 hours with some additional hours added on as needed, to an erratic schedule of irregular hours, to on-call hours only, to numerous consecutive days worked with no time off, to time off cancelled without notice (Ehrenreich and Hochschild, 2002; Parreñas, 2001). These time intrusions are especially burdensome for live-in migrant domestic workers. However, even in arrangements in which the worker does not live-in, time intrusions are problematic, especially in urban areas, where non-live-in domestic workers often endure gruelingly long commutes via multiple modes of transportation (Parreñas, 2001).

Like schedules, living conditions for domestic workers who reside in the home of their employers vary widely. Such arrangements include living in private lockable rooms, sleeping areas in a communal living space, and living in unsafe and inadequate quarters, some of which may be makeshift spaces exposed to the elements (Cohen-Mansfield et al., 2013). Live-in arrangements are particularly notorious for extremely low pay, significant time impositions, and high rates of physical and sexual abuse (Parreñas, 2001; OHCHR, 2010). Due to migrants' limited bargaining power and exacerbated vulnerability attributable to precarious documentation status and language barriers, it is migrants and not local domestic workers who are more likely to accept live-in arrangements.

More often than not, migrant domestic workers are not compensated for working overtime, a consequence of the lack of boundaries between employees' work and personal time (Cohen-Mansfield et al., 2013; Parreñas, 2001). The blurring of work/life boundaries holds especially true in live-in arrangements, where domestic workers are all too often expected to constantly remain on-call, even on days off (Cohen-Mansfield et al., 2013).

Due to long hours of hard labor and minimal rest, migrant domestic workers are likely to endure overexertion and fatigue (Cohen-Mansfield et al., 2013). Common health complications include chronic back pain due to standing and performing manual labor for extended periods of time and respiratory problems attributable to inhaling fumes from cleaning products (Malhotra et al., 2013; Smith, 2011). Migrant domestic workers also are likely to endure untreated mental health complications (e.g., anxiety, stress, and depression) (Lau, Cheng, Chow, Ungvari, and Leung, 2009; Sales and Santana, 2003; Santana, Loomis, and Newman, 2001). Furthermore, many of these workers report feeling secluded from the outside world. They work in "double isolation," laboring in homes with minimal human contact apart from their employers while also experiencing social isolation outside of work due to language barriers, cultural differences, and precarious documentation status (Cohen-Mansfield et al., 2013; OHCHR, 2010). In extreme cases of isolation, workers are kept in slavery-like conditions—situations that may be linked to human trafficking (OHCHR, 2010).

An equally exploitative scenario is the *kafala* (sponsorship) system prevalent in the Gulf region. This system strips workers of all rights and documentation, rendering the worker legally bound and economically indebted to her employer, the "sponsor" (Pande, 2013).

For those migrant domestic workers who provide personal caregiving to members of the household, unsafe work conditions are of particular concern. In addition to the lack of safety equipment, more often than not, domestic workers do not receive formal training on safety precautions of working with clients living with illness or disease. Depending on the condition, this may render these workers unprotected and at a significant risk for contracting illness (Malhotra et al., 2013). As a condition of employment, employers may require domestic workers to present evidence of negative health tests for illnesses such as tuberculosis or HIV (Human Rights Watch, 2011). However, due to power dynamics between the worker and her employer, domestic workers are often unable to require the same information from employers.

It is not surprising that given the work terms and conditions that migrant domestic workers endure, they have limited opportunities for job advancement or securing gainful employment within the formal economy. Opportunities for obtaining professional training (e.g., paraprofessional or childcare training) or participating in certification programs (e.g., standardized domestic worker certification) are impeded by barriers such as literacy level, fluency in the local language, and documentation status (Ehrenreich and Hochschild, 2002; Cohen-Mansfield et al., 2013). At the same time, such opportunities are few and far between in many countries and communities. Enhanced training for and professionalization of care work would enhance domestic workers' expertise and, in turn, improve the quality of direct and indirect care provided. However, given the low wages and the common view in host countries that migrant domestic workers exist as a "cheap and expendable" labor force (Ogaya, 2004), it is reasonable to assume that most employers and third-party agencies would be unwilling to pay the costs associated with such training, as there appears to be no economic advantage or incentive for incurring such costs. Migrant domestic workers, meanwhile, are likely not to know about such programs when they exist, due in part to these workers' social isolation. And even if they were to know about the availability of such opportunities, they lack the requisite time and economic resources required to participate in them.

Policy Responses

Given the increasing demand, decreasing supply, and conflicting pressures on women when it comes to care work, education, and paid employment, policy responses to a complicated and growing global problem are a concern. With the exception of selected grassroots and collective organizations that advocate for migrant domestic workers while also attempting to secure adequate employment terms and conditions on their behalf (e.g., National Domestic Workers Alliance), the work relationships in which these women find themselves tend to be almost completely dictated by employers and third-party intermediaries (ILO, 2013b; OHCHR, 2010; Parreñas, 2001). Although few select studies report that for some women domestic work can be both a gateway into the formal labor market and a tool of economic independence (e.g., Sugita, 2010), overwhelming evidence suggests that domestic work, particularly for migrant women, is deeply exploitative (e.g., Ehrenreich and Hochschild, 2002; Human Rights Watch, 2011; ILO 2013a; Ramirez-Machado, 2013).

The precarious and oftentimes dangerous working conditions that migrant domestic workers endure are largely due to their exclusion from labor laws and regulations as well as the lack of enforcement where such laws exist. The absence of contracts pervades migrant domestic work, and even when work agreements are in place, they are oftentimes informal, unenforceable, and do not discuss a worker's rights (Cohen-Mansfield et al., 2013; OHCHR, 2010; Parreñas, 2001). Moreover, in most countries, domestic work is not acknowledged as "real work" by the law, thus rendering it unregulated (Cohen-Mansfield et al., 2013; OHCHR, 2010). Therefore, domestic workers in general often are not covered by any generic and basic employment protections simply because they are not recognized as members of the workforce (Cohen-Mansfield et al., 2013; OHCHR, 2010). Within this context of no or minimal legal protection, migrant domestic workers are unlikely to seek restitution or retribution for exploitation or employer wrongdoing nor are they likely to pursue new employment for fear of losing their current work, being deported, or enduring physical harm (Parreñas, 2001; Ramirez-Machado, 2003).

This is not to say that formal protection of domestic workers is nonexistent. However, even in countries such as Canada or Singapore where formal regulation of domestic work is in place (e.g., in the form of basic wages, paid holidays, and guaranteed sick leave), these benefits are not always provided in full (Cohen-Mansfield, Garms-Homolová, and Bentwich, 2013). Ensuring that workers enjoy codified and guaranteed benefits and protections requires strict and consistent enforcement of penalties when employers violate the parameters of protective legislation. Yet across the globe, we see employers' unwillingness to comply with laws and officials ignoring legal infractions or, at most, minimally punishing those who violate the laws. This situation is exacerbated when workers are undocumented or prevented from having access to their passports or their home country's representatives within the host country. This context coupled with migrant domestic workers' unawareness of their own rights and legal protections contribute to the lack of enforcing worker protections even where they are codified.

Discussion and Recommendations for Practice

Every day, tens of millions of female migrant domestic workers across the globe wake up and find themselves employed in dangerous, underpaid, and unprotected jobs. Given the growing demand for domestic workers who provide personal assistance and care, the conditions and terms of work that domestic workers endure are, and will continue to be, issues of inherent concern for social workers and practitioners in other helping professions (Harrison and Melville, 2009). Social workers often are involved in working with individuals or very small groups, providing to those persons advocacy, support, services, or relief. While micro-level assistance is critical and not to be disregarded, global issues such as migrant domestic work and, more broadly, the global care chain, require practitioners to stretch beyond micro-level interventions in order to engage in and lobby for a broader action and change. As such, issues of migration and labor call for larger-scale efforts at national and international policy levels—efforts that should be led by practitioners who understand the day-to-day realities that these women live. Social workers are well positioned to answer this call, given their training on the micro, meso, and macro layers of human well-being (Green and McDermott, 2010). And while no doubt globalization has exacerbated many of the inequities that impact women's livelihoods, it also has opened the door for practitioners to join forces across borders, advocating for (and alongside) vulnerable populations (Harrison and Melville, 2009, p.79). Today, more than ever, social workers have access to tools and resources that encourage and support broad-based social mobilization, lobbying efforts, and international dialogue and information exchange (Harrison and Melville, 2009).

When working for and with migrant domestic workers to secure large-scale change, many critical areas present an opportunity to deliver tangible improvements. One of the most pressing is advocating for enforceable employment contacts applicable to this labor sector. Previous data illustrate two salient points. First, labor protections, when they exist at all, are far and few between. Second, where labor protections do exist, enforcement is meager and ineffective. Through lobbying and direct policy efforts as well as working in a collaborative interdisciplinary context, social workers are in a strong position to promote employment contacts designed to protect migrant domestic workers economically, socially, politically, culturally, and sexually. Employment contracts must ensure that a migrant domestic worker is not left without resources, rights, or options. At the same time, there must be assurances that the resources and infrastructure required to enforce those contracts are solidly in place. No contract is of any value unless it is accompanied by a robust commitment to fully enforce the civil and criminal penalties and consequences associated with violating the terms of the contract. As such, advocates must ensure that work contracts and terms of employment carry stringent enforcement clauses. Employment contracts or models of employment that offer little protection and lack strong enforcement mechanisms inherently support the employer, thus reinforcing the invisibility of the employee and discounting her rights and protections. Finally, a requisite stipulation in all contracts must be protections from deportation.

Practitioners also must begin to design models of domestic work that offer economic protections to this female-dominated labor sector. These protections are especially important because domestic workers—particularly migrants—are among the first to be relieved of their duties or fired when the economic conditions of the employer-family change. Domestic workers are essential but disposable and, if need be, easily replaceable. This is particularly true of migrant workers because they have little opportunity or leverage to seek retribution for mistreatment. When one set of domestic workers is fired due to economic exigencies another group can, and will be, hired when there is an economic resurgence. Currently, practitioners are exploring new models of domestic work such as collective and cooperative domestic worker enterprises (Cheney, Santa Cruz, Peredo, and Nazareno, 2014; ILO, 2013b; Roulstone and Hwang, 2015). However, more research on such alternative employment models is needed in order to evaluate their impact and viability.

Practitioners, advocates, and researchers alike must also take on the responsibility of providing a conceptual shift in how domestic work and migrant domestic workers are seen. Specifically, it is imperative to guarantee that care and domestic work are no longer seen in a paternalistic or family-like model. Instead of recognizing the human and economic impact of the work and workers, all too often the nomenclature of domestic and care work involves talking about the work as an act of love and the workers being like familial maternal figures (UN Women, 2015). Rather than allow employers to speak of these workers as "part of the family," advocates must begin referring to domestic workers in professional terms that reflect a more formal model of employer-employee relations. It is the "like family" model that allows for and exacerbates time infringements, low pay, exploitation, erratic schedules, and long arduous hours that are far beyond any reasonable call to duty.

Finally, as we sought to demonstrate in this chapter, domestic work, as we know it today, requires that workers in addition to providing traditional household help also must perform unskilled medically driven care and assistance with daily activities. Given that the need for such care will only increase with current demographic shifts, we posit a change in terminology. Rather than domestic work and domestic worker we suggest a more accurate reflection of the realities of this employment are the terms *domestic and care work* and *domestic and care worker*. Going foreword in academic and policy arenas, this expanded definition and change in terminology is required because of the changing demographics, family needs, and realities of the work performed by this labor sector.

CONCLUSION

As long as the global commitment to increasing voice, agency, and power among females vis-à-vis enhanced access to educational and economic opportunities is the norm, it is poor females from poor areas of the world—the left behind women and girls—that are the most likely to become migrant domestic workers. These females are the people least likely to reap benefits from global and national policies aimed at diminishing inequity and inequality. They also are least apt to significantly partake in any increased access to educational and economic opportunities. However, they will provide needed domestic care, albeit not fully meeting demand, most likely in highly exploitative jobs that remain outside of the regulatory and legal reaches of authorities. This situation necessitates advocacy and intervention from practitioners, as without it, most female migrant domestic workers will not be protected from an assortment of abuses.

REFERENCES

African Development Bank. (2011). *The middle of the pyramid: Dynamics of the middle class in Africa*. Abidjan: African Development Bank.

Agree, E. M. (2014). The potential for technology to enhance independence for those aging with a disability. *Disability and Health Journal*, 7(1), S33-S39.

Cheney, G., Santa Cruz, I., Peredo, A. M., and Nazareno, E. (2014). Worker cooperatives as an organizational alternative: Challenges, achievements and promise in business governance and ownership. *Organization*, 21(5), 591-603.

Cohen-Mansfield, J., Garms-Homolová, V., and Bentwich, M. (2013). Migrant home attendants: Regulation and practice in seven countries. *American Journal of Public Health*, 103(12), e30-e39.

Ehrenreich, B., and Hochschild, A. R. (2002). *Global woman: Nannies, maids, and sex workers in the new economy*. New York: Metropolitan Books.

Green, D., and McDermott, F. (2010). Social work from inside and between complex systems: Perspectives on person-in-environment for today's social work. *British Journal of Social Work*, 40(8), 2414-2430.

Harrison, G., and Melville, R. (2009). *Rethinking social work in a global world*. London: Palgrave Macmillan.

Hill, M. A., and King, E. (1995). Women's education and economic well-being. *Feminist Economics*, 1(2), 21-46.

Hochschild, A. (1997). The time bind. *Working US*, 1(2), 21-29.

Hochschild, A., and Machung, A. (2012). *The second shift: Working families and the revolution at home*. New York: Penguin.

Hu, F. B. (2011). Globalization of diabetes: The role of diet, lifestyle, and genes. *Diabetes Care*, 34(6), 1249-1257.

Human Rights Watch. (2011). *"They deceived us at every step": Abuse of Cambodian domestic workers migrating to Malaysia*. New York: Human Rights Watch.

International Labor Organization (ILO). (2013a). *Domestic workers across the world: Global and regional statistics and the extent of legal protection*. Geneva: International Labor Organization (ILO).

International Labor Organization (ILO). (2013b). *Cooperatives offer migrant workers options for better lives*. Geneva: International Labor Organization (ILO).

International Labor Organization (ILO). (2011). *Domestic workers convention*. (ILO Convention No. 189). Geneva: International Labor Organization (ILO).

Jenkins, S. P., and O'Leary, N. C. (1995). Modeling domestic work time. *Journal of Population Economics*, 8(3), 265-279.

Klasen, S. (2002). Low schooling for girls, slower growth for all? Cross-country evidence on the effect of gender inequality in education on economic development. *The World Bank Economic Review*, 16(3), 345-373.

Lau, P. W., Cheng, J. G., Chow, D. L., Ungvari, G. S., and Leung, C. M. (2009). Acute psychiatric disorders in foreign domestic workers in Hong Kong: A pilot study. *International Journal of Social Psychiatry*, 55(6), 569-576.

Lessa, I., and Rocha, C. (2012). Food security and gender mainstreaming: Possibilities for social transformation in Brazil. *International Social Work*, 55(3), 337-352.

LeVine, R., LeVine, S., and Schnell, B. (2001). "Improve the women": Mass schooling, female literacy, and worldwide social change. *Harvard Educational Review*, 71(1), 1-51.

Lunenfeld, B., and Stratton, P. (2013). The clinical consequences of an ageing world and preventive strategies. *Best Practice and Research Clinical Obstetrics and Gynecology*, 27(5), 643-659.

Malhotra, R., Arambepola, C., Tarun, S., de Silva, V., Kishore, J., and Østbye, T. (2013). Health issues of female foreign domestic workers: a systematic review of the scientific and gray literature. *International Journal of Occupational and Environmental Health*, 19(4), 261-277.

Mayosi, B. M., Flisher, A. J., Lalloo, U. G., Sitas, F., Tollman, S. M., and Bradshaw, D. (2009). The burden of non-communicable diseases in South Africa. *The Lancet*, 374(9693), 934-947.

Mirkin, B. and Weinberger, M. B. (2001). The demography of population ageing. *UN Population Bulletin*, 42/43, 41-48.

National Institute on Aging. (2011). *Global health and aging*. Bethesda, MD: National Institute on Aging.

Nelson, R. (2012). Combating global health worker shortages. *The American Journal of Nursing*, 112(12), 17-18.

Ogaya, C. (2004). Filipino domestic workers and the creation of new subjectivities. *Asian and Pacific Migration Journal*, 13(3), 381-404.

Organization for Economic Cooperation and Development (OECD). 2009. *Promoting pro-poor growth: Employment.* Paris: Organization for Economic Cooperation and Development (OECD).

Ortiz, I., and Cummins, M. (2013). *The age of austerity: A review of public expenditures and adjustment measures in 181 countries*. Geneva: International Labor Organization (ILO).

Pande, A. (2013). "The paper that you have in your hand is my freedom": Migrant domestic work and the sponsorship (Kafala) system in Lebanon. *International Migration Review*, 47(2), 414-441.

Parreñas, R. S. (2001). *Servants of globalization: Women, migration and domestic work*. Palo Alto, CA: Stanford University Press.

Pew Research Center. (2014). *Attitudes about aging: A global perspective.* Washington, D.C.: Pew Research Center.

Ramirez-Machado, J. M. (2003). *Domestic work, conditions of work and employment: A legal perspective.* Geneva: International Labor Organization (ILO).

Roulstone, A., and Hwang, S. K. (2015). Disabled people, choices and collective organisation: Examining the potential of cooperatives in future social support. *Disability and Society*, 30(6), 849-864.

Rubinow, I. M. (1906). The problem of domestic service. *The Journal of Political Economy*, 14(8), 502-519.

Sales, E. C., and Santana, V. S. (2003). Depressive and anxiety symptoms among housemaids. *American Journal of Industrial Medicine*, 44(6), 685-691.

Santana, V. S., Loomis, D. P., and Newman, B. (2001). Housework, paid work and psychiatric symptoms. *Revista de Saúde Pública*, 35(1), 16-22.

Shutes, I. (2011). *Social care for older people and demand for migrant workers.* Oxford: The Migration Observatory, Centre on Migration, Policy and Society, Oxford University.

Smith, P. R. (2011). The pitfalls of home: Protecting the health and safety of paid domestic workers. *Canadian Journal of Women and the Law*, 23(1), 309-339.

Sugita, S. (2010). Social care and women's labor participation in Lebanon. *Al-Raida*, 128, 31-37.

Sweeting, H., Bhaskar, A., Benzeval, M., Popham, F., and Hunt, K. (2014). Changing gender roles and attitudes and their implications for well-being around the new millennium. *Social Psychiatry and Psychiatric Epidemiology*, 49(5), 791-809.

UN Women. (2015). *Transforming economies, realizing rights: Progress of the world's women report 2015-2016*. New York: UN Women.

UN Women. (2013). *Contributions of migrant domestic workers to sustainable development.* Bangkok: UN Women.

United Nations Office of the High Commissioner for Human Rights (OHCHR). (2010). *Rights of migrant domestic workers in Europe.* Geneva: OHCHR.

Van Hooren, F. J. (2012). Varieties of migrant care work: Comparing patterns of migrant labour in social care. *Journal of European Social Policy*, 22(2), 133-147.

Wagner, K. H., and Brath, H. (2012). A global view on the development of non communicable diseases. *Preventive Medicine*, 54, S38-S41.

Walsh, K. and Shutes, I. (2013). Care relationships, quality of care, and migrant workers caring for older people. *Ageing and Society*, 33(3), 393-420.

World Bank (2011). *World Development Report 2012: Gender Equality and Development*. Washington, D.C.: World Bank.

World Health Organization (WHO). (2011). *World report on disability*. Geneva: World Health Organization (WHO).

In: Migrant Workers
Editors: Qingwen Xu and Lucy P. Jordan
ISBN: 978-1-63485-272-2

Chapter 3

SOCIAL SUPPORT, ACCULTURATION, AND FINANCIAL STABILITY AMONG MEXICAN ECONOMIC MIGRANTS

Aimee Hilado[1,*], Philip Young Hong[2], Maria Vidal de Haymes[2] and Marta Lundy[2]
[1]Social Work Program, Northeastern Illinois University, Chicago, IL, US
[2]School of Social Work, Loyola University, Chicago, IL, US

ABSTRACT

The pursuit of economic opportunities is one major factor behind migration patterns worldwide. Attempting to escape excruciating hardships, economic migrants are met with the need to achieve stability and advancement through employment as they acculturate to the norms of their new society. In this context, social support networks become critical to economic advancement and adjustment for new immigrants. These networks are social relationships that afford both emotional and material resources that facilitate a number of benefits beyond success in finding a job. Literature suggests that migrants accessing social support networks report a greater sense of self-efficacy, greater interpersonal competencies, and enhanced acculturation adjustment supporting the formation and internalization of a social identity that aligns with their new community. Moreover, migrants accessing informal, less structured social support systems showed greater difficulty in economic adaptation and higher levels of psychological distress. This chapter provides an overview of the interconnections between social support, economic pursuit, and economic stability among migrant populations. Acculturation and economic adaptation theories are presented as well as a thorough discussion of social support structures that both promote and inhibit adjustment and economic stability among migrant populations. Using findings from a study involving 125 Mexican-born adults who migrated to Chicago, Illinois, we provide empirical evidence showing greater economic stability and acculturation levels among those participants receiving social support resources. Practice and policy implications are included, building on the study findings. Specifically, we discuss the value of community-based networks and economic stability, and suggest directions for future research.

* Corresponding author: Aimee Hilado, Social Work Program, Northeastern Illinois University, 5500 North St. Louis Avenue, Chicago, IL 60625, US. Email: a-hiladovillalpando3@neiu. edu.

INTRODUCTION

The pursuit of economic opportunities is a major factor behind migration patterns worldwide. For those whose primary reason for migration is economic pursuit—economic migrants—are met with a dual charge to achieve financial stability and advancement through employment while acculturating to the norms of their new society. Social support networks have been shown to be a critical factor in supporting economic advancement and adjustment for migrant workers. These networks are social relationships that afford both emotional and material resources to facilitate success in finding a job. Network members not only share information on job openings to new arrivals (Calvo-Armengol and Jackson, 2004) but also provide referrals to employers (Montgomery, 1991; Dustmann, Glitz and Schöenberg, 2011), subsequently leading to successful job offers (Goel and Lang, 2009).

The benefits of social support networks extend beyond the job search and are associated with positive health and wellbeing outcomes including lower stress levels throughout the immigration process, improved mental health symptoms to buffer/mediate against adjustment distress, and increased help-seeking behaviors that promote overall health (Berkman, 1984; Cohen, and Wills, 1985; Dalgard and Thapa, 2007; Lin, Ensel, Simeone, and Kuo, 1979; Kim, Kreps, and Shin, 2015; Salinero-Fort, del Otero-Sanz, Martín-Madrazo, de Burgos-Lunar, et al., 2011). Migrant workers accessing social support networks have also reported a greater sense of self-efficacy and greater interpersonal competencies (Balaji, Claussen, Smith, Visser, et al., 2007; Jasinskaja-Lahti, Liebkind, Jaakkola, and Reuter, 2006; Birman, Trickett, and Vinokurov, 2002). This is in addition to positive acculturation wherein immigrants internalize a social identity that aligns with his/her new community while maintaining his/her own culture of origin. Despite the benefits, not all social support systems are the same and the outcomes vary.

This chapter begins with an overview of acculturation theories. Acculturation provides the foundation for examining the interconnections between social support and financial stability, as a key process of social integration. We then provide an examination of social support structures that both promote and inhibit adjustment and financial stability among migrant workers. To test these hypotheses, we conducted a study involving 125 Mexican-born adults who migrated to Chicago, Illinois in the United States (US). While each migrant story is unique, our study findings offer a framework for better understanding of what can support adjustment and self-sustainability across diverse immigrant populations highlighting the use of social support networks. The chapter concludes with practice implications that build on the literature and study findings for possible applications across diverse service settings and transnational communities.

LITERATURE REVIEW

Acculturation theory. Acculturation is a key element of each migrant's story. For economic migrants, the degree to which they acculturate to the new home country can directly influence financial stability, i.e., changes in behaviors on the part of individuals in response to changes in the economic environment leading to self-sufficiency through employment. Acculturation is the process of adapting and/or adopting the cultural traits or social patterns of another group and it is both a physical and psychological process. According to Berry (1997), "cultural groups and their individual members, in both the dominant and non-dominant situations, must deal with the issue of how to acculturate [to a new environment]" (p. 7) and he cites two major issues — cultural maintenance and contact and participation — as key elements of the acculturative process that must be worked out daily. Cultural maintenance is defined as "to what extent are cultural identity and characteristics considered to be important, and their maintenance strived for" (Berry, 1997, p. 9) while contact and participation are defined as "to what extent should they become involved in other cultural groups, or remain primarily among themselves" (Berry, 1997, p. 9).

Level of acculturation can serve as a powerful indicator of adjustment and adaptation of economic migrants, and both the immigrant and the receiving society feel the impact of acculturation. When examining the dynamics of cultural maintenance and contact and participation, the effects of acculturation on the immigrant and receiving society become clearer. For the immigrant, there is the delicate balance of maintaining one's culture of origin while participating in a new culture with values, beliefs and ways of being that contrast from the familiar. As for the receiving community, the level of acculturation of a new immigrant will determine the degree of integration into the various sectors of society from the workforce to political participation.

Acculturation models outline the different phases and types of adjustment experienced by new immigrants. Some models describe the acculturation patterns along a continuum that spans from individuals and groups that completely reject the host country's culture to individuals and groups who experience full assimilation involving the rejection of one's home culture (Berry, 1997). Other models such as Lysgaard's (1955) U-Curve Theory of Adjustment illustrate the highs and lows of the initial adjustment period for new immigrants, a period that marks the beginning of the acculturation process for new arrivals. And while the research on the acculturation patterns that result in the most optimal outcomes across health, mental health, economic and social dimensions is not conclusive, there is a general consensus in the value of maintaining some of one's culture of origin while adapting and adopting qualities of a new culture to create a more globalized identity (Suarez-Orozco and Qin-Hillard, 2004). For economic migrants, cultural maintenance and contact and participation are salient acculturation processes that play a key role in economic adaptation and overall adjustment to a new country.

Social support and the social support network. Humans are social beings existing within relationships that develop through interactions with one another. This social quality manifests itself in the human desire to make connections with others, which is particularly important for migrant workers entering new communities. Social support and social support networks, two terms often used interchangeably, depict this human quality of meeting needs through group connections. The terms can be defined broadly but for the purpose of this study, the terms "social support services," "social resources," "social support," "community resources," and "social service referrals" all apply to the same concept of using social relationships to locate, procure, or provide diverse financial, educational and/or emotional resources to support individual and group functioning (Balaji, et al., 2007; Keel and Drew, 2004; Thompson and Peebles-Wilkins, 1992). Social support networks vary in size, density (i.e., the degree of connectedness between members), the level of social engagement involved, and the level of access to resources and material goods (Berkman and Glass, 2000). Social support, in turn, is a provision of networks that can include close contacts or a group tied by a special bond (Balaji et al., 2007; Berkman and Glass, 2000).

The use of social support is influenced by a number of factors. Cultural practices and norms (Somhlaba, and Wait, 2008; Payne, 2005), gender, education levels, and socioeconomic status (Thompson and Peebles-Wilkins, 1992), and the perceived quality of the support and/or network (Olstad, Sexton, and Sogaard, 2001) are important variables that lead to support seeking behaviors. The use of social support affects the way people cope and adjust to life's stressful situations (Kim, Sherman and Taylor, 2008), such as transitions including acculturation to a new social environment.

The literature provides evidence of the benefits of social support networks specific to Latino immigrant populations in the United States. Social support buffers against the negative effects of acculturative stress and its negative impact on physical health (Salgado, Cataneda, Talavera, and Lindsay, 2012; Shobe, Coffman, and Dmochowski, 2009; Viruell-Fuentes and Schulz, 2009). Social support is also cited to improve poor mental health symptoms (e.g., depression) and emotional distress among newly arrived Latino immigrants (Hansen, and Aranda, 2012; Orenelas and Perreira, 2011). Additionally, Latino families were more likely to rely on social support networks for navigating other areas of adjustment including public child welfare systems (Ayon, 2011) and engaging parents in public school systems (Henry, Plunket and Sands, 2011) with positive outcomes for the entire family.

Challenges with social support networks among Latino immigrants are also documented. Language is related to the degree to which social support networks were accessed. For example, non-English speakers were less likely to use networks to assist with finding employment (Turney and Kao, 2009). Additionally, non-English speakers reported lower levels of perceived social support, with implications for the degree to which their social and economic needs were met, with further implications for adjustment (Turney and Kao, 2009). Fernandez and Fernandez-Mateo (2006) found that Latinos, particularly those who lacked English-language skills, reported no benefits from individual social support networks and that they struggled with obtaining employment. Latino immigrants with employment were more likely to experience job stress and overall poor functioning when they perceived they were receiving low social support, felt they were of low socioeconomic status, and feared a lack of job control and security (Perez, Franzini, Freeman, Jue and Peek, 2011). Lastly, employment was related to access to healthcare and without it, ones health was viewed as compromised (Shobe et al., 2009). Here we can see both elements of economic adaptation and poor outcomes related to negative outcomes or perceptions related to social support networks.

Financial stability. The influence of social support begins even before an economic migrant leaves home in pursuit of economic opportunities. Social support networks in the country of origin and in the receiving host country have been increasingly understood as critical to transnational migration (Faist and Ozveren, 2004; Castles and Miller, 2003; Jordan and Duvell, 2003). Networks in the country of origin and receiving country provide a bridge that either encourages or hinders migration and determines the level of adaptation in a receiving country (Raghuram, Henry, and Bornat, 2010). For new immigrants, social support networks that bridge the transnational divide become an important source of social support upon arriving in a receiving country, giving access to informational and emotional resources that allow them to adjust in a new environment (Ryan, Sales, Tilki, and Siara, 2008; Stewart, Anderson, Beiser, Mwakarima, Neufeld, Simich and Spitzer, 2008; Jasinskaja-Lahti, 2006, Castles and Miller, 2003; Jordan and Duvell, 2003).

It is suggested that social support networks in receiving countries may not be easy to access upon arrival (Ryan et al., 2003), yet they are extremely important during the critical initial adjustment period (i.e., the first three to six months upon arrival). The presence of social networks mitigates the negative effects of not having adequate economic resources upon arrival (Potocky-Tripodi, 2004; Putnam, 2000). For migrant workers, economic resources are paramount in the pursuit of employment opportunities to help new arrivals settle and begin the process of building a life in a new country. The quality of the social support network has direct implications for how well new immigrants adapt and stabilize socially and economically (Ryan et al., 2008; Stewart et al., 2008; Putnam, 2000). For economic migrants, financial stability is a primary goal thus finding networks that can provide resources (employment information, recommendations, etc.) becomes a priority.

Financial stability itself can be assessed by a number of indicators including employment status, income, earnings, and welfare utilization (Potocky-Tripodi, 2004). The most important factors that contribute to financial stability include household composition, various acculturation indicators, gender, networks, competencies, shared norms, and social trust that facilitate and are coordinated for mutual benefits (Potocky-Tripodi, 2004). To a certain degree, a social support network could facilitate several areas of economic adaptation including the increase in human capital that could lead to a job. According to Garcia-Ramirez et al. (2005), immigrants were better able to secure a job when they had access to support networks connecting them with opportunities wherein the social support network served as a vehicle to gain more economic opportunities.

Granovetter (2002) suggests labor market experiences are, in part, related to the nature of the networks and the strength of the ties within those networks. Ethnic ties, language, class ties and shared skills were all components of network ties that were seen to strengthen the bond between members (Harvey, 2008; Kim et al., 2008, Anthias 2007; Granovetter, 2002) while fear of perceived social stigma against one's ethnic group when accessing support, language barriers, and rigid requirements that may exist for joining more established organizational networks could weaken connections (Ahmed, Steward, Teng, Wahoush and Gagnon, 2008; Hernandez-Plaza, Pozo, and Alonso-Morilljo, 2004). Ultimately, the stronger the support connections, the more likely there would be an easier transition into employment opportunities in the receiving country; thus, greater financial stability (Raghuram et al., 2010).

Building on these ideas, Putnam (1995) offers the perspective that social trust and norms are developed within the framework of a social network that can in turn facilitate coordination for a mutual benefit. Furthermore, recent findings suggest that economic success in the labor market is positively associated with psychological empowerment for low-income jobseekers (Hong, 2013; Hong, Choi, and Polanin, 2014; Hong, Lewis, and Choi, 2014; Hong, Sheriff, and Naeger, 2009). According to Garcia-Ramirez et al. (2005), immigrants with a positive self-concept of their professional competence, who held internal attributions about their employment and who engaged in an active job search — all related indicators of psychological empowerment — were more likely to be employed.

Taking all these together, social support networks can serve as critical vehicles that maintain the connection to culture of origin while helping new arrivals engage and facilitate connections that could support financial stability (Potocky-Tripodi, 2004). Social support networks can also develop human and social capital (Putnam, 1995) while facilitating psychological empowerment, all of which has been seen to improve employment status among economic migrants. And ultimately, social support networks can be a catalyst for economic attainment and advancement through securing stable employment (Garcia-Ramirez et al., 2005), which leads to financial stability among this group.

METHODS

This study examines the relationships among social support, acculturation, and financial stability among Mexican migrants living in Chicago. The study sheds light on an area less understood in the literature. Specifically, it focuses on the relationship between social support networks and financial stability, which has implications on the overall health and wellbeing of immigrant populations. The research question that guides this study is: To what extent are social support networks associated with acculturation and employment stability among Mexican migrants in Chicago? It is hypothesized that social support would be positively related to acculturation and financial stability. It is further hypothesized that economic pursuit at the onset of immigration has a positive effect on acculturation and financial stability.

Data Collection. The data were collected during the period of 2007-2008 as part of a larger study that examined the dynamics, resources, organization, structure and wellbeing of Mexican migrants and their families. In collaboration with a national study of the Mexican family, *Diagnostico de la Familia,* conducted in Mexico by the Sistema Nacional para el Desarrollo Integral de la Familia (SNDIF), the Mexican federal government's principal human service agency, the present study was conducted in Chicago, Illinois. Chicago is home to the nation's second largest Mexican concentration (Zong and Batalova, 2014) and has a long and varied history of receiving Mexican migrants from different regions, thus making it an ideal site for a study of Mexican immigrant families.

Sample. Participants in the study met the following criteria: (a) currently resided in the United States; (b) born in Mexico and migrated to the United States; and 3) over the age of 18. The sample for the survey was derived from individuals who were seeking assistance at the Mexican Consulate in Chicago. The assistance of the Consulate was solicited because they provided the best vehicle to access a convenience sample of Mexican immigrants in the Chicago area. The Chicago Consulate is one of the largest and most active Mexican consulate in the US, serving over 700,000 Mexican nationals and offering a broad array services that include: the issuing of visas, passports, and matricula consular (Consular issued identification cards); the retrieval of vital documents from Mexico such as marriage, birth and death certificates; assistance with locating family members; legal information and assistance in labor, civil, and criminal matters; assistance in deportation and repatriation cases; homeownership promotion programs; and application for All Kids, the Illinois state program for all uninsured children of low income, regardless of immigration status (Ramirez, 2010). Because of the broad range of services that the Consulate provides, this site allowed for extraordinary access to all segments of the Mexican immigrant population, including recent and more established migrants of all immigration and socio-economic statuses.

Interval sampling was conducted to select individuals waiting for consular services each day over a six-month period until 125 interviews were completed. Once an individual was selected, s/he was approached and asked if s/he was willing to take part in the interview. Only one member of a household was selected. A short screening protocol was used to ensure that the individual met the criterion for inclusion and that s/he had not already been interviewed in Mexico as well as to make sure we did not interview the same person at the Consulate more than once. Data was collected via individual interviews (approximately 1.5 hours long) in a separate room in the Consulate facilities to ensure privacy. While participants had the option of conducting the interview in Spanish or English, all chose Spanish. The interviews were conducted by a trained bilingual Mexican doctoral student. All survey participants received a $20 gift card for their time.

Variables and Instruments. The survey instrument consists of a questionnaire and several scales. Survey instruments and interview guides were available in English and in Spanish. All of the scales used in the study were available in English and Spanish and the questionnaire was translated and pre-tested. The following instruments were administered to all participants: Demographic and Family Dynamics Questionnaire, and Short Acculturation Scale for Hispanics (SASH).

Demographic and Family Dynamics Questionnaire: This questionnaire included a number of variables of interest that assessed the following constructs: the structure of the domestic group; occupational and educational dynamics characteristics of family members, family dynamics including the formation and dissolution of unions; intrafamily relations; and extra family relations (between the family nucleus and kin and nearby friends; networks of intra and intergenerational solidarity and social support). The questionnaire also collected information on diverse characteristics (education, occupation, place of residence, etc.) and questions regarding income sources (both formal and informal, public and private). Most of these items were previously included the SNDIF *Diagnostico* study, however additional questions regarding the migratory history and experience of the participants were added in the present study.

- The Short Acculturation Scale for Hispanics (SASH). The SASH scale (Marín, et al., 1987) was used to assess the level of acculturation. This scale includes 12 items related to three factors: (a) language use (b) media and (c) ethnic social relations. Marín, Sabogal, Marín, Otero-Sabogal, and Perez-Stable (1987) reported an Alpha coefficient of .92 and this sample presented a score of .88, indicating good reliability.

FINDINGS

Roughly half of the sample were women (53%) and similarly almost one half were married (48%). Thirty-seven percent had no children while the remaining 63% had from one to three children. The age range of the participants spanned from 17-63 years with an average age of 31.4 with varying levels of education (Elementary – 25%; Secondary – 22%; High school – 30%; Professional –14%; No education – 11%) (see Table 1 for detailed results).

Migration Experience. Economic pursuit as the reason for migration received the largest response in the sample (65%) while the second most popular response was family reunification (21%). The majority of respondents made the decision to migrate on his/her own (51%), but made the journey with other family members (56%). The arrival destination for migrant workers was largely determined by family reunification (46%) followed by employment recruitment (34%) (see Table 2). These responses allowed us to closely examine diversity in social supports since we had participants who migrated for economic reasons and whose decision making process was influenced, to a certain degree, on obtaining employment stability; a premise of our research study.

Social support. We wanted to understand the circumstances around when and why social support networks were accessed and when participants provided social support to others, Table 3 outlines some of the questions asked referring to instances when social support was received and offered, including helping with ill family members or members who had passed away. We also asked questions related to economic problems and the degree to which support was given or received within the last 12 months. Fifty-six percent of the participants cited giving social support to family, neighbors and friends within the year while only 35% reported receiving support.

Financial stability. To understand economic adaptation among the sample of Mexican immigrants, we asked a number of questions related to type of employment (based on hours per week and payment type) and the type of assistance received to obtain a job. In our sample, 72% of the sample reported receiving help to get a job and that in many cases (49%), the contact worked at the prospective place of employment and made an internal recommendation. Of the jobs secured by the sample, 77% were working for money with an average of 45.6 hours per week and 80.4% were in full-time positions. However, as many as 34% of respondents reported having serious economic and 18% reported having work-related problems.

Moreover, we found that participants who needed specific resources had their needs met through social support networks. As the services were critical supports for adjustment and obtaining and maintaining employment, again we see the value of networks. The following table outlines the specific needs in the sample population and the degree to which those needs were met through social support networks.

Table 1. Description of Demographic Variables

Variables	N	Percentage
Gender		
Female	65	52.8
Marital Status		
Married	59	48.0
Cohabitating	25	20.3
Number of Children		
0	45	36.6
1	20	16.3
2	21	17.1
3	21	17.1
Gender (Mean)	31.4	
Education		
Elementary (Grade 1-6)	30	24.6
Secondary (Grade 7-9)	27	22.1
Preparatory or High school (Grade 10-12)	37	30.3
Professional	17	13.9
None	14	11.2

Table 2. Description of Migration Experience Variables

Variables	N	Percentage
Reason for Immigration		
Economic	77	65.0
Reunite with family	25	21.2
Displaced	1	0.8
Study	4	3.4
Other	11	9.3
Made Decision to Migrate ...		
On his/her own	61	51.1
With his/her family	40	34.5
Other	16	13.4
Made the Journey ...		
Alone	24	20.2
With his/her partner	17	14.3
With other family member(s)	67	56.3
Other	10	8.2
Deciding on the place of destination in the US		
Recruited to work here	41	33.9
Wanted to reunite with family	56	46.3
Heard there were jobs here	6	5.0
Other	18	14.9

Table 3. Description of Social Support Variables

Variables	N	Percentage
Has helped family members, neighbors, and friends when they:		
Suffered the death of a loved one	78	36.1
Suffered a serious illness	60	49.2
Had an accident	48	40.0
Had serious economic problems	43	36.1
Has given help to a family, neighbors and friends in the last 12 months:		
Yes	66	55.5
Received help from family members, neighbors, and friends when they:		
Suffered the death of a loved one		
Suffered a serious illness	48	39.3
Had an accident	33	27.0
Had serious economic problems	25	20.7
Had serious work problems	43	35.2
Experienced domestic violence	22	18.0
	19	15.6
Has received help from family members, neighbors, and friends in the last 12 months:		
Yes	43	35.2

A series of independent group t-tests were conducted to examine the bivariate relationships among the variables of interest. We found several statistically significant relationships among social support, acculturation and financial stability. In detail, participants who received social support in the last 12 months were able to work significantly longer hours than those who did not receive any social support (t (117) = -1.75, $p < .10$); significant difference in working hours also were evident between migrant workers who received help in finding a job and those who did not (t (73.75) = -4.02, $p < .001$), both implying a relationship between social supports and financial stability. As for social support and acculturation, participants who used social support to address economic problems reported a higher acculturation level than those who did not seek support in the same situation (t (105) = -1.85, $p < .10$). Additionally, participants showed significantly lower acculturation level when economic reasons motivated immigration compared to those who migrated for other reasons (t (60.18) = 2.462, $p < .05$), This significance in acculturation level is further apparent between those who migrated to a specific destination for economic reasons and those who migrated to destinations without a clear purpose (t (100.3)= 1.81, $p < .10$). There were no significant differences in economic stability when economic pursuit was a factor in immigration.

Table 4. Description of Financial Stability Variables

Variables	N	Percentage
Work for money	92	76.7
Average number of hours at work (mean)	45.6	
Full-time job	74	80.4
Received help getting this job	73	79.3
From friend	37	50.7
Type of help received getting this job		
He/she worked in the business and made recommendation	36	49.3
He/she didn't work in the business but recommended	21	28.8
Problems Experienced		
Serious economic problems	43	34.4
Serious work problems	22	17.6

Table 5. Services Needed Versus Services Received

Variables	Need	Received
Employment agency	33 (27.5%)	30 (90.9%)
Job/vocational training	44 (36.7%)	44 (100%)
Educational classes	49 (40.8%)	47 (97.9%)
Parent training	12 (10%)	12 (100%)
Childcare/daycare	8 (6.8%)	8 (100%)
After-school programming	15 (12.5%)	15 (100%)
Regular medical care	35 (29.4%)	35 (100%)

DISCUSSION

Results from the study indicate that Mexican immigrants are using social support networks for acculturation and to help navigate their way towards financial stability. In this study, those who reported using social supports were more likely to demonstrate financial stability as measured by hours of work. And immigrants using social supports for economic problems and finding employment showed a higher level of acculturation that suggests overall better adjustment. Economic migration (i.e., economic reasons for immigration and for choosing destination) was negatively associated with acculturation and did not demonstrate a significant association with economic stability as anticipated.

We initially reasoned that a migrant worker who was driven to leave his/her country to pursue economic opportunities would show higher levels of acculturation and economic stability simply because of the driving force underlying the migration would be clear and the migrant worker would use targeted strategies to be successful. Social support networks could be a crucial tool for economic migrants to obtain job referrals or more knowledge about markets that could result in a job. Moreover, the process of using social support networks to learn and adjust quickly to the job market would result in higher levels of acculturation; the migrant would naturally learn about different cultural groups and adopt/adapt as needed to fit the job market but also learn more about the new community in the process.

The study does provide evident to support our original a hypothesis, led us to a different argument. Economic pursuit can be a powerful catalyst to leave one's home country but adjustment to a new country and finding a stable job (i.e., financial stability) are more complicated than simply the desire to migrate in search of economic opportunities. Acculturation and financial stability may have more to do with social-emotional adaptation and economic integration. Lower levels of acculturation among migrant workers might imply higher level of dependency on social networks for supports since their own capacity of securing economic stability might be weak. Through social supports, economic migrants may become more capable of preparing themselves (e.g., learning English, obtaining marketable skills, etc.) for economic opportunities and thus work-ready jobseekers.

We cannot overemphasize the relevance of social support networks in the lives of economic migrants. The key is to enhance the effectiveness of these networks and tailor them to be most useful among immigrant populations. This would include recognizing the role of social support networks as a vehicle for cultural connections and a provider of concrete resources that could support adjustment to the larger society. Hernández-Plaza, Alonso-Morillejo and Pozo-Muñoz (2006) offered a practical framework of social support interventions with migrant populations that integrates support found in both informal and formal networks: dyadic interventions, social network interventions, mutual aid groups and community interventions. First, an emphasis on the interpersonal exchanges of help and resources in dyadic interactions by incorporating new sources of support in immigrants' social networks is crucial. Secondly and related to social network interventions, the identification and mobilization of existing informal sources of resources in migrant communities is necessary to improve supportive exchanges among migrant and native groups. The third level involves mutual aid groups that can serve as a new link between community members as a way of creating and improving social support exchanges. Finally, community based interventions emphasizing the immigrants' participation in the identification of collective needs, the development of strategies to address those needs, and implementation of actions to meet them are considered critical.

Building on above framework, the development and nurturance of informal social networks are crucial to migrants' economic security, adjustment and acculturation and family wellbeing. Increased connections between native and migrant groups in the production of informal networks will further bolster the delivery of resources and supporting network members. At the same time, social services need to more accessible to new immigrants both linguistically and culturally so that new immigrants will feel comfortable seeking support in these settings. Additionally, an increased emphasis on creating opportunities to build leadership within the arriving populations to strengthen community-based interventions may help to improve the likelihood that migrant workers will access services. Further, the development of mutual aid groups can be a powerful venue and resource. These mutual aid organizations are where community service providers can provide guidance, and immigration policies and budgets can allocate resources to establish and maintain such programs. Mutual aid associations can access state funding in certain state such as Illinois but the resources are limited, thus attention to this area could be essential.

The utilization of social support networks that are most impactful among migrant populations is also important to our discussion. Hernández-Plaza and colleagues (2006) contribute valuable insights into how service providers and researchers can continue supporting the vital role social support networks play in migrant groups. Their work focused on the ways in which immigrants turn to informal networks rather than formal organizational memberships to overcome barriers because of the greater accessibility, shared norms, and greater flexibility. On the other hand whileInformal social support systems, are accessible to many migrant workers, exclusive use of informal networks may limit their access to job opportunities only within the confines of ethnic enclaves and/or precarious jobs. Given this reality, strengthening the informal support system in direct practice with migrant populations is suggested (Hernández-Plaza, Alonso-Morillejo, and Pozo-Muñoz, 2006). Stakeholders can provide guidance to potential leaders in the community who could organize informal networks to align with more structured social services in the area or support community leaders in establishing mutual aid groups to work directly with migrant workers.

CONCLUSION

Social support networks and acculturation operate in tandem; the networks provide a vehicle for contact maintenance to one's culture of origin while also serving as a valuable resource to connect with others in the new location. The acculturative process is supported by the presence of a network that can provide resources to aid in adjustment and reaching economic goals. Although we discuss the relevance of social support in helping financial stability (important for migrant workers), we cannot forget there is also a social-emotional and cultural benefit to having these systems in the lives of economic migrants that extends beyond the economic benefits. Ultimately, the role of social support networks cannot be underestimated in the lives of migrants in a new country. The presence of these networks is related to diverse positive outcomes across dimensions of acculturation and financial stability in the lives of recent immigrants.

In the 21st century global migration is well-established as individuals and families continue to migrate for better life opportunities. For those who leave their countries of origin in pursuit of financial stability, we can have a better appreciation for the resources that are necessary to support positive outcomes. The complex interplay between social support networks and acculturation that influences financial stability is just one example of how one resource — social support networks — can impact so many other areas of adjustment for economic migrants. Our hope for any immigrant is that he or she finds wellness in the process of seeking new life opportunities. In this vein, there must be a continued recognition of the influence of social support networks to ensure acculturation and economic success that could potentially provide overall wellness for economic migrants in their receiving countries.

REFERENCES

Ahmed, A., Steward, D.E., Teng, L., Wahoush, O., and Gagnon, A.J. (2008). Experience of immigrant new mothers with symptoms of depression. *Archives of Women's Mental Health*, 11, 295-303.

Antias, F. (2007). Ethnic ties, social capital and the question of mobilisability. *The Sociological Review*, 55(4), 788-805.

Ayon, C. (2011). Latino families and the public child welfare system: Examining the role of social support networks. *Children and Youth Services Review*, 33 (10), 2061-2066.

Balaji, A.B., Claussen, A.H., Smith, D.C., Visser, S.N., Morales, M.J., and Perou, R. (2007). Social support networks and maternal mental health and wellbeing. *Journal of Women's Health*, 16(10), 1386-1396.

Berkman, L.F. (1984). Assessing the physical health effects of social networks and social support. *Annual Review of Public Health*, 5, 413-432.

Berkman, L.F. and Glass, T. (2000). Social integration, social networks, social support, and health. In: L.F. Berkman and I. Kawachi (eds.), *Social epidemiology* (pp. 137-173). New York: Oxford University Press.

Berry, J.W. (1997). Immigration, acculturation, and adaptation. *Applied Psychology: An International Review*, 46(1), 5-68.

Birman, D., Trickette, E.J., and Vinokurov, A. (2002). Acculturation and adaptation of Soviet Jewish refugee adolescents: Predictors of adjustment across life domains. American *Journal of Community Psychology*, 30(5), 585-607.

Calvo-Armengol, A. and Jackson, M.O. (2004). The effects of social networks on employment and inequality. *American Economic Review*, 94, 426-454.

Castles, S., and Miller, M. (2003). *The age of migration: International population movements in the modern world.* Basingstoke: Palgrave.

Cohen, S., and Wills, T. A. (1985). Stress, social support, and the buffering hypothesis. *Psychological bulletin*, 98, 310-357.

Dalgard, O. S., and Thapa, S. B. (2007). Immigration, social integration and mental health in Norway, with focus on gender differences. *Clinical Practice and Epidemiology in Mental Health*, 3(1), 24.

Dustmann, C., Glitz, A., and Schöenberg, U. (2011). Referral-based job search networks (IZA Discussion Paper No. 5777). Institute for the Study of Labor: Bonn, Germany.

Faist, T, and E. Ozveren (Eds.) (2004). *Transnational social spaces: Agents, networks, and institutions*. Aldershot: Ashgate.

Fernandez, R.M. and Fernandez-Mateo, I. (2006). Networks, race, and hiring. *American Sociological Review*, 71 (1), 42-71.

Garcia-Ramirez, M., Martinez, M.F., Balcazar, F.E., Suarez-Balcazar, Y., Albar, M., Dominguez, E., and Santolaya, F.J. (2005). Psychosocial empowerment and social support factors associated with the employment status of immigrant welfare recipients. *Journal of Community Psychology*, 33(6), 673-690.

Goel, D., and Lang, K. (2009). Social ties and the job search of recent immigrants (*NBER Working Papers 15186*). National Bureau of Economic Research: Cambridge, MA.

Granovetter, M. (2002). 'The strength of weak ties,' reprinted in J. Scott (ed.) *Social Networks* (pp. 60-80). New York: Routledge.

Hansen, M.C. and Aranda, M.P. (2012). Sociocultural influences on mental health service use by Latino older adults for emotional distress: Exploring the mediating and moderating role of informal social support. *Social Science and Medicine*, 75(12), 2134-2142.

Harvey, W. (2008). Strong or weak ties: British and Indian expatriate scientists finding jobs in Boston. *Global Networks*, 8(4), 453-473.

Henry, C.S., Plunkett, S.W., and Sands, T. (2011). Family structure, parental involvement, and academic motivation in Latino adolescents. *Journal of Divorce and Remarriage*, 52(6), 370-390.

Hernández-Plaza, S., Alonso-Morillejo, E. and Pozo-Muñoz, C. (2006). Social Support Interventions in Migrant Populations. *The British Journal of Social Work*, 36(7), 1151-1169.

Hernandez-Plaza, S., Pozo, C., and Alonso-Morillejo, E. (2004). The role of informal social support in needs assessment: Proposal and application of a model to assess immigrants' needs in the south of Spain. *Journal of Community and Applied Social Psychology*, 14, 284-298.

Hong, P.Y.P., Lewis, D., and Choi, S. (2014). Employment hope as an empowerment pathway to self-sufficiency among ex-offenders. *Journal of Offender Rehabilitation*, 53, 317-333.

Hong, P.Y.P., Choi, S., Polanin, J.R. (2014). A multi-sample confirmatory factor analysis of the Short Employment Hope Scale (EHS-14). *Journal of Social Service Research*, 40, 339-352.

Hong, P.Y.P. (2013). Toward a client-centered benchmark for self-sufficiency: Evaluating the 'process' of becoming job ready. *Journal of Community Practice*, 21, 356-378.

Hong, P.Y.P., Sheriff, A., and Naeger, S. (2009). A bottom-up definition of self-sufficiency: Voices from low-income jobseekers. *Qualitative Social Work, 8,* 357-376.

Jasinskaja-Lahti, I., Liebkind, K., Jaakkola, M., and Reuter, A. (2006). Perceived discrimination, social support networks, and psychological wellbeing among three immigrant groups. *Journal of Cross-Cultural Psychology*, 37, 293-311.

Jordan, B. and Duvell, F. (2003). *Migration: The boundaries of equality and justice.* Cambridge: Polity.

Keel, M.R. and Drew, N.M. (2004). The settlement experiences of refugees from the former Yugoslavia: Acculturation, ethnic identity, ethnicity, community and social network development. *Community, Work and Family*, 7(1), 95-115.

Kim, H.S., Sherman, D.K., and Taylor, S.E. (2008). Culture and social support. *American Psychologists*, 63(6), 518-526.

Kim, W., Kreps, G. L., and Shin, C. N. (2015). The role of social support and social networks in health information–seeking behavior among Korean Americans: a qualitative study. *International journal for equity in health*, 14(1), 40.

Marín, G., Sabogal, F., Marín, B. V., Otero-Sabogal, R., and Perez-Stable, E. J. (1987). Development of a short acculturation scale for Hispanics. *Hispanic Journal of Behavioral Sciences*, 9, 183-205.

Lin, N., Ensel, W. M., Simeone, R. S., and Kuo, W. (1979). Social support, stressful life events, and illness: A model and an empirical test. *Journal of Health and Social Behavior*, 20, 108-119.

Montgomery, J.D. (1991). Social networks and labor market outcomes: Towards an economic analysis. *American Economic Review*, 81, 1408-18.

Ornela, I.J., and Perreira, K.M. (2011). The role of migration in the development of depressive symptoms amont Latino immigrant parents in the US. *Social Science and Medicine*, 73(8), 1169-1177.

Payne, M. (2005). *Modern social work theory* (3rd Ed.). Lyceum Books Inc.: Chicago, Illinois.

Perez, N. Franzini, L., Freeman, D.H., Ju, H., and Peek, K. (2011). A population-based study of job stress in Mexican Americans, non-Hispanic Blacks, and non-Hispanic Whites. *Hispanic journal of Behavioral Sciences*, 33(2), 221-233.

Piedmont, R. L. (2007). *The Trauma Symptom Inventory*. Loyola College in Maryland.

Potocky-Tripodi, M. (2002). *Best practices for social work with refugees and immigrants*. New York: Columbia University Press.

Putnam, R.D. (2000). *Bowling alone: The collapse and revival of American community*. New York: Simon and Schuster.

Raghuram, P., Henry, L., and Bornat, J. (2010). Difference and distinction? Non-migrant and migrant networks. *Sociology*, 44(4), 623-641.

Ramirez, M. (May 4, 2010). Mexican Consulate goes where the people are. Chicago Tribune. Retrieved from: http://articles.chicagotribune.com/2010-05-04/news/ct-x-w-0505-mobile-consulate-20100504_1_mobile-consulate -mexican-consulate-consulate-officers.

Ryan, L., Sales, R., Tilki, M., and Siara, B. (2008). Social networks, social support and social capital: The experience of recent polish migrants in London. *Sociology*, 42(4), 672-690.

Salgado, H., Castaneda, S., Talavera, G., and Lindsay, S. (2012). The role of social support and acculturative stress in health-related quality of life among day laborers in Northern San Diego. *Journal of Immigrant and Minority Health*, 14(3), 379-385.

Salinero-Fort, M. Á., del Otero-Sanz, L., Martín-Madrazo, C., de Burgos-Lunar, C., Chico-Moraleja, R. M., Rodés-Soldevila, B., … Gómez-Campelo, P. (2011). The relationship between social support and self-reported health status in immigrants: an adjusted analysis in the Madrid Cross Sectional Study. *BMC Family Practice*, 12, 46.

Shobe, M.A., Coffman, M.J, and Dmochowski, J. (2009). Achieving the American Dream: Facilitators and barriers to health and mental health for Latino immigrants. *Journal of Evidence-Based Social Work*, 6(1), 92-110.

Somhlaba, N.Z., and Wait, J.W. (2008). Psychological adjustment to conjugal bereavement: Do social networks aid coping following spousal death? *Omega*, 57(4), 341-366.

Stewart, M., Anderson, J., Beiser, M., Mwakarimba, E., Neufeld, A., Simich, L., and Spitzer, D. (2008). Multicultural meanings of social support among immigrants and refugees. *International Migration*, 46(3), 123-159.

Thompson, M.S. and Peebles-Wilkins, W. (1992). The impact of formal, informal, and societal support networks on the psychological wellbeing of black adolescent mothers. *National Association of Social Workers*, 37(4), 322-328.

Turney, K. and Kao, G. (2009). Assessing the private safety net: social support among minority immigrant parents. *Sociological Quarterly*, 50(4), 666-692.

Viruell-Fuentes, E.A. and Schulz, A.J. (2009). Toward a dynamic conceptualization of social ties and context: Implications for understanding immigrant and Latino health. *American Journal of Public Health*, 99(12), 2167-2175.

Zong, J. andBatalova, J. (2014). Mexican immigrants in the United States. Washington, D.C.: Migration Policy Institute. Retrieved from http://www.migrationpolicy.org/article/mexican-immigrants-united-states.

In: Migrant Workers
Editors: Qingwen Xu and Lucy P. Jordan
ISBN: 978-1-63485-272-2

Chapter 4

HIV/AIDS AND MIGRATION IN SUB-SAHARAN AFRICA

Soma Sen[1,*] and Jemel P. Aguilar[2]
[1]School of Social Work, San Jose State University, San Jose, CA, US
[2]University of Saint Joseph, West Hartford, CT, US

ABSTRACT

The third phase of the Global AIDS pandemic is characterized by social, cultural, and economic causes and consequences of HIV infection. These causes and consequences are relevant to both HIV itself as well as to HIV prevention and treatment. Thus scholars link poverty, powerlessness, and social instability to Global AIDS in that more than 95% of global HIV infections are in developing, or "resource-poor," countries with two-thirds of AIDS infections occurring in Sub-Saharan Africa. Despite efforts to understand the social factors leading to HIV infection, a majority of HIV interventions are currently designed primarily after public health models that focus on individual behavior modification and consequently pay little attention to the socioeconomic environment in which HIV transmission occurs. With the growing migrant population in Sub-Saharan Africa, widespread evidence indicates that the socioeconomic environment in which migrant populations live and work increase their risk for poor health in general and HIV transmission in particular. While being a migrant in and of itself does not constitute a risk factor, certain activities and conditions associated with the migration process increase migrants' vulnerability to HIV. This chapter examines how migration acts as a conduit for disease transmission in Sub-Saharan Africa and argues that social disruption and stress from migration lead to high-risk behaviors among migrants that amplify the likelihood of HIV transmission. Drawing on social capital theory, a culturally relevant, macro-level prevention model is proposed to supplement current prevention programs.

* Corresponding author: Soma Sen, School of Social Work, San Jose State University, One Washington Square, San Jose, CA 95192, US. Email: soma.sen@sjsu.edu.

Introduction

In the year 2012, the Joint United Nations Programme on HIV/AIDS estimates that 35.3 million people worldwide are living with HIV and 2.3 million new infections (UNAIDS, 2013). In the same year, 1.6 million people succumbed to AIDS globally, leaving behind anguished orphans, family members, and ravaged communities. The greatest burden of this disease is felt by developing countries. The United Nations characterizes AIDS and the migration of millions of people in resource poor countries as two of the most critical issues facing HIV work today. Migration is the movement of a person or group of persons from one place to another either temporarily or permanently and for a multitude of voluntary or involuntary reasons (Brummer, 2002; Hope, 2001). While being a migrant in and of itself is not a risk factor for HIV/AIDS, the processes and circumstances that accompany migration substantially increase migrants' vulnerability to HIV. In this chapter we present the case of Sub-Saharan Africa and elaborate how migration and HIV/AIDS are connected.

Sub-Saharan Africa (SSA), geographically and politically denotes the area and twenty one countries of the African continent that lie to the south of the *Sahara* Desert, including Angola, Burundi, Chad, Gambia to name a few. In Sub-Saharan Africa, migration is a part of the overall labor market system, and features a variety of movements, mostly intraregional: migrant workers, undocumented migrants, nomads, frontier workers, refugees, and highly skilled professionals (Adepoju, 2000). In recent decades, worsening socio-economic and political conditions in the region including rapid population growth, economic depression, conflicts, political instability, widespread poverty and deepening unemployment have been the common factors for in any kind migration (http://www.iom/int), and have been particularly associated with increased migration in Sub-Saharan Africa region. For a long time, labor migration as manifested by gendered migration has been dominating; sponsored, selective male migrants have supplied the needed cheap labors for the region's mining industry. Such mine workers constitute a highly mobile population who move back and forth between their destination and home communities on a frequent basis, often once a month for two or three days (Brummer, 2002; Hope, 2001), thus, according to the International Office of Migration (IOM), making the migration process both fluid and cyclical.

Migration and HIV Risks

The link between migration and HIV in developing countries is well documented and is a result of both macro or structural factors as well as micro or individual factors (Haour-Knipe, 2003; Shtarkshall and Soskolone, 2000). As early as late 20th century, theorists had identified unique structural factors such as colonization, international debt crisis, poverty, urbanization, and government policies that explain the migration and HIV epidemic connection (Lurie, 2001; Webb, 1997). In addition, regional conflicts, globalization, environmental disasters, and a global reduction in public spending on healthcare and education have also compounded the issue. War and conflict create situations in which civilians are subjected to mass displacement, human rights violations, sexual violence and poverty, all conditions that increase their vulnerability to HIV. Evidences indicate that of the 17 countries with the highest AIDS rates, 13 are in war torn regions of the world. For example, in Sierra Leone,

HIV rates increased from 27% to 71% during its decade long civil war. Eleven percent of Nigeria's peacekeepers returned home from conflict torn regions as HIV positive (UNAIDS, 2004).

Globalization and the current global economic order are characterized by unequal distribution of resources and increasing economic disparity between the global South and the global North (Polack, 2004). These disparities lead to conditions of poverty and unemployment in many developing countries forcing individuals to migrate. More recently, migrant workers have been responding to unprecedented economic growth, liberal economic policies and less restrictive immigration policies. However, such rapid movement of population has not been supported adequately by existing infrastructure of the host countries or communities and as a result the labor migrants are forced to live and work in deplorable conditions. Such migrants are seen primarily as a source of labor and host governments or places of employments (such as mining and agricultural fields) have not been inclined to invest in these individuals. In fact, when economic situations have declined, these migrant workers have been expelled from the host communities and forced to return to their communities of origin. These migrants are susceptible to many health problems including HIV. Risk factors include substandard living arrangements, high rates of alcohol use, sex with multiple partners and with commercial sex workers. For example, in South African mining companies that primarily employ migrant workers, HIV infection rate is about 18%. In Senegal, where 82% of men between 20 and 40 years of age travel for employment purposes, labor mobility has been the only significant factor to be associated with HIV (UNAIDS, 2004).

Meanwhile, environmental disasters occurring in developing countries have led to increased population mobility and subsequently the risk of communicable diseases including HIV. In the case of 2004 floods of Bangladesh, in Dhaka alone, 1.5 million people were forced to leave their homes. Immediately outbreaks of diarrhea, typhoid, and jaundice were reported. These conditions further aggravated the pre-existing conditions created by poverty, lack of healthcare and increased the risk for HIV transmission. In addition to natural disasters, millions of individuals every year are displaced from their homes as a result of development projects such as highways and dams. These projects disproportionally impact already vulnerable populations including indigenous groups of people, the rural population, and the urban poor. Development projects often destroy agricultural bases and uproot communities thus forcing individuals to leave their communities in search for employment in their own country or abroad (Polack, 2004). These development associated displaced individuals often lack adequate government-sponsored relocation services, and face same vulnerabilities as labor migrants, thus consequently are at risk for HIV (World Health Organization, 2003; UNAIDS, 2004).

Thus it is important to note that for many developing countries, globalization has created a cycle of structural poverty and poor health. These countries received loans from the International Monetary Funds and the World Bank for various economic development projects (such as construction of dams and roadways), which have resulted in a heavy burden of debt repayment and structural adjustment policies (Polack, 2004). Such policies prescribed by global financial institutions syphon funds from social development initiatives such as education and health care and have made it very difficult for these countries to tackle health problems like HIV. The reduction in public health expenditures impacts the migrant population even more drastically because migrants are often the group to be excluded from the health care system of the host country. When many migrant workers live and work in conditions that increase their HIV risk, they have no way of accessing health care services.

Irrespective of reasons for migration, migrants are often marginalized and stigmatized throughout the migration process. They are subject to discrimination, xenophobia, and exploitation in host societies and have limited access to legal or social recourses. In addition, multiple factors stemming from cultural transitions, social disruptions, and financial and other adjustments typically associated with the migration process would interact with each other to create environments conducive for HIV transmission among migrants. The possible friction between migrants and the host culture can create confusion and mistrust causing psychological stress that might increase risk behaviors such as unprotected sex and intravenous drug use, while at the same time reduce their engagement with health care providers (Weine and Kashube, 2012). The less than optimal environment makes migrants particularly vulnerable to poor health outcomes including HIV risk.

Besides the above mentioned macro level structural and environmental factors that impact a migrant's HIV risk, Brockerhoff and Biddlecom (1999) identify three micro or individual level factors that might explain their HIV risk as well. These are factors related to a migrant's sexual behavior; namely her/his pre-migration characteristics, changes in individual characteristics as a result of migration, and exposure to new physical and social environments due to migration. Figure 1 explains the relationship between migration and risk behaviors. Some pre-migration individual characteristics include sex, age, marital status, level of education, and socio-economic status. It is anticipated that the migration process changes some of these individual characteristics; the most commonly cited are having a regular sexual partner, connections with family, as well as the migrant's economic status. Migration is also associated with a changed socio-cultural environment that connects with high risk sexual behaviors (Brockerhoff and Biddlecom, 1999). Specifically the lack of social support has been linked to risk-taking behaviors that might result from the stressors of being in a new environment (Campbell and Williams, 1999; Weine and Kashuba, 2010).

These micro and macro level factors interact with each other to create circumstances rife with limited access to health care, poor working and living conditions, poverty, powerlessness and social instability that migrants often find themselves in. To complicate matters further, often host countries are not interested in investing in health care for migrant workers and many national health care plans exclude migrants completely or limit their care.

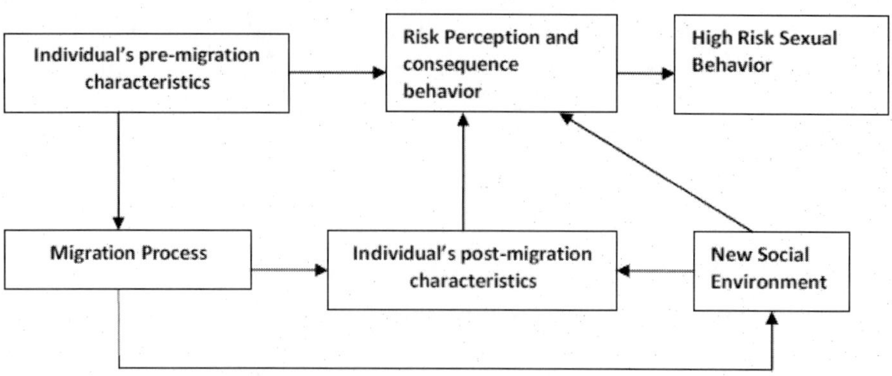

Brokerhoff and Biddlecom, 1999.

Figure 1. The influence of migration on high risk behaviors.

HIV AND MIGRATION IN SUB-SAHARAN AFRICA

Given the relationship between migration and HIV, HIV risks and prevalence among migrant workers in Sub-Saharan Africa (SSA) draw special attention here. Labor migrants or migrant workers are individuals engaged in remunerated activities in places other than the individuals' place of origin (UNAIDS, 2013). In SSA, labor migration can be international (crossing the country boundaries) or national (within the country boundaries) or regional (rural-urban). Examples of labor migrants include mine workers, agricultural workers, and others; the rural-urban flow of migrant labors within national and regional boundaries represents the predominant pattern of migration in SSA (Black, 2004). Much of the established literature that focuses on HIV/AIDS and migration in SSA is from late 1990s to early and mid-2000s. This was the time when social epidemiology of HIV/AIDS was beginning to gain ground and structural factors such as migration and poverty were being explored as factors impacting the prevalence and incidence of the infection. Available etiological literature examines the relationship between HIV/AIDS and migration, and takes a closer look at migrants' vulnerability and HIV related risky behaviors.

In 2011 there were an estimated 23.5 million people living with HIV in Sub-Saharan Africa. This has increased since 2009, when an estimated 22.5 million people were living with HIV. The increase in people living with HIV could be partly due to a decrease in AIDS-related deaths in the region. There were 1.2 million deaths due to AIDS in 2011. Almost 70% of people living with HIV worldwide live in Sub-Saharan Africa. In fact, just three countries—Nigeria, South Africa and Uganda—account for 48% of all new HIV infections in the world. Uniquely, HIV transmission in Sub-Saharan Africa is predominantly through heterosexual encounters (UAIDS, 2012).

HIV research on Sub-Saharan Africa has indicated that labor migrants are no longer the agents of spreading HIV as it was the case at the inception of the disease, but instead are targeted as a group who are at high risk for contracting the infection (Decosas, 1995; Hunt, 1996; Lurie et al., 2003; Lurie, 2000). Although migration forms an integral part of the African labor market and is primarily driven by economic reasons, Sub-Saharan Africa in contrast to North Africa has a unique migration pattern of its own. Migrants from this region tend to stay on the continent, moving within the region or their country. The major host countries within Sub-Saharan Africa are Côte d'Ivoire, Gabon, Botswana, and South Africa. The main sending countries are Mali, Burkina Faso, Zimbabwe, Mozambique, and Lesotho. In the Western parts of Sub-Saharan Africa migrants primarily work as manual laborers on cotton, cocoa, and coffee plantations. In the South African region migrants have been characterized by contract labor, predominantly within the mining industry (de Haan, 2000).

Migrant workers in Sub-Saharan Africa are predominantly male (Black, 2004). Generally young men (25-49 years) leave their rural homes in search of work in urban areas within the national boundaries. In a new unfamiliar urban environment, away from the rural cultural norms and village traditions, they may engage in sexual activities with high-risk individuals, such as sex workers, thereby exposing themselves to the virus. Thus they might carry the acquired virus and upon returning to their host communities might infect their rural partners (Lurie, 2000). Studies that address this situation all arrive at the same conclusion that it is the social disruption, which characterizes migration, determines the migrant male workers' vulnerability to HIV and then eventually to AIDS (Brummer, 2002; Caldwell, Caldwell and

Quiggin, 1989; Decosas, Kane and Anarfi, 1995; Hunt, 1996 and 1989). Migration has a deleterious effect on family and social relations. Doyal as early as in 1981 stated that in the case of male migrants, the disruption of personal foundations attributed to family life often led to the disintegration of established marital and sexual patterns. In SSA, many employers that hired migrants supported such disintegration of marital and sexual patterns by providing sex workers to migrants after paydays. In many cases, employers brought a convoy of 30 to 40 sex workers to migrant camps soon after migrants were paid. This phenomenon of frequenting sex-workers is not confined to miners and plantation workers only, but is true for many migrant workers.

Available etiological literature on the relationship between HIV/AIDS and migration in the context of Sub-Saharan Africa can be generally divided into two areas: one that emphasizes agency (i.e., individual characteristics) and the other that emphasizes structure (economic and political). Theories on individual factors come from anthropological studies (Caldwell et al., 1989) and focus on the cultural or ideological reasons behind the disease progression. Caldwell, Caldwell and Quiggin (1989) contended that African cultural factors such as polygyny, linkage through lineage rather than conjugal bonds, and stress on reproduction create weak marriage ties. They reported that in the SSA culture it was not unusual for men to have more than one sexual partner. These already weak marital ties have been further weakened due to migration. Weak marital ties along with the cultural acceptance of the norm that one can have more than one sexual partner, then increases a migrant's risk of HIV exposure.

Theories that look to structural factors shaping the relationship between HIV/AIDS and migration come from the Marxist traditions. Marxists look at colonialism in combination with labor market theory and world systems theory to explain not only the creation of migrant labor, but also how this leads to poor health outcomes among migrants. Those who follow the Marxist tradition are of the view that colonialism and apartheid created the migrant labor system in Africa. This migrant labor theory propounds that due to economic reasons (for example hut and head taxes imposed upon African Blacks), individuals often had to leave their rural base in order to reduce the financial burden created by taxation. These migrants worked in mines and plantations without adequate health facilities or proper living conditions. The employers did not encourage movement of migrants with their families. For instance, in South Africa, the Native Land Act of 1913 allowed Black South Africans to temporarily live in white areas and work for the mining companies and at the end of the migration season, these men were expected to return to their rural bases. Such structural factors caused long periods of separation between the migrant and his family (Hunt, 1996).

Both theoretical orientations are somewhat reductionist in nature as they try to describe the relationship between migration and HIV in a simplistic manner (Hunt, 1996). Brummer (2002) provides a more complex picture and posits that any theory that aims to explore the relationship between migration and HIV needs to take into account the interaction among the individual migrant's characteristics, the cultural factors that shape him (and in which he is embedded), and the socio-political and economic context within which the migration takes place. In case of Sub-Saharan Africa, a critical contextual factor that fuels migration is poverty.

MIGRANTS' VULNERABILITY AND HIV-RELATED RISK BEHAVIORS

The relationship between labor migration and HIV in SSA is validated by empirical evidences about migrants' unique vulnerability to HIV. Literature has identified social disruption and isolation as main factors that increase migrants' risk behaviors and thus vulnerability to HIV. Several studies have indicated that migrants are at a greater risk of HIV/AIDS along with other sexually transmitted diseases than non-migrants in all of Africa (Decosas et al., 1995; Jochelson, Mothibeli and Leger, 1991; Lurie, Williams, Zuma, Mkaya-Mwamburi, et al., 2003). Studies done in Uganda, South Africa, Botswana, and Senegal also pointed to a strong association between migration and HIV (Decosas and Adrien, 1997, Pison, Le Guenno, Lagarde, Enel, et al., 1993). A study on male factory workers in Zimbabwe indicated that male migrant workers who lived apart from their wives and had multiple sexual partners were more likely to be HIV-positive compared to their non-migrant counterparts (Mbizo et al., 1996). All these studies have arrived at the same conclusion that social disruption as a result of migration was associated with migrants' vulnerability to HIV. This vulnerability, however, is not causally linked to mobility per se. As Decosas and Adrien (1997) argued, it was the events (e.g., separation from the family) and circumstances (e.g., urban working conditions) related to migration process that have increased the risk of HIV transmission. Even though the situations encountered and risky behaviors engaged in during migration may differ from one individual to another and from one place to another, such vulnerabilities among migrant workers are common. Compounding such circumstances is the fact that HIV/AIDS education, health services and condoms are not always available to the migrant population (Decosas and Adrien, 1997). Additional vulnerability results from sex with multiple partners which is often the result of alienation, loneliness, separation from the family, and breakdown of traditional family values. Hunt (1996) aptly stated these "causative factors, all derived from the migrant labor system, [lead] to massive explosion of STDS and illnesses [AIDS] in the African population" (p. 1294).

Both the World Health Organization (WHO) and the Joint United Nations Programme on HIV/AIDS (UNAIDS) reported that unsafe sexual practices have been responsible for the vast majority of HIV infections in Sub-Saharan Africa (Lobe, 2003). Historically it was the spread of HIV among individuals in Africa who were neither homosexual nor intravenous drug users that led to the realization that the infection could be spread through heterosexual intercourse. In fact evidence indicates that heterosexual intercourse accounts for the majority of the disease prevalence among Sub-Saharan Africans; transmission through blood transfusion and infection transmitted through infected needle account for a very low percentage of infections (Clumeck, Mascart-Lemone, De Maubeuge, Brenez and Marcelis, 1983; Morison, 2001).

Risk behaviors such as unprotected heterosexual intercourse, age of first intercourse, and multiple sexual partners (Bockerhoff and Biddlecom, 1999) have been primary factors accounting for sub-Saharan HIV transmission. Buve and colleagues (2001) found out that the spread of HIV was through unprotected sexual intercourse between sex workers and their male clients, the same male clients and their regular female partners, and these female partners and other males with whom they have sexual relationships. In the early nineties, health researchers started to explore the nature of these sexual networks. Their assumption was that it is not so important to know how many sexual partners an individual might have as it is to know who they are. For example, an individual might have four sexual partners, but the network is closed. She/he thus is less at risk of getting infected than an individual who has two sexual partners and the network is open, in which partners can have many other partners (Orubuloye et al., 1995). As migrant laborers' sexual networks tend to be open, their sexual activities increases the risk of intra- and extra-network transmissions.

CURRENT EFFORTS

Given the knowledge that heterosexual transmission has been the primary means HIV transmission among migrant men in Sub-Saharan Africa (Painter, 2001), most of the early and even current intervention programs target individual's sexual practices. As a result, the nature of current prevention and intervention programs and HIV-related policies implemented in Sub-Saharan Africa continue to focus on individual level interventions and a vast majority of prevention models emphasize biomedical interventions. Typically, primary aims of these intervention strategies have been to increase condom use, decrease the number of sexual partners, increase knowledge regarding HIV/AIDS, and increase the provision of STD treatment (Williams, MacPhail, Cambell, Tajaard, et al., 2000).

Even though such strategic efforts have had some success, the pitfalls of these programs are clear including decontextualization and reductionism. Decontextualization occurs when the contexts that influence sexual decisions, such as economics, tradition, culture, and politics, are not taken into account. Reductionism stems from decontextualization because it views individuals and their health behavior as separate from their social contexts. Conventional health behavior models in western societies postulate that knowledge translates into action (McKenzie and Jurs, 1993). Based on the knowledge to action models, it is expected that the more an individual knows about health risks, the more risk averse he/she would become; and people would make rational choices regarding their sexual behavior. However, research on HIV interventions in SSA challenges such models, since increase in awareness have not always translated into behavior change (Makinwa, 2007). In addition, most migrant workers are not aware of the array of choices available to them in order to make rational decisions (Harrison, Smit and Myer, 2000). The rational choice explanatory model that underscores informed decision making on part of an individual in the face of accurate and comprehensive health knowledge might fall short of accurate prediction of behavior (Hutchison and Charlesworth, 2011 in the context of SSA.

Unfortunately most of the HIV-related prevention and intervention programs in SSA fail to consider the broader country context as well as the detailed context within which sex is negotiated between migrant workers and their partners. Concurring to the argument proposed by Campbell and Williams (1999), HIV should be viewed as a social and developmental issue as opposed to a primarily biomedical and/or an individual behavioral problem. In line with studies highlighting the individualistic notions of risk, Campbell and Williams (1999) link social capital and risky sexual behaviors. For instance, the migrant that came from surrounding rural areas and toiled in the gold mines of Johannesburg missed family and their living conditions (a single sex hotel where 90% of the workers live) provided very little in terms of social support; away from parental supervision, village elders, rural norms, and living the extremely high stress life as a miner made drinking and sex seem to be two of the most common diversionary activities that were easily available to this group of migrant workers.

Based on the literature discussed thus far we posit that migration leads to social disruption which in turn increases migrants' vulnerability for contracting HIV. Evidences also suggest that purely individual level prevention and interventions targeting behavior modification are not enough to curb the scourge of HIV in Sub-Saharan Africa. From what the field of research has offered, thereafter, we put forth a theoretical model based on social capital theory (see Figure 2) to supplement interventions that addresses social disruptions associated with migration process. In this model, social capital is understood as the institutions, relationships, and norms that shape the quality and quantity of an individual's social interactions; it is not just the sum of the institutions that underpin a society — it is the glue that holds the individual members of a society together (Serageldin, 1998). The central tenet of social capital is the membership in a certain group that confers benefits and obligations for the individual (Portes, 1998). In the context of HIV and migration in SSA, social disruption associated with migration process contributes to declining social capital, which has been manifested by decreased social identity, lack of trust in the receiving community, losing traditional norms and culture, and changed social networks.

The social capital theory oriented framework is particularly relevant in SSA given its history of colonialism, and long-term struggles with poverty and income disparity. While people in SSA nations migrated as an economic survival strategy (Kothari, 2002) and family financial security mechanism (Adepjou, 2000; Schrider and Knerr, 2000), relationships between migration and poverty became bi-directional; that is, structural poverty motivates migration as a buffer against economic vicissitudes in SSA and meanwhile migration might increase the financial vulnerability for migrant workers as they sending remittance and those left behind as they becoming too dependent on it (Waddington, 2003). Thus, social disruption and declining social capital seems to be inevitable and an unhealthy route for migrant workers.

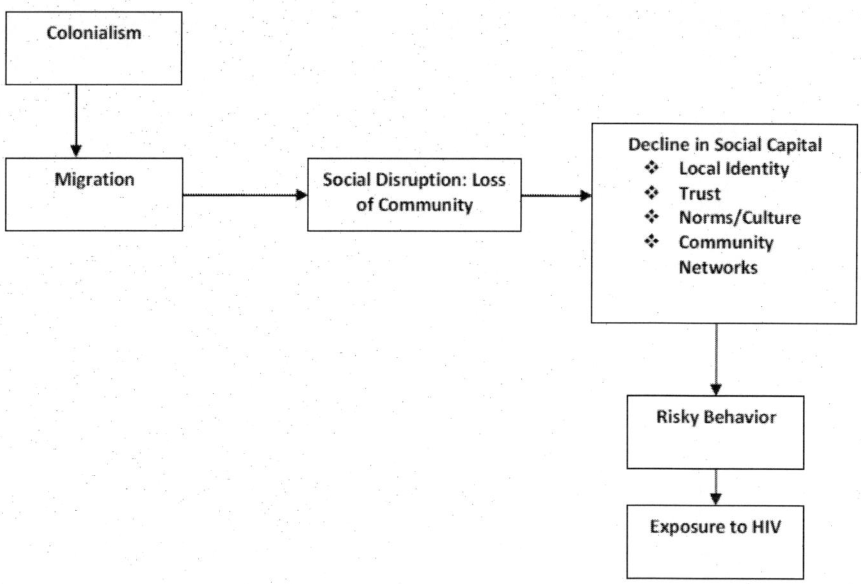

Figure 2. Colonialism, Migration and HIV.

In addition, links between social capital and health came into prominence through income inequality and health inequality literature; income inequality led to a lack of investment in social capital which in turn led to higher mortality rates among the poor (Kawachi and Kennedy, 1997). Lynch and Kaplan (1997) maintained that income and other resource inequalities were indicators of other latent inequalities in the socio-political structures that adversely affect the poor. (Pevalin and Rose's work (2004) emphasized the links among social capital, social support, and health. Therefore, in both ex-migration and immigration related to SSA nations, social capital would arguably be essential to individual health. For instance, Campbell and colleagues (2002) drew on Freire's critical consciousness as a way of increasing social identity and social capital among a group of school children in South Africa and then employed peer education as an HIV prevention strategy. Sen, Aguilar and Goldbach (2010) in their study on migrant men in Angola demonstrated that migrant men have a lower level of social capital and this lower level of social capital is associated with higher levels of HIV risk behaviors.

Practice Implication: Leadership Mobilization Model

Based on the theoretical framework regarding HIV, social capital, and positive health outcomes, we propose a prevention model that aims at increasing social capital and social networks among migrants and the communities in which they reside as a way of combating HIV/AIDS. Various types of mobilization models are used throughout the Sub-Saharan Africa to organize communities to combat against HIV/AIDS (Gregson, Terceira, Mushati, Nyamukapa, and Campbell, 2004; Low-Beer and Stoneburner, 2003). Among the most promising ones, Leadership Mobilization Models (LMM) becomes prominent. LMM in general seeks to create a united front in the fight for public policy enforcement and reforms where necessary, advocate for funding to combat the proliferation of the disease, increase education and knowledge, and utilize social power and assets within community organizations to advocate for resources to slow the progression of the disease. In specific, we are proposing a LMM that is based on the "*Council of Elders*" model for community reform (Amram, 1900) and adopts concepts from social capital theories as its foundational framework. This model has been presented as an HIV prevention model for South Africa (Sen, Aguilar and Bacchus, 2010). And given the socio-cultural and other contextual similarities across South African and Sub-Saharan African nations at large, it is expected that this model can be easily transferred to the Sub-Saharan context.

This model aims at mobilizing social capital of the leaders in the clergy, public policy, health promotion, medicine, and community-based or non-governmental organizations. The goal is to bring together local leaders in the community and educate them about their potential role in the fight against HIV transmission. Through the mobilization of the leadership this model aims at increasing the integration of migrants in the host communities. The underlying assumption is that better integration implies higher social capital of migrants and a resultant decline in social isolation, re-establishment of cultural norms and traditions, increased access to social and health-related resources, and ultimately a decline in sexually risky behaviors.

Core elements or activities of the LMM include: (1) identifying, educating, and mobilizing African community leadership; (2) facilitating collaborations with all community entities and exploring collaborations with other non-traditional entities who also have a stake in addressing the problem; and (3) creating action plans that respond to World Health Organization's, World Bank's, and the CDC's initiatives to identify high-risk populations, increase testing, provide continuum of care for HIV positive individuals, and reduce the spread of HIV infection.

Unlike traditionally individualistic models of HIV intervention and prevention, LMM builds on the collectiveness embedded within Sub-Saharan men's lives. In contrast to the existing HIV prevention and intervention programs that encourage individual decision-making based on health-related information, the LMM makes use of indigenous leadership existent within a community (bonding social capital) to carry the cultural traditions from rural areas into the migrant communities. This carryover permits the cultural strictures that regulate marital and sexual behavior to continue regulating migrant workers' sexual behaviors despite the incredible distances between urban communities in which they work and the rural villages these men migrate from. This carryover also facilitates collaboration with other entities and stakeholders outside the community (bridging social capital), thus increasing the collective bargaining power of the surrounding communities to advocate for better living and working conditions as well as access to health care for the migrants and sex workers.

LMM is predicated on a set necessary competencies and skills. First, leadership must possess several core competencies, which include the capacity to: work with African community leaders, collaborate with and engage other governmental and non-governmental organization leaders, and understand the role and value of macro or *structural intervention*. Although the LMM is a community based macro level intervention, leaders must also understand the role and value of individual behavioral interventions. Second, it is necessary that each participating organization should themselves have a sound infrastructure to support accomplishing LMM tasks including: facilitating collaborations among various stakeholders, teaching HIV prevention skills to migrants, conducting social marketing campaigns, developing and implementing action plans, and monitoring and evaluation to ensure quality, integrity and accountability of the model.

Effective LMM depends on the first step of establishing an Advisory Committee — "*Council of Elders*," which would help identify leaders on an on-going basis. The members of the council are often village elders who are highly respected in the community. Identified leaders would be trained and educated to increase the awareness of HIV and migration and their impacts on local communities, to enhance the leadership capacity in aligning or realigning resources to target the problem, and to develop a collective disposition of working with other leaders and community stakeholders. The third step of LMM is the development of action plans in which action items are to be identified collectively by members of the Advisory Committee. Action plans are the result of prioritizing local community needs, selecting the three most important issues to act upon (in the case of HIV and migration the three issues would be public health, community integration, and community cohesion), and producing a strategy to implement action items that delineates roles and responsibilities of each leader. Leaders must also reach consensus regarding the collaborations needed and the resources required to accomplish each identified goal. The final step of the LMM is monitoring or evaluation of progress. The leadership will be held accountable to produce regular evaluation reports concerning the implementation and impact of the action plans. Such evaluations will assess the capacity of the leadership to affect changes at the macro level, which translates into significant and sustainable changes in how HIV is addressed in local communities where migrants reside.

CONCLUSION

HIV/AIDS is currently one of the most devastating health conditions affecting the health of millions throughout the world. A significant proportion of these individuals reside in Sub Saharan Africa. The health and social implications of HIV/AIDS on human development are extensive and have resulted in an expanded national and international effort to respond to the HIV/AIDS epidemic with increased funding and expansion of prevention, care and intervention activities. As the literature points out the connection between migration and HIV/AIDS has been explored extensively and it has been established that the social disruption that accompanies migration is an important mediating factor in this relationship. However, most of the interventions designed have looked at behavioral modifications. It is hoped that the culturally grounded social capital theory based Leadership Mobilization Model proposed here would supplement the existing prevention and intervention programs. This model also reflects social work missions of upholding social justice and empowerment by shifting the burden of the disease from a purely individual level and placing it in the environment and by exploring the solutions from within the community itself.

REFERENCES

Adepoju, A. (2000). Issues and recent trends in international migration in Sub-Saharan Africa. *International Social Science Journal*, 52(165), 383-394.

Aguilar, J. P. and Sen, S. (2009). Framing social capital for macro social work practice. *Journal of Community Practice*, 17(4), 424-443.

Amram, D. W. (1900). The Zekenim, or Council of Elders. *Journal of Biblical Literature*. 19, 34-52.

Bourdieu, P. (1986). The forms of capital. In: J. Richardson (Ed.), *Handbook of theory and research for the sociology of education* (pp. 241-258). New York, NY: Greenwood.

Brokerhoff, M. and Biddlecom, A. (1999). Migration, sexual behavior and the risk of HIV in Kenya. *International Migration Review*, 33(4), 0833-0856.

Brummer, D. (2002). *Labour migration and HIV/AIDS in Southern Africa*. International Organisation for Migration, Regional Office for Southern Africa, Pretoria.

Buve, A. et al. (2001). Multicenter study on factors determining the difference in rate of spread of HIV in sub-Saharan Africa: Methods and prevalence of HIV infection. *AIDS*, 15 (suppl. 4), 5-14.

Caldwell, J.C., Caldwell, P. and Quiggin, P. (1989). The social context of AIDS in Sub-Saharan Africa. *Population and Development Review* 15(2), 185-234.

Campbell, C. and Williams, B. (1999). Beyond the biomedical and behavioral: Towards an integrated approach to HIV prevention in the Southern African mining industry. *Social Science and Medicine*, 48(11), 1625-1639.

Campbell, C., Williams, B., and Gilgen, D. (2002). Is social capital a useful conceptual tool for exploring community level influences on HIV infection? An exploratory case study from South Africa. *AIDS Care*, 14, 41-54.

Coleman, J. S. (1990). *Foundations of Social Theory.* Cambridge Massachusetts, Harvard University Press.

Clumeck, N., Mascart-Lemone, F., DeMaubeuge, J. Brenez, D. Marcelis, L. (1983). Acquired Immune Deficiency Syndrome in black Africans. *Lancet*, 1, 642.

de Haan, A. (2000). Migrants, livelihood and rights: The relevance of migration in development policies. *Social Development Working Paper no. 4*, Department for International Development, London. Retreived from http://62.189.42.51/DFIDstage/Pubs/files/sdd_migwp4.pdf.

Decosas, J., Kane, F., and Anarfi, J. (1995). Migration and AIDS. *Lancet*, 346, 826-828.

Decosas, J. and Adrien, A. (1997). Migration and HIV. *AIDS*, 11(Supplement A), 77-84.

Doyal, L., Hunt, G., and Mellor, J. (1981). Your life in their hands: migrant workers in the national health service. *Critical Social Policy*, 1, 54-71.

Fee, E. and Krieger, N. (1993). Understanding AIDS historical interpretation and the limits of biomedical individualism. *American Journal of Public Health*, **83**(10), 1477-1486.

Gregson, S., Terceira, N., Mushati, P., Nyamukapa, C., and Campbell, C. (2004). Community group participation: Can it help young women to avoid HIV? An exploratory study of social capital and school education in Rural Zimbabwe. *Social Science and Medicine*, 58, 2119-2132.

Harrison, A., Smit, J.A., Myer, L. (2000). Prevention of HIV/AIDS in South Africa: A review of behavior change interventions, evidence, and options for the future. *South African Journal of Science*, 96(6), 285-290.

Haour-Knipe, M. (2003). *Sexual health of mobile and migrant population.* Geneva: International Office of Migration.

Hawe, P. and Shiell, A. (2000). Social capital and health promotion: A review. *Social Science and Medicine*, 51(6), 871-885.

Hope, K. R. (2001). Population mobility and multi-partner sex in Botswana: Implications for the spread of HIV/AIDS. *African Journal of Reproductive Health*, 5(3), 73-83.

Hutchison, E. D., and Charlesworth, L. W. (2011). Theoretical perspectives on human behavior. In: E. D. Hutchison (Ed.), *Dimensions of human behavior: Person and environment* (4th ed., pp. 34-69). Thousand Oaks, CA: Sage.

Hunt, C. W. (1996). Social vs. biological: Theories on the transmission of AIDS in Africa. *Social Science and Medicine*, 42(9), 1283-1296.

Jochelson, K., Mothibeli, M. and Leger, J. (1991). Human immunodeficiency virus and migrant labor in South Africa. *International Journal of Health Services*, 21, 157-173.

Joffe, H. (1996). AIDS research and prevention: A social representational approach. *British Journal of Medical Psychology*, 69, 169-190.

Kawachi, I. and Kennedy, B. P. (1997). Health and social cohesion: Why care about income inequality? *British Medical Journal*, 314, 1037-1040.

Kawachi, I. and Kennedy, B. P. (1999). Income inequality and health: Pathways and mechanisms. *Health Services Research*, 34, 215-227.

Kippax, S. and Crawfdord, J. (1993). *Flaws in the theory of reasoned action.* In: D. Terry, C. Gallios, and M. McCamish, (Eds.). The theory of reasoned action: Its application to AIDS-preventive behavior, 253-269. Oxford England: Pergamon.

Low-Beer, D. and Stoneburner, R. L. (2003). Behavior and communication change in reducing HIV: Is Uganda unique? *African Journal of AIDS Research*, 2, 9-21.

Lurie, M. (2000). Migration and AIDS in Southern Africa: A review. *South African Journal of Science*, 96(6), 343-355.

Lurie, M., Williams, D., Zuma, K., Mkaya-Mwamburi, D., Garnett, G., Sturm, A., Sweat, M., Gitteslsohn, J., and Abdool Karim, S. (2003). The impact of migration on HIV-1 transmission in South Africa: A Study of migrant men and their partners. *Sexually Transmitted Diseases*, 30(2), 149-156.

Lynch, J. W. and Kaplan, G. A. (1997). Editorial: Whither studies on the socioeconomic foundations of population health. *American Journal of Public Health*, 87, 1409-1410.

Makinwa, B. (2001). Communication framework for HIV/AIDS: A new direction. Paper presented at the VIII International Communication for Development Roundtable, Managua, Nicaragua.

Mbizo, M.T., Machekano, R., McFarland, W. R. S., Bassett, M., Latif, A., and Katzenstein, D. (1996). HIV seroincidence and correlates of seroconversion in a cohort of male factory workers in Harare, Zimbabwe. *AIDS*, 10, 895-901.

Morison, L. (2001). Global epidemiology of HIV/AIDS. *British Medical Bulletin*, 58(1), 7-18.

Muntaner, C., Lynch, J., and Smith, G.D. (2000). Social capital and the third way in public health. *Critical Public Health*, 10(2), 107-124.

Painter, T. M. (2001). *Voluntary counseling and testing for couples: High leverage intervention for HIV/AIDS prevention in Sub-Saharan Africa*. National Center for HIV, STD and TB Prevention, Division of HIV/AIDS Prevention, Center for Disease Control. Atlanta, Georgia.

Pevalin, D.J., and Rose, D. (2003). *Social capital for health: Investigating the links between social capital and health using the British Household Panel Survey.* London, England: Health Development Agency. ISBN 1-84279-129-X.

Orubuloye, I.O., Omoniyi, O.P., and Shokunbi, W.A. (1995). Sexual networking, STDs and HIV/AIDS in four urban goals in Nigeria. *Health Transmission Review*, 5 supplement, 123-129.

Pison, G., Le Guenno, B., Lagarde, E., Enel, C., and Seck, C. (1993). Seasonal migration: a risk factor for HIV in rural Senegal. *Journal of Acquired Immunodeficiency Syndrome*, 6, 196-200.

Polack, R. J. (2004). Social justice and the global economy: New challenges for social work in the 21st century. *Social work*, 49(2), 281-290.

Portes, A. (1998). Social capital: its origins and applications in modern sociology. *Annual Review of Sociology*, 24, 1-24.

Portes, A. and Landolt, P (1996). The downside of social capital. *The American Prospect*, 26, 18-21.

Putnam, R. D. (1995). Tuning in, tuning out: The strange disappearance of social capital in America. *Political Science and Politics*, 28(4), 664-683.

Quinn, T.C. (1994). Population migration and the spread of Types 1 and 2 Human Immunodeficiency Virus. *Proceedings of the National Academy of Sciences*, 91, 2407-2414.

Sen, S., Aguilar, J., and Bacchus, D (2010). Migration, poverty, and HIV risk of infection: An application of social capital theory. *Journal of Human Behavior in the Social Environment*, 20(7), 897-908.

Sen, S., Aguilar, J. and Goldbach, J. (2010). Social capital: A buffer against HIV/AIDS among migrant men in Sub-Saharan Africa. *Journal of HIV/AIDS and Social Services*, 9 (2), 190-211.

Serageldin, I. (1998). Social capital: The missing link? *Social Capital Initiative, Working Paper No. 3*. The World Bank Group.

Shtarkshall, R. and Soskolone, V. (2000). *Migrant population and HIV/AIDS: The development and implementation of programmes: Theory, methodology, and practice*. UNESCO/UNAIDS: Geneva.

UNAIDS (2004). Report on the Global AIDS Epidemic. Geneva.

UNAIDS (2013). Report on the Global AIDS Epidemic. Geneva.

Weine, S. M. and Kashube, A. B. (2012). Labor migration and HIV risk: A systematic review. *AIDS and Behavior* 16, 1605-1621.

Williams, B. G., MacPhail, C. Cambell, C., Tajaard, D. Gouws, E., Meoma, S., Mzaidume, Z. and Rosego, B. (2000). The Carletonville-Mothusimpilo project: Limiting transmission of HIV through community-based interventions. *South African Journal of Science*, 96(6), 351-360.

Woolcock, M. (1998). Social capital and economic development: Toward a theoretical synthesis and policy framework. *Theory and Society* 27, 151-208.

Woolcock, M. and Narayan, D. (2000). Social capital: Implications for development theory, research, and policy. *The World Bank Research Observer* 15(2), 225-249.

World Bank (2007). HIV/AIDS in Africa. Regional Brief. Retrieved from http://web.world bank.org/.

World Health Organization (2003). *International migration, health and human rights*. Geneva.

In: Migrant Workers
Editors: Qingwen Xu and Lucy P. Jordan
ISBN: 978-1-63485-272-2

Chapter 5

ASSESSING PSYCHOSOCIAL STRESS OF PUERTO RICAN WOMEN IN THE UNITED STATES: THE HISPANIC WOMEN'S SOCIAL STRESSOR SCALE

Yong Li[1,*], Blanca M. Ramos[2] and Young Do[3]
[1]Department of Social Work, Plattsburgh State University of New York, Plattsburgh, NY, US
[2]School of Social Welfare, University at Albany, State University of New York, New York, US
[3]Hospitality House, TC, Inc., Albany, New York, US

ABSTRACT

Puerto Rican women have experienced psychosocial stress as they face myriad individual, familial, and societal stressors that could contribute to negative mental health outcomes. These stressors are associated with their migration experience and often complex and multidimensional. However, research remains scant in relation to the measurement of psychosocial stress among Puerto Rican women thus intervention and prevention efforts could be inappropriate or inadequate. To bridge this gap, the chapter examined the underlying factor structure of the Hispanic Women's Social Stressor Scale (HWSSS) in a sample of 153 Puerto Rican women in upstate New York. The findings indicate the HWSSS has good reliability and validity, and produces a five-factor underlying structure: (a) employment, (b) socioeconomic status, (c) acculturation, (d) parental, and (e) familial. The correlations between all subscales and depressive symptoms were significant, thus providing evidence that the HWSSS has good criterion validity in this sample of Puerto Rican women. In addition, the emerged factor structure was notably different from that of the original HWSSS developed for women of Mexican heritage. Of special interest, stressors related to employment, familial strain, and acculturation appear more salient among Puerto Rican women. The findings underscore

* Corresponding author: Yong Li, Department of Social Work, SUNY Plattsburgh, 101 Broad St., Plattsburgh, NY 12901, US. Email: yli009@plattsburgh.edu.

the need to consider gender and unique Hispanic subgroup characteristics in mental health practice and migration research.

INTRODUCTION

The Puerto Rican population is the second largest Hispanic subgroup living in the United States mainland (Ennis, Ríos-Vargas, and Albert, 2011). According to the Census Bureau's American Community Survey, this population was estimated to be 4.9 million in 2011 (Brown and Patten, 2013). About two thirds were born in the mainland and nearly half are concentrated in the New York metropolitan area and the state of Florida (Collazo, Ryan, and Bauman, 2010). Compared to the US Hispanic population overall, they speak English more proficiently, are slightly older, and are less likely to be married (Brown and Patten, 2013). In addition, unlike the other Hispanic subgroups, Puerto Ricans are characterized by their unique legal status; they are US citizens at birth. Therefore, they are migrants rather than immigrants (Guarnaccia, 1997).

Puerto Ricans have a long history of migrating between the island and the mainland, and the post-war great wave of migration was the response of affordable air travels between the island and the mainland, as well as the huge demand of cheap labor by US companies. In the recent decade, the search for economic opportunities is still the most commonly given explanation for Puerto Ricans' migration (Cohn, Patten and Lopez, 2014). Migration for this group often takes place following a circular pattern between the island of Puerto Rico and the mainland (Ramos, 1992). Indeed, among the recent migration wave, mainland-born Puerto Ricans have taken disproportionate larger section of departures (Cohn et al., 2014). Although their ability to migrate in both directions appears to reduce migration related stress, their circular migration also gives rise to new stressors. This involves facing a 'neither here nor there' situation and thus a sense of loss of cultural identity (Guarnaccia, Martinez, and Acosta, 2005).

Few studies have focused on the mental health of Puerto Ricans in the mainland, particularly Puerto Rican women. Comparative studies that have investigated the mental health of different Hispanic subgroups in the United States generally agree that Puerto Ricans are more likely to experience mental health problems and to be diagnosed with psychiatric disorders attributed in part to low levels of education, few economic resources, and relatively poor health outcomes due to their circular migration patterns (Alegría, Mulvaney-Day, Torres, Polo, et al., 2007; Sánchez, Cardemil, Connell, Ferreira, et al., 2014; Guarnaccia, et al., 2005; US Department of Health and Human Services, 2001). Empirical evidence on the mental health of Hispanic women indicates that Puerto Rican women had the highest rates on depression and substance abuse compared to those from other Hispanic subgroups (Ai, Appel, Huang, and Lee, 2012).

SOCIAL STRESSORS AND HISPANIC MENTAL HEALTH

Researchers have examined the correlates of the mental health problems among Hispanics and highlighted the role of social stressors. They often note that the social stressors facing Hispanics are multidimensional. Caplan (2007) identified three dimensions of stressors facing Hispanic migrants: instrumental or environmental, social and interpersonal, and societal. Instrumental or environmental stressors are related to challenges and difficulties in obtaining the goods and services to meet basic needs in the arriving society (e.g., employment, access to health care, and language abilities). Social and interpersonal stressors include difficulties due to migration associated changes in relationships, roles, behaviors, and cultural norms (e.g., loss of family and social support, and intergenerational conflicts). Societal stressors are those stemming from discrimination and political and historical forces due to minority and migration status. These stressors may ensue as individual, family, and societal factors interact (Guarnaccia, 1997). Factors at the individual level may include socioeconomic resources, social skills, knowledge of the host culture, and social support. Societal factors may include the characteristics of the host society such as its economy, social and class structures, and attitudes toward immigrants (Guarnaccia, 1997).

Although Puerto Ricans on the mainland are US citizen migrants, they still share similar stressors identified above for Hispanic immigrants. Compared with other US Hispanics, Puerto Ricans overall are worse off on several indicators of well-being; they are concentrated in lower-skilled, low-paying jobs, have lower median household income, and are more likely to live in poverty (Brown and Patten, 2013; Cohn et al., 2014). Puerto Ricans also experience high levels of prejudice and discrimination (Guarnaccia, 1997). Research on Puerto Rican women suggests that they experience additional social inequalities associated with sexism and racism; economic oppression, racial and gender discrimination, cultural conflict, and the loss of social support systems often place them at risk for psychosocial stress and psychological stress (Ramos, 2012; Roschelle, 2002). Those women living in New York State, for example, tend to be even poorer than Puerto Rican women on the mainland (Bose, 2006). Older Puerto Rican women have been found to live in deteriorating housing conditions and unsafe neighborhoods (Ramos, 2007). For newly migrated Puerto Rican women, stressors related to traditional gender roles are not uncommon. Working Puerto Rican women have experienced not only employment related stressors but also stressors associated with prescribed family caregiving responsibilities expected to be met simultaneously. These, in turn, can be exacerbated by existing and impending economic strains (Ramos, 2012; Ramos and Carlson, 2004).

The multidimensional stressors Hispanics face have been found to predict negative mental health outcomes. Stacciarini and colleagues (2015), for instance, reported positive associations between mental health problems and family stressors (such as mother-child relationships, family separation, and family conflict) and community stressors (such as social isolation) among Hispanic mothers in rural communities. Discrimination and socioeconomic stressors have been linked to psychological distress including depressive symptoms among Hispanics (Ayón, Marsiglia, and Bermudez-Parsai, 2010; Leung, LaChapelle, Scinta, and Olvera, 2014; Moradi and Risco, 2006). Among Puerto Ricans, discrimination stressors have also been associated with mental health problems (Lee and Ferraro, 2009). Torres and Wallace (2013) found that among Puerto Rican women having to migrate (as opposed to wanting to migrate) was associated with increased psychological distress. Available literature with a focus on Puerto Rican women is sporadic and more research is sorely needed.

ASSESSING SOCIAL STRESS AMONG HISPANICS

Effective intervention and prevention programs depend on an accurate and culturally appropriate assessment of social stress for Puerto Rican women, the measures that take into account the complex, multidimensional nature of stressors they are likely to experience and their interactions with those that are gender and Hispanic subgroup specific. By and large, for now, the instruments frequently used to assess social stress among Hispanics do not capture gender and/or Puerto Ricans' unique situations. Commonly used assessment tools include the Hispanic Stress Inventory (HIS) developed by Cervantes, Padilla and Salgado de Snyder (1991), which has an immigrant version (73 items) and a US born version (59 items). Both versions assess occupational stress, parental stress, marital stress, and family/culture stress. The immigrant version also assesses immigration stress. Evidence supports the reliability and validity of the HSI (Cervantes et al., 1991). In an effort to shorten the HSI, Cavazos-Rehg and colleagues (2006) validated a 17-item HSI in a sample of adult Hispanic immigrants residing in a large Midwestern city. Their findings suggested an intrafamilial-extrafamilial structure that was associated with Hispanic immigrant stress. The Social, Attitudinal, Familial, and Environmental Acculturative Stress Scale (SAFE), another widely adopted tool, developed by Mena, Padilla and Maldonado (1987) also measures acculturation stress in these dimensions. Evidence supports that the SAFE has both reliability and validity among different generations of Hispanic college students (Fuertes and Westbrook, 1996; Mena, et al., 1987).

The Hispanic Women's Social Stressor Scale (HWSSS) is specially developed to measure social stress among Hispanic immigrant women (Goodkind, Gonzales, Malcoe, and Espinosa, 2008). The HWSSS incorporates the unique stressors related to traditional gender roles and role strain immigrant women often encounter/face. Compared to immigrant men, Hispanic women may experience the same stressors to a greater extent. The HWSSS has been validated with first and second generation immigrant women of Mexican heritage living in the Southwestern United States. Goodkind and colleagues (2008) conducted a factor analysis of the HWSSS which revealed six subscales: (a) immigration, (b) socioeconomic, (c) racism-related, (d) familial, (e) parental, and (f) employment. Although the HWSSS takes into account gender specific stressors, this instrument has not been validated with women from other Hispanic subgroups, including Puerto Rican women. The present study seeks to help bridge this gap in the literature.

Our study examines the underlying factor structure of the HWSSS and its psychometric properties to render an instrument that more accurately assesses social stress among Puerto Rican migrant women. Based on the review of the literature, we expect that the factor structure (i.e., construct validity) identified in the study would be slightly different from what have been reported in Goodkind and colleagues' study (2008) with Mexican immigrant women. Using the subscales derived from our data, we also examined the internal consistency reliability of the HWSSS. Finally, we report the criterion validity of the subscales using depressive symptoms and anxiety sensitivity as two criterion measures.

METHODS

Data Collection and Sample

The study utilizes a cross-sectional design to assess social stressors and mental health in in a community sample of women of Puerto Rican heritage in upstate New York. Participants completed a survey in an English or Spanish version based on their language preference. About 48% of the participants preferred the English version of the survey while 52% preferred the Spanish version. Participants were compensated for their time.

Participants were recruited from Hispanic communities in three small cities in upstate New York. Local church officials, community agencies, and other advocates helped identify potential women to be included in the study. Participants (N = 153) were primarily born in Puerto Rico (72%) with a mean age of 33.6 years old. Most participants were in the US labor force (80%). Among them, about 45% worked full-time or part-time, or were self-employed; 38% were unemployed; and 8% were students. Seventy three percent of the participants had an annual household income below $24,999, and 42% had not completed high school.

Measures

We used the HWSSS to measure social stressors, a 41-item scale with Likert-type responses that measures the degree to which a respondent experienced a particular stressor in the past year. If the participants had not experienced the stressor, the item was coded as, "did not happen/does not apply." Otherwise, participants indicated their experiences on a 4-point scale (1 = "not at all stressful," 2 = "a little stressful," 3 = "somewhat stressful," and 4 = "very stressful"). Consistent with Goodkind and colleagues' study (2008), we combined the "did not happen/does not apply" category with the "not at all stressful" category to indicate no stressor. Goodkind and colleagues (2008) reported that the HWSSS demonstrated good internal consistency reliability, construct validity, convergent validity, and criteria validity among Mexican immigrant women. In our study, three items were removed from the scale that pertained to fears of deportation due to the fact that Puerto Ricans are US citizens and do not experience those elements of immigration (e.g., "thinking you or family members might be deported"). Therefore, this modified version of the HWSSS in the current study had 38 items.

To examine the criterion validity, we used the Center for Epidemiological Studies Depression Scale (CES-D; Radloff, 1977) and the Anxiety Sensitivity Index (ASI; Reiss, Peterson, Gursky, and McNally, 1986) to assess mental health among Puerto Rican women. The CES-D is a 20-item self-report diagnostic scale which measures depressive symptomology during the past week (e.g., "I felt depressed"). Response options range from 0 to 3 for each item (0 = "rarely or none of the time," 1 = "some or little of the time," 2 = "moderately or much of the time," 3 = "most or almost all the time"). Research has suggested that it has high internal consistency and good validity (Lewinsohn, Seeley, Roberts, and Allen, 1997). It has also been validated among Hispanic women (Posner, Stewart, Marín, and Pérez-Stable, 2001).

The ASI is a 16-item scale which measures fear of anxiety and physical sensations related to anxiety (e.g., "It is important to me not to appear nervous"). It uses a 5-point Likert-type response scale ranging from 0 ("very little") to 4 ("very much"). Research has shown that it has good reliability and validity (Peterson and Heilbronner, 1987; Reiss, 1991). It has been reported to have both convergent validity and discriminant validity among island Puerto Ricans (Cintrón, Carter, Suchday, Sbrocco, and Gray, 2005).

Data Analysis Strategies

Exploratory factor analysis was used to examine the underlying factor structure of the HWSSS. To determine the number of factors to retain for rotation, we used the Kaiser's eigenvalue >1 rule (Kaiser, 1960) and the minimum average partials test (MAP; Velicer, 1976). We used maximum likelihood (ML) to derive the factors and the Geomin rotation method to allow for correlations between factors. Only items with a loading at .40 or higher are considered as loaded on their factors (Ferguson and Cox, 1993). If an item is loaded on two factors with a loading difference smaller than .20, the item is considered as cross-loaded and removed from the analysis; subsequently, the processes of extraction and rotation are repeated with it removed (Ferguson and Cox, 1993). In addition, Cronbach's α was calculated as a measure of the internal consistency reliability. Finally, we conducted correlation analyses to examine the criterion validity of the HWSSS. The factor analysis was conducted in Mplus 6.12 and all other analyses were conducted in STATA 12.0.

RESULTS

Puerto Rican women reported a little, somewhat, or very stressful on most items of the HWSSS. As shown in Table 1, the three items on which women reported the highest stress level included "not having enough money to pay debts," "conflicts among family members," and "not having enough money for basic necessities such as food for your family or shoes for your children." The percentage of women reporting "very stressful" on these three items was also the highest (see Table 1).

Table 1. Descriptive statistics for the HWSSS items in Puerto Rican women

	Item	Range	Mean	SD	Very Stressful (%)
1	Living with relatives	1-4	2.28	1.18	24.3
2	Having trouble balancing work and family	1-4	2.32	1.19	24.0
3	Not being able to spend as much time with your children as you wanted because you had to work	1-4	2.22	1.29	27.9
4	Having to deal with co-workers' or supervisors' negative stereotypes about Hispanic women at your job	1-4	2.03	1.25	21.5
5	Feeling lonely and isolated	1-4	2.41	1.25	28.8
6	Feeling your children were not safe in your neighborhood	1-4	1.99	1.25	23.3

	Item	Range	Mean	SD	Very Stressful (%)
7	Not having enough money to pay debts	1-4	2.88	1.20	44.2
8	Not having the same job opportunities as Anglo women	1-4	2.36	1.29	31.1
9	Not being understood in stores or offices because you could not speak English well	1-4	2.01	1.23	20.6
10	Your children being influenced by bad friends	1-4	2.01	1.18	18.4
11	Not being able to afford to live in the neighborhood you want	1-4	2.27	1.29	27.6
12	Having to be careful about the quality of your work so others would not think you were lazy	1-4	1.90	1.11	13.6
13	Feeling the need to learn English	1-4	2.06	1.23	21.2
14	Your children being exposed to drugs or alcohol	1-4	1.87	1.23	19.9
15	Your husband or partner having a hard time finding a job or being forced to accept a low paying job	1-4	1.80	1.19	17.6
16	Being treated as if you don't deserve medical care of social services by staff because you are Hispanic	1-4	1.84	1.17	16.9
17	Having to wait longer than others or being treated poorly because you could not speak English well	1-4	1.76	1.14	14.8
18	Feeling family members were losing their religion	1-4	1.82	1.10	12.9
19	Your concern about not being able to pay for medical care for your children	1-4	1.73	1.15	15.1
20	Being paid less or having a hard time getting promotions or raises because you are Puerto Rican	1-4	1.97	1.22	19.3
21	Being concerned about the welfare of family or friends in Puerto Rico	1-4	2.38	1.23	29.1
22	Not having enough money for basic necessities such as food for your family or shoes for your children	1-4	2.44	1.31	35.6
23	Having doctors or hospital staff look down on your or treat you poorly because you are Puerto Rican	1-4	1.90	1.16	15.2
24	Not knowing who to trust for good information or help	1-4	2.32	1.21	24.3
25	Your children receiving poor school reports or grades	1-4	1.81	1.16	15.5
26	Not understanding US values and customs	1-4	1.91	1.14	15.0
27	Family members not putting family first	1-4	2.18	1.26	25.2
28	You having a hard time finding a job or being forced to accept a low paying job	1-4	2.14	1.30	16.4
29	Your children being placed in lower classes or having fewer school opportunities because they are Puerto Rican	1-4	1.56	1.02	9.46
30	Missing the help and support of your family in Puerto Rico	1-4	2.02	1.23	21.3
31	Your children not respecting you as they should	1-4	1.90	1.25	22.1
32	Being ignored or getting poor service at stores or offices because you are Puerto Rican	1-4	2.07	1.22	21.0
33	Being a single parent	1-4	1.93	1.29	23.8
34	Losing the status or independence you had in Puerto Rico	1-4	1.74	1.12	14.7
35	Feeling that people close to you were less concerned than you about morals	1-4	2.11	1.22	22.3
36	Conflicts among family members	1-4	2.57	1.26	34.5
37	Having to depend on others for transportation or to get simple errands done	1-4	2.26	1.33	31.6
38	Your job	1-4	2.10	1.26	25.2

The factor structure and factor loadings of the HWSSS in our sample are presented in Table 2. Although the Kaiser's rule yielded eight eigenvalues greater than one, the minimum average partials test suggested that six factors should be extracted. We decided to retain six factors because researchers have recommended the MAP test over the Kaiser's rule (e.g., Courtney, 2013). Additionally, this number is consistent with the original validation study on the HWSSS (Goodkind et al., 2008).

According to our factor loading criteria, our first EFA revealed three cross-loading items (i.e., items 16, 19, and 28). We removed these items and reran the EFA subsequently. Results indicated that seven items did not load on any factor (items 1, 15, 18, 24, 31, 32, and 34). Therefore we removed these seven items in subsequent analysis. In addition, item 29 ("Your children being placed in lower classes or having fewer school opportunities because they are Puerto Rican") was dropped because it was the only item loaded on a sixth factor. Finally, item 23 ("Having doctors or hospital staff look down on you or treat you poorly because you are Puerto Rican") was dropped because it was somewhat irrelevant to the theme of Factor 1.

Consequently, 26 items were subjected to principal axis factoring to assess the dimensionality for the data. The mean of the Kaiser-Meyer-Olkin measure was .87 which is well above the recommended threshold of .6 (Kaiser, 1974). This indicates the correlations were sufficiently large for exploratory factor analysis. Six factors were extracted, but only five of them are reported here for interpretation purposes. The five factors explained 64.59% of the variance, which is a 3.85% drop from that explained by the six-factor structure. Table 2 presents the information on the factor loadings. Specifically, six items were loaded on Factor 1, which was labeled employment-related stressors (e.g., "Having trouble balancing work and family"). Six items made up Factor 2 and were named socioeconomic stressors (e.g., "Not having enough money to pay debts"). Factor 3 consisted of four items reflecting acculturation-related stressors (i.e., "Feeling the need to learn English"). Factor 4 had five items and reflected stressors related to parental responsibilities (e.g., "Feeling your children were not safe in your neighborhood"). Finally, Factor 5 included five items related to familial support and relationships (e.g., "Conflicts among family members").

All five subscales had adequate reliability: α = .86, .77, .84, .83, and .84, respectively. Meanwhile, they were all correlated (see Table 3), indicating using the oblique type of rotation (i.e., Geomin) is appropriate. Finally, the correlations between the five subscales and depressive symptoms and anxiety sensitivity were all significant, except for that between the employment stressor and anxiety sensitivity (see Table 3), thus providing evidence that the HWSSS has good criterion validity among Puerto Rican women.

DISCUSSION

The aim of this study is to examine the psychometric properties of the HWSSS in a community sample of Puerto Rican women living in upstate New York. Our findings indicate that the HWSSS has good reliability and validity in this sample. Specifically, we found that the HWSSS measures social stressors in the following five dimensions: (a) employment, (b) socioeconomic status, (c) acculturation, (d) parental, and (e) familial. In general, these findings align with previous research on social stressors among Hispanics (e.g., Caplan, 2007).

Table 2. Factor Loadings of the HWSSS in Puerto Rican Women

	Factor				
Scale Item	EMP	SES	ACC	PAR	FAM
Factor 1: Employment (EMP)					
2. Having trouble balancing work and family	**0.44**	0.29	-0.10	0.26	0.02
4. Having to deal with co-workers' or supervisors' negative stereotypes about Hispanic women at your job	**0.80**	0.06	0.02	0.05	-0.11
8. Not having the same job opportunities as Anglo women	**0.64**	0.25	0.25	-0.18	-0.07
12. Having to be careful about the quality of your work so others would not think you were lazy	**0.52**	-0.06	0.30	0.04	0.16
20. Being paid less or having a hard time getting promotions or raises because you are Puerto Rican	**0.81**	-0.07	-0.02	0.06	0.04
38. Your job	**0.52**	-0.02	-0.05	0.18	0.17
Factor 2: Socio-economic Status (SES)					
5. Feeling lonely and isolated	0.03	**0.44**	0.12	-0.03	0.20
7. Not having enough money to pay debts	0.16	**0.59**	-0.03	0.12	-0.05
11. Not being able to afford to live in the neighborhood you want	0.02	**0.47**	-0.11	0.20	0.23
22. Not having enough money for basic necessities such as food for your family or shoes for your children	0.02	**0.60**	0.00	0.01	-0.06
33. Being a single parent	-0.14	**0.46**	0.00	-0.04	0.08
37. Having to depend on others for transportation or to get simple errands done	-0.23	**0.57**	0.19	0.07	0.08
Factor 3: Acculturation (ACC)					
9. Not being understood in stores or offices because you could not speak English well	0.06	0.01	**0.93**	0.04	-0.05
13. Feeling the need to learn English	-0.08	0.03	**0.84**	0.01	-0.03
17. Having to wait longer than others or being treated poorly because you could not speak English well	0.25	0.14	**0.53**	-0.16	0.04
26. Not understanding US values and customs	-0.08	-0.08	**0.49**	0.11	0.37
Factor 4: Parental (PAR)					
3. Not being able to spend as much time with your children as you wanted because you had to work	0.34	0.02	0.12	**0.40**	0.02

Table 2. (Continued)

	Factor				
Scale Item	EMP	SES	ACC	PAR	FAM
6. Feeling your children were not safe in your neighborhood	0.02	0.24	0.08	**0.69**	-0.15
10. Your children being influenced by bad friends	0.08	0.05	-0.05	**0.74**	0.02
14. Your children being exposed to drugs or alcohol	0.15	-0.10	-0.01	**0.64**	0.10
25. Your children receiving poor school reports or grades	-0.06	0.03	0.02	**0.74**	-0.03
Factor 5: Familial (FAM)					
21. Being concerned about the welfare of family or friends in Puerto Rico	0.09	-0.02	0.19	0.02	**0.57**
27. Family members not putting family first	0.02	0.18	-0.03	0.15	**0.69**
30. Missing the help and support of your family in Puerto Rico	0.08	0.00	0.36	-0.07	**0.53**
35. Feeling that people close to you were less concerned than you about morals	-0.03	0.28	0.05	0.05	**0.44**
36. Conflicts among family members	0.02	0.33	-0.01	-0.01	**0.63**

Note: Extraction method: maximum likelihood; Rotation Method: the oblique with geomin method. Factor loadings of .40 and above are bolded to indicate items that fit the inclusion criteria for the factor.

Table 3. Correlations between the factors of the HWSSS in Puerto Rican Women

	1	2	3	4	Depression	Anxiety
1. Employment					$.33^{***}$	.11
2. Socio-economic Status	2.27^{*}				$.55^{***}$	$.24^{**}$
3. Acculturation	4.46^{***}	3.60^{***}			$.39^{***}$	$.17^{*}$
4. Parental	2.24^{*}	3.49^{***}	2.76^{**}		$.19^{*}$	$.19^{*}$
5. Familial	4.02^{***}	3.26^{**}	3.92^{***}	4.30^{***}	$.42^{***}$	$.22^{**}$

Note: *$p < .05$, **$p < .01$, ***$p < .001$.

Our study also suggests that almost all the dimensions of the HWSSS were correlated with mental health outcomes among Puerto Rican women. This is consistent with previous research that has linked social stressors to mental health among Hispanics, including Puerto Ricans (e.g., Lee and Ferraro, 2009; Leung et al., 2014; Stacciarini, Smith, Garvan, Wiens, and Cottler, 2015).

Since Puerto Ricans are not immigrants, we expected this study would yield a slightly different factor structure from the one reported by Goodkind and colleagues (2008), the original validation study of the HWSSS conducted with women of Mexican heritage. We found evidence that generally supports what we expected. As discussed previously, Goodkind and colleagues (2008) identified six factors: (a) immigration, (b) socioeconomic, (c) racism-related, (d) familial, (e) parental, and (f) employment. In our analysis, although most items of the HWSSS were loaded on the same factor or on a similar factor identified in the original study, it is important to note the following discrepancies.

First, our factor analysis did not yield a racism or discrimination factor. Items loaded on this factor in Goodkind and colleagues' (2008) study were either dropped or loaded on other factors in our study. For instance, item 12 ("Having to be careful about the quality of your work so others would not think you were lazy") and item 20 ("Being paid less or having a hard time getting promotions or raises because you are Puerto Rican") were loaded on employment in our study. Nevertheless, this finding does not suggest that Puerto Rican women did not experience discrimination. Instead, it suggests that Puerto Rican women may experience more employment related racism or discrimination. This finding was supported by the fact that two other items loaded on employment in our study also reflect racism (e.g., item 4, "having to deal with co-workers' or supervisors' negative stereotypes about Hispanic women at your job"). Therefore, it is consistent with previous research indicating that Hispanics generally experience racism and discrimination in the United States (e.g., Pérez, Fortuna, and Alegria, 2008), but also suggests Puerto Ricans may face additional employment related stressors.

Second, we were not able to identify an immigration factor in the study. In the original validation study (Goodkind, et al., 2008), 12 items were loaded on the immigration factor. In our study, all these items were either dropped or loaded on other factors. For instance, item 8 ("Not having the same job opportunities as Anglo women") was loaded on employment in our study, which again supports our earlier notion that Puerto Rican women may experience more employment-related racism instead of immigration-related discrimination. Similarly, two other items were loaded on familial stress in this study (e.g., item 21, "being concerned about the welfare of family or friends in Puerto Rico"). This suggests that Puerto Rican women may face more familial strain as a result of separation with their families and friends. In addition, four other items loaded on immigration stressor in the original study were loaded on a new factor in our study. Since these four items were focused on language and culture, we labeled the factor acculturation stressor. These discrepancies suggest that our study produced more salient social stressors experienced by Puerto Rican women (e.g., stressors of employment, familial concern, and acculturation). In the literature, immigration-related stress has been linked to acculturation, family dynamics, and employment (e.g., Arbona et al., 2010; Mitrani, Santisteban, and Muir, 2004). Instead of a more general immigration factor, our study is more sensitive in identifying specific factors of underlying immigration-related stress.

Third, item 3 ("Not being able to spend as much time with your children as you wanted because you had to work") was loaded on employment in the original study, but on parental stressors in our study. This represents the struggle between work and caregiving responsibilities. For Puerto Rican women, parental responsibilities seem to lead to more stress. Finally, item 11 ("Not being able to afford to live in the neighborhood you want") was loaded on socioeconomic stress in our study, but dropped in the original study. Gookind and colleagues (2006) did not report why they dropped the item, but neighborhood characteristics have been used as part of a multi-level measure to assess socioeconomic status (Chen and Paterson, 2006).

Study Limitations

The study has a few limitations. First, our sample is a convenient community sample and thus not representative of all the Puerto Rican women in the mainland. Future research could use nationally representative samples. To validate the results of the current study, confirmatory factor analysis is also warranted. Second, the sample size is not large. One rule of thumb regarding the ratio between the sample size and the number of items is 10:1 or higher in the EFA (Osborne and Costello, 2004). Our ratio is substantially lower than this recommended criterion. However, researchers have also suggested that a minimum of 150 cases should be sufficient (Tabachnick and Fidell, 2012). Third, although this study provides evidence on the construct validity and criterion validity of the HWSSS in Puerto Rican women, it is not clear whether the scale has concurrent validity. Future research could examine the psychometric properties of the HWSSS with a larger sample of Puerto Rican women. If the factor structure found in this study is confirmed, then the next step could be to examine the concurrent validity by comparing the HWSSS to another measure of social stress.

CONCLUSION

Culturally responsive preventions and interventions must take into account the individual, familial, and societal stressors that may contribute to negative mental health outcomes. This approach is consistent with the person-in-environment perspective and calls for interventions at the micro, meso, and macro levels (Potocky-Tripodi, 2002). In this study we identified a factor structure that is, by in large, aligned with the findings reported in Goodkind and colleagues' (2008) study. Both studies highlight the role of employment, socioeconomic status, acculturation, parental stress, and familial support in shaping the stressful experiences of Mexican immigrant and Puerto Rican women. That is, despite their US citizenship, Puerto Rican women are no different from Mexican female immigrants. Their experiences in the United States are profoundly shaped by gender, race and culture related struggles, and prejudice and discrimination.

From this study, Puerto Rican women have a unique set of employment related stressors, particularly those stemming from racism and competing gender role expectations and job responsibilities. Early scholars indicated that despite their primary reason of migration, Puerto Rican women were migrating to work that included a wide range of reproductive and productive labor, because of their obligation or desire to meet gender responsibilities (Ellis, Conway and Bailey, 1996). Whalen (1998), in writing the oral history of Puerto Rican women during the post-war great wave of migration, argued that the sexual divisions of labor within and beyond the household made Puerto Rican women all becoming labor migrants; they participated in paid employments, informal economic activities, and/or household and community work, whether paid or unpaid, which were expected by their culture and for the family and community survival. Sadly saying, today's Puerto Rican women have not gained much ground in terms of gender, work, family and migration. For effective prevention and intervention programs to improve mental health among Puerto Rican women, an active holistic approach to address stressors from instrumental or environmental (e.g., family supporting services), social and interpersonal (e.g., gendered culture changes), and societal (e.g., equal employment and pay) dimensions would be essential.

REFERENCES

Ai, A. L., Appel, H. B., Huang, B., and Lee, K. (2012). Overall health and healthcare utilization among Latino American women in the United States. *Journal of Women's Health*, 21(8), 878-885.

Alegría, M., Mulvaney-Day, N., Torres, M., Polo, A., Cao, Z., and Canino, G. (2007). Prevalence of psychiatric disorders across Latino subgroups in the United States. *American Journal of Public Health*, 97(1), 68-75.

Arbona, C., Olvera, N., Rodriguez, N., Hagan, J., Linares, A., and Wiesner, M. (2010). Acculturative stress among documented and undocumented Latino immigrants in the United States. *Hispanic Journal of Behavioral Sciences*, 32(3), 362-384.

Ayón, C., Marsiglia, F. F., and Bermudez-Parsai, M. (2010). Latino family mental health: Exploring the role of discrimination and familismo. *Journal of Community Psychology*, 38(6), 742-756.

Bose, C. E. (2006). *Changes in economic status: City variations among Latino New Yorkers, 2000-2005*. New York Latino Research and Resources Network. Retrieved from http://www.albany.edu/news/imagesdispersion.pdf.

Brown, A., and Patten, E. (2013). *Hispanics of Puerto Rican origin in the United States, 2011*. Retrieved from http://www.pewhispanic.org/2013/06/19/hispanics-of-puerto-rican-origin-in-the-united-states-2011/.

Caplan, S. (2007). Latinos, acculturation, and acculturative stress: A dimensional concept analysis. *Policy, Politics and Nursing Practice*, 8(2), 93-106.

Cavazos-Rehg, P. A., Zayas, L. H., Walker, M. S., and Fisher, E. B. (2006). Evaluating an abbreviated version of the Hispanic Stress Inventory for immigrants. *Hispanic Journal of Behavioral Sciences*, 28(4), 498-515.

Cervantes, R. C., Padilla, A. M., and Salgado de Snyder, N. (1991). The Hispanic Stress Inventory: A culturally relevant approach to psychosocial assessment. *Psychological Assessment*, 3(3), 438-447.

Chen, E., and Paterson, L. Q. (2006). Neighborhood, family, and subjective socioeconomic status: How do they relate to adolescent health? *Health Psychology: Official Journal of the Division of Health Psychology, American Psychological Association*, 25(6), 704-714.

Cintrón, J. A., Carter, M. M., Suchday, S., Sbrocco, T., and Gray, J. (2005). Factor structure and construct validity of the Anxiety Sensitivity Index among island Puerto Ricans. *Journal of Anxiety Disorders*, 19(1), 51-68.

Cohn, D., Patten, E., and Lopez, M. H. (2014). *Puerto Rican population declines on island, grows on US mainland.* Pew Research Center. Retrieved from http://www.pewhispanic.org/2014/08/11/puerto-rican-population-declines-on-island-grows-on-u-s-mainland/.

Collazo, S. G., Ryan, C. L., and Bauman, K. J. (2010). *Profile of the Puerto Rican population in United States and Puerto Rico: 2008*. Presented at the Annual Meeting of the

Population Association of America, Dallas, TX. Retrieved from https://www.census.gov/hhes/socdemo/education/data/acs/paa2010/Collazo_Ryan_Bauman_PAA2010_Paper.pdf.

Courtney, M. G. R. (2013). Determining the number of factors to retain in EFA: using the SPSS R-Menu v2. 0 to make more judicious estimations. *Practical Assessment, Research and Evaluation*, 18(8), 1-14.

Ellis, M., Conway, D., and Bailey, A. J. (1996). The circular migration of Puerto Rican women: Towards a gendered explanation. *International Migration*, 34(1), 31-64.

Ennis, S. R., Ríos-Vargas, M., and Albert, N. G. (2011). *The Hispanic population: 2010 (2010 Census Briefs C2010BR-04)*. Washington, DC: United States Census Bureau.

Ferguson, E., and Cox, T. (1993). Exploratory factor analysis: A users' guide. *International Journal of Selection and Assessment*, 1(2), 84-94.

Fuertes, J. N., and Westbrook, F. D. (1996). Using the Social, Attitudinal, Familial, and Environmental (S.A.F.E.) Acculturation Stress Scale to assess the adjustment needs of Hispanic college students. *Measurement and Evaluation in Counseling and Development*, 29(2), 67-76.

Goodkind, J. R., Gonzales, M., Malcoe, L. H., and Espinosa, J. (2008). The Hispanic Women's Social Stressor Scale: Understanding the multiple social stressors of US- and Mexico-born Hispanic women. *Hispanic Journal of Behavioral Sciences*, 30(2), 200-229.

Guarnaccia, P. J. (1997). Social stress and psychological distress among Latinos in the United States. In: I. Al-Issa and M. Tousignant (Eds.), *Ethnicity, Immigration, and Psychopathology* (pp. 71-83). New York: Plenum Press.

Guarnaccia, P. J., Martinez, I., and Acosta, H. (2005). Mental health in the Hispanic immigrant community. *Journal of Immigrant and Refugee Services*, 3(1-2), 21-46.

Kaiser, H. F. (1960). The application of electronic computers to factor analysis. *Educational and Psychological Measurement*, 20, 141-151. http://doi.org/10.1177/001316446002000116.

Kaiser, H. F. (1974). An index of factorial simplicity. *Psychometrika*, 39(1), 31-36.

Lee, M.-A., and Ferraro, K. F. (2009). Perceived discrimination and health among Puerto Rican and Mexican Americans: buffering effect of the Lazo matrimonial? *Social Science and Medicine (1982)*, 68(11), 1966-1974.

Leung, P., LaChapelle, A. R., Scinta, A., and Olvera, N. (2014). Factors Contributing to Depressive Symptoms among Mexican Americans and Latinos. *Social Work*, 59(1), 42-51.

Lewinsohn, P. M., Seeley, J. R., Roberts, R. E., and Allen, N. B. (1997). Center for Epidemiologic Studies Depression Scale (CES-D) as a screening instrument for depression among community-residing older adults. *Psychology and Aging*, 12(2), 277-287.

Mena, F. J., Padilla, A. M., and Maldonado, M. (1987). Acculturative Stress and Specific Coping Strategies among Immigrant and Later Generation College Students. *Hispanic Journal of Behavioral Sciences*, 9(2), 207-225.

Mitrani, V. B., Santisteban, D. A., and Muir, J. A. (2004). Addressing immigration-related separations in Hispanic families with a behavior-problem adolescent. *American Journal of Orthopsychiatry*, 74(3), 219-229.

Moradi, B., and Risco, C. (2006). Perceived discrimination experiences and mental health of Latina/o American persons. *Journal of Counseling Psychology*, 53(4), 411-421.

Osborne, J. W., and Costello, A. B. (2004). Sample size and subject to item ratio in principal components analysis. *Practical Assessment, Research and Evaluation*, 9(11), 8 pages. Retrieved from http://PAREonline.net/getvn.asp?v=9&n=11.

Pérez, D. J., Fortuna, L., and Alegria, M. (2008). Prevalence and correlates of everyday discrimination among US Latinos. *Journal of Community Psychology*, 36(4), 421-433.

Peterson, R. A., and Heilbronner, R. L. (1987). The anxiety sensitivity index: Construct validity and factor analytic structure. *Journal of Anxiety Disorders*, 1(2), 117-121.

Posner, S. F., Stewart, A. L., Marín, G., and Pérez-Stable, E. J. (2001). Factor variability of the Center for Epidemiological Studies Depression Scale (CES-D) among urban Latinos. *Ethnicity and Health*, 6(2), 137-144.

Potocky-Tripodi, M. (2002). *Best practices for social work with refugees and immigrants*. New York: Columbia University Press.

Radloff, L. S. (1977). The CES-D scale: A self-report depression scale for research in the general population. *Applied Psychological Measurement*, 1(3), 385-401.

Ramos, F. (1992). Out-migration and return migration of Puerto Ricans. In: G. J. Borjas and R. B. Freeman (Eds.), *Immigration and the workforce: Economic consequences for the United States and source areas* (pp. 49-66). Chicago, IL: University of Chicago Press.

Ramos, B. M. (2007). Housing disparities, caregiving, and their impact for older Puerto Ricans. *Journal of Gerontological Social Work*, 49(1-2), 47-64.

Ramos, B. M. (2012). Psychosocial stress, social inequality, and mental health in Puerto Rican women in upstate New York. *Centro Journal*, 24(2). Retrieved from http://www.redalyc.org/articulo.oa?id=37730308003.

Ramos, B. M., and Carlson, B. E. (2004). Lifetime abuse and mental health distress among English-speaking Latinas. *Affilia*, 19(3), 239-256.

Reiss, S. (1991). Expectancy model of fear, anxiety, and panic. *Clinical Psychology Review*, 11(2), 141-153.

Reiss, S., Peterson, R. A., Gursky, D. M., and McNally, R. J. (1986). Anxiety sensitivity, anxiety frequency and the prediction of fearfulness. *Behaviour Research and Therapy*, 24 (1), 1-8.

Roschelle, A. R. (2002). The tattered web of kinship: Black white differences in social support in a Puerto Rican community. In: M. Durr (Ed.), *The new politics of race: From Du Bois to the 21st Century* (pp. 113-136). Westport, CT: Greenwood Publishing Group.

Sánchez, M., Cardemil, E., Connell, J., Ferreira, J., Handler, J. S., Melo, T., … Rivera, I. (2014). Brave new world: Mental health experiences of Puerto Ricans, immigrant Latinos, and Brazilians in Massachusetts. *Cultural Diversity and Ethnic Minority Psychology*, 20(1), 16-26.

Stacciarini, J.-M. R., Smith, R., Garvan, C. W., Wiens, B., and Cottler, L. B. (2015). Rural Latinos' mental wellbeing: A mixed-methods pilot study of family, environment and social isolation factors. *Community Mental Health Journal*, 51(4), 404-413.

Tabachnick, B. G., and Fidell, L. S. (2012). *Using multivariate statistics* (6th ed.). Upper Saddle River, NJ: Pearson.

Torres, J. M., and Wallace, S. P. (2013). Migration circumstances, psychological distress, and self-rated physical health for Latino immigrants in the United States. *American Journal of Public Health*, 103(9), 1619-1627.

US Department of Health and Human Services. (2001). *Mental health: Culture, race, and ethnicity-A supplement to mental health: A report of the Surgeon General*. Rockville,

MD: US Department of Health and Human Services, Substance Abuse and Mental Health Services Administration, Center for Mental Health Services. Retrieved from http://www.ncbi.nlm.nih.gov/books/NBK44243/.

Velicer, W. F. (1976). Determining the number of components from the matrix of partial correlations. *Psychometrika*, 41(3), 321-327.

Whalen, C. T. (1998). Labor migrants or submissive wives: Competing narratives of Puerto Rican women in the post-world war II era. In: Rodriguez, F. V. M. and Delgado, L. C. (Ed.), *Puerto Rican women's history: New perspective* (pp. 277-252). New York: Routledge.

PART II: INTERNAL MIGRATION AND RIGHTS TO WELFARE

In: Migrant Workers
Editors: Qingwen Xu and Lucy P. Jordan

ISBN: 978-1-63485-272-2

Chapter 6

POOR LIVING AND WORKING CONDITIONS, SOCIAL ISOLATION, AND COPING STRATEGIES OF MIGRANT LABORERS IN HANOI, VIETNAM

Trang Mai Le[1], Tuan-Anh Nguyen[2] and Huong Ngoc Nguyen[3,*]
[1]Department of Social Work, Trade Union University, Vietnam
[2]Department of Social Work, Vietnam National University, Hanoi, Vietnam
[3]College of Social Work, University of South Carolina, Columbia, SC, US

ABSTRACT

This study examines the impact of living and working environments on physical and mental health of rural-to-urban migrant laborers in Hanoi, Vietnam. Data were collected through in-depth interviews with 84 migrant laborers. Three major themes emerged from the data. First, most migrant laborers endured very poor living and working conditions without health insurance or benefits, and many developed physical health problems. Second, most migrant laborers felt socially isolated as "outsiders" of the city, some experienced visible discrimination due to their status as migrants, leading to migrant laborers constantly feeling lonely, anxious, and homesick. Finally, since their economic and social resources in the city were very limited, most migrant laborers coped with physical and psychological health issues primarily by remaining very mindful about diet and sleep habits, and minimize risky behaviors. If they did fall sick, they often chose self-treatment or returning to their home town for treatment in order to cut medical cost. In all, migrant laborers in Hanoi, Vietnam experienced a very difficult life; yet, most chose to endure this life to make money to support family in their home town.

[*] Corresponding author: Huong Ngoc Nguyen, College of Social Work, University of South Carolina, Columbia, SC 29208, US. Email: hnguyen@mailbox.sc.edu.

INTRODUCTION

In Vietnam, the term "migrant laborers" (*lao dong di cu*) has been used to indicate laborers who migrate internally from one region to another within Vietnam. In the late 1980s and early 1990s, this term often signified waves of people who moved from their home towns to "new economic zones" (*khu kinh te moi*) in accordance with appointment and/or recommendations of the central and local government. In this movement, people often moved the entire family to the central highlands or new farming zones in order to open up new agricultural areas. However, in the last decade, the term "migrant laborers" in Vietnam has shifted its meaning to denote primarily people who moved temporarily from rural areas to urban areas or industrial zones near big cities to look for jobs (Dang and Nguyen, 1998). According to the 1999 Census, about 4.5 million Vietnamese migrated within the country; by 2009, the number of internal migrants rose sharply to 6.6 million (United Nations Population Fund [UNFPA], 2010). This new wave of rural-to-urban migrants responded to fast urbanization in Vietnam where about 45% of the population was predicted to be living in urban areas in 2020 compared to only 25% in 1999 (UNFPA, 2010). Unlike the migrant laborers in the 1990s, many migrant laborers of the 2000s in Vietnam kept permanent residence and family at their home villages while they alone moved to the city to seek employment and used the income earned in the city to support the family back home. These migrants were sometimes called "pendulum migrants" since they constantly swing back and forth between home village and the city as two living environments (Nguyen, Hardesty, and Khuat, 2013). In big cities like Hanoi or Ho Chi Minh City, rural-to-urban migrant laborers became more and more instrumental to the daily functioning of the city since they supplied low-level workers to fill up low-level jobs in the city including construction workers, street vendors, retail shop-keepers, manual laborers, and house-maids.

While internal migrants became an increasingly important social phenomenon in Vietnam, research about this group remained scarce, especially research focusing on their physical and mental health. Thus far, most studies on internal migrants focused on economic and social impact of their movements to the sending and receiving locations as well as Vietnam's overall socioeconomic development (United Nations [UN] Vietnam, 2010; Institute for Social Development Studies [ISDS], 2011; International Organization for Migration [IOM], 2012). In 2004, Vietnamese government conducted the first national survey on internal migration. The study found that the majority of migrants knew someone in their new environments; yet 75% of them reported having difficulties settling down in their new environments, for which they mainly relied on personal relationships and social networks to deal with rather than on social services (UNPFA, 2008). In this study, 62% of migrants lived in temporary poor housing with limiting access to clean water, 60% of them worked at low-level jobs requiring no or very little prior training. Yet, overall, 80% of the migrants in this first national survey reported that their life was "much better" or "better than their life before migration. Housing is where migrants had the least satisfaction, followed by education and health care.

With regard to internal migrants' health, the focus has been general health assessment (UNFPA, 2007) or primarily core public health issues such as HIV/AIDS, tuberculosis, or reproductive health (Dang, 2008; Nguyen and White, 2007; Rushing, 2006; Rydstrom, 2006; UNFPA, 2010, 2012). These studies fit in the larger literature about public health concerns of internal migration in developing countries across the globe (Bond and Dover, 1997; Brockeroff and Biddlecom, 1999; Coast 2006; Lurie, 2006; Yang, 2010; Yang and Xia, 2006; Ma and Chenge, 2010). In many of these studies, the underlying concern was that since migrant laborers moved freely between regions of the country, they became key transmitters of diseases, particularly sexually transmitted diseases. This likelihood was exacerbated by the fact that, living far away from their normal familial and social networks, migrant laborers were more likely to involve in risky sexual behaviors. However, a few qualitative studies using a small sample size of migrant laborers suggested that this assumption was not guaranteed. Nguyen, Hardesty, and Hong (2011, 2013) argued that while migrant laborers did develop sexually transmitted diseases or other sexual health issues, these problems rooted in their unhealthy and unsanitary living and working conditions, rather than their risky sexual behaviors. Most migrants in the 2004 survey reported having "normal health"; two third of them had no health insurance and relied primarily on self-treatment when they got sick.

In all, there is a gap in the literature about physical and psychological health of internal migrants in Vietnam, particularly rural-to-urban migrant laborers working at low-level, low-income jobs. To begin filling this knowledge gap, in this paper, we asked three open questions: (1) How do living and working conditions impact Vietnamese migrant laborer's physical health?; (2) How do living and working conditions impact Vietnamese migrant laborers' psychological/mental health?; and (3) What are migrant laborers' strategies in coping with health problems? It should be noted that the concepts of "mental health" in this study were understood broadly and in accordance with Vietnamese culture. Since most Vietnamese people are not familiar with clinical definitions and symptoms of mental disorders, the exploration of migrant laborers' mental health in this study mostly focused on general emotional well-being, experiences of social relationships, social isolation, stress, anxiety, and prolonged negative emotions (e.g., loneliness, homesickness, fear). We also focused our study on migrant laborers who worked at low-level, low-income jobs such as street vendors, construction workers, or retailers.

METHODS

Data Collection. Data for this paper come from in-depth interviews with 84 migrant laborers in Hanoi, Vietnam as part of a larger mixed-method study on migrant laborers in Hanoi and Ho Chi Minh City. The study was funded by the National Foundation for Science and technology (Nafosted). In-depth interviews were conducted from April 2013 to April 2014 with 19 male and 67 females. Key characteristics of the sample were described in Table 1.

A group of graduate students in sociology from Vietnam National University were trained to conduct in-depth interviews with migrant laborers. Once trained, the graduate students were guided to approach migrant laborers in areas with high concentration of migrant laborers, using several approaches. One approach was to visit neighborhoods known to have high concentration of migrant laborers renting out rooms or spaces to live. Another approach was to stand on busy streets or visit corner markets where migrant laborers worked as street vendors selling fruits, vegetables, snacks, etc. Finally, trainees also used snowball sampling, using migrating students or migrant laborers they met as references. In all cases, once a migrant laborer was located, the trainee would approach to explain about the study and obtained verbal consent before conducting the interview. Most interviews were audio-taped with consent from migrant laborers.

Because of the diverse ways of locating migrant laborers, locations for interviews varied. Of the 84 migrant laborers participating in this study, about 22% of the interviews were conducted at laborers' residential settings, 17% at work place, 17% at a place mutually agreed upon by the interviewer and laborers (e.g., coffee shops or restaurants), and the rest used a combination of all the above settings. Some interviews would start at one place and then had to move to another place to continue. For example, a migrant laborer selling fruits on the street might agree to be interviewed on the street, then she would have to walk on when she saw the police approach or have customer. On average, the interviews last one hour. Besides demographic information (gender, age, home residence, time living in Hanoi, etc.) the interview questions focused on migrant laborers' living and working conditions, their challenges in living in Hanoi, the status of their physical and mental health, and their strategies when facing health problems.

Participants in this study came from diverse locations around Hanoi, ranging from half an hour to day-long travel. On average, they had been living as migrant laborers in Hanoi for 60 months (5 years) with the longest time being 144 months (12 years) and the shortest being 1 month. Participants in this study did various jobs but could be grouped into three major categories: service jobs such as house-keepers (27%), retail jobs, such as street vendors (46%), and industrial work such as welder, brick-layers (15%).

Table 1. Participants Descriptions (N = 84)

Characteristics	Valid N (Missing)	Mean	SD	Min	Max	Frequency (%)
Age	84 (0)	37.87		17	63	
Gender	84 (0)					
Female						65 (77.38)
Male						19 (22.62)
Months living in the city	73 (11)	53.32	3761	1	144	
Average working hours/ day	38 (46)	11.89	3.59	6	20	
Income/month (million VND)	56 (28)	3.5	1.28	1.0	7.0	
Marriage status	84 (0)					
Single						21 (25)
Married						62 (73.81)
Bereaved						1 (1.19)
Current main job	84 (0)					
Industrial workers						13 (15.48)
Officers						3 (3.58)
Service workers						23 (27.38)
Retail sellers/mobile vendors						39 (46.43)
Temporary workers						6 (7.14)

Data Analysis. Interviews were transcribed into Microsoft Word documents by the trainees in order to secure accuracy of the interviews. Transcriptions were then submitted to the team of principal investigator (PI) and co-PIs. For this paper, two researchers independently conducted line-by-line coding from the transcriptions, using the following initial themes: living conditions, working conditions, physical health, and mental health. We looked for themes reflecting the relationships between migrant laborers' living and working conditions and their physical and mental health. Once line-by-line coding was completed, we developed major themes based on the coding.

RESULTS

Migrant Laborers' Physical Health

Poor housing. All migrant laborers in this study rented rather than owning a home in Hanoi. To save expenses on housing, they often chose to rent in areas far from the city center and/or "slum" areas. Ninh, a street-vendor selling fruits in Thanh Xuan District revealed that she rented a room in the slum areas under Long Bien bridge, which is across the town from her "*working area*." She shared the room with three other migrant laborers who were also street vendors. Even though she described her room as "*sloppy, dark, dirty, and always wet... I have to share the toilet and kitchen with 5 or 6 other rooms*" but she insisted on enduring this housing situation because "*it's cheap, I don't need much, I only need a place to crash*." Like Ninh, the top priority in housing decisions of migrant laborers in this study is not the comfort, security, or resources in the area but the low rent, which often runs between 1.5 million to 2 million Vietnamese dong (US$75-100) per month for a room about 10 square feet. They accepted poor housing in exchange to the money they could save to send back to the family at home.

> "...People who rent here are mostly migrant laborers working in the city. Each room is about 130 square feet, just one floor, shared bathroom, it's pretty shabby. Sometimes power and water will be cut. But what can I do? Other places would be more expensive, I won't have money to cover my expenses, there are so many things I need to spend money on, if I don't buckle up, I won't have money to send my children." (Thom, female, selling sweet potatoes on the street)

With "saving" as the central goal, most migrant laborers did not live alone but shared a room with family members or 3-4 other migrant laborers. Some was so keen on saving that they rented on a day-to-day basis rather than monthly, so that they could save even just a night or two on rent. In this day-to-day renting arrangement, they would get a bed in a room shared with up to 10 people. Ms. Lanh, a 59-year-old street vendor, revealed:

> "I am only here in the evening. During day time, I am selling on the streets. I pay 15,000 dong per day (US75cents). You stay a night, you pay for a night. You don't pay for the whole month. You pay water separate, electricity included. I have to buy water for each night. About 5000 *dong* per night will be enough for me."

Even though migrant laborers in this study did not seem to place priority in housing, stating that they only needed "*a place to crash*," many of them were exposed to health hazards in their residential settings and were concerned about these hazards. Ms. An, a vegetables vendor at a corner market said that she was sharing a "*terrible room*," about 120 square feet, with three other women. The room was close to a huge city dumpster, thus she had to endure terrible odors all the time, plus mosquitos, flies, rats, and other disease-carrying insects and animals. She got sick frequently since moving here but she hadn't been able to find another place to rent.

> "[The room] leaks and always wet, it's hot in the summer and cold in the winter. Sewage system is terrible, we have clog-ups all the times, then dirty water will spill all over. Utilities are expensive but they often cut the power and don't really provide clean water. There's trash everywhere around the house, it's very filthy and very noisy too."

Poor living conditions were particularly dangerous for women in this study. A number of them reported developing gynecological diseases due to using water drawn from open wells instead of sanitized city water. For male migrant laborers, the negative impact of poor housing conditions was most obvious with those working in construction. These workers did not rent but lived in temporary huts on the construction sites, built from steel structure and covered by aluminum roof. They slept on wooden planks with 13-15 people sharing one hut. Bao, a construction worker from Thanh Hoa, a province few hours from Hanoi, said that it was very uncomfortable to live in those huts since "*it is too hot in the summer and the floor will get wet when it rains*." He also said that sharing a small space with so many people "*easily led to the spreading of all sorts of diseases*." All participants in this study agreed that poor living conditions greatly affected their physical health but their limited income prevented them from seeking better housing.

Long and difficult working hours. In addition to poor living conditions, most migrant laborers also endured poor working conditions including long and difficult working hours, physically and emotionally draining tasks, and exposure to toxics. The majority of laborers in this study worked in "un-official" sector such as day laborers, bricklayers, street vendors, house-keepers, security people, etc., which required little or no training but was demanded unusual work hours. Ms. Thuy, 42, who had been living and working as a bread-seller in Hanoi for four years, was a typical example. Her work day started at 4 am when she started to bake the first batch of bread loaves. At 8 am, she carried the freshly baked loaves of bread to train or bus stations to sell them to travelers. At noon, she returned to the bakery to sell to people on the streets. Her afternoon shift started at 1 pm when she baked the afternoon batch of bread. After 5 pm, she again went out on the streets to sell bread until 10 pm. Altogether, she worked between 14 and 18 hours each day without holidays.

Among the migrant laborers, the ones working the longest hours were street vendors, security staff, house-keepers, and waiters or waitresses at restaurants. They were also the group that faced high risks of health problems. Mr. Hoc, 60, a guard at a parking lot said that he worked every day from 9 am to 10 pm, sitting on the streets to guard cars and motorbikes, enduring the sun, rain, dust, and street noise. Ms. Tham, a 54-year-old waitress cum cleaner at an inexpensive restaurant, faced different challenges compared to Mr. Hoc. She had to get up every day at 6:30 am to start the kitchen; then throughout the day, she carried food trays, cleaned the tables, and washed dishes until 11 pm, when the restaurant closed. With only few hours of sleep each night and a lot of heavy lifting during the day, she reported feeling chronic pain in her joints and body, leading to insomnia, which worsened the problem. Similar to Ms. Tham, Mr. Nam, 25, worked and lived at a restaurant serving students. His working hours lasted from 5:30 am to 10 pm. Nam said that since it was a students' restaurant, there was not much space, thus he had to move around carrying weight in awkward positions. Moreover, since the restaurant cooked mostly with a kind of mud-coal mixture, which produced toxic smoke, he often felt tired, sometimes suffocated with smoke and smells of food in a small space.

Street vendors probably had the toughest jobs since they must get up before dawn go to the wholesale markets to buy their goods before spending their days walking the streets of Hanoi, trying to sell off all the good they had bought at dawn. Lan, a 49-year-old woman selling fruits on the streets revealed that she got up every day at 3 am in the morning to ride her bike to the wholesale fruit market on the other side of the city, then carried two heavy baskets of fruits to sell all over the city.

> "Sometimes it rains, sometimes it's too hot, I'm always on the streets, it's dusty. When I get home, it's already 11 pm. After I take a shower, it's midnight. I have at most 3 hours of sleep each night. It's very tiring."

> "I think I work more than 12 hours a day and mostly by walking. I think I walk about 15 kilometers a day (nearly 10 miles). I get up around 5 am to go get the fruits, then I return to my room to wash them, put them into the baskets. It's about 7 am when I am done, then I start walking around Phung Khoang market and all over Thanh Xuan district. Around 11:30 am, I have lunch and rest a little, then I sit on the pavement selling fruits until around 4 pm. If there is still fruits left, I will walk around trying to sell them. If I sell everything off early, then I can end the day early; if I can't, then I will keep walking around selling. I have to try. It's sad if I can't sell them all."

Most street vendors shared similar stories as that of Ms. Lan mentioned above. They had to carry heavy loads for long hours, walked a lot, or sat around all day long, which explained why some of them developed arthritis, back pain, and other issues with posture.

Unhealthy working conditions with no safety measures. Besides long working hours with physically draining tasks, migrant laborers' working environment posed high risks for their health. Some in fact worked directly in chemically dangerous environment. Ms. Hue, a woman from Ha Nam who had been living in Hanoi for 3 years, worked at a factory making plastic raincoats. Her daily task was to use an electronic soldering-iron to glue different parts of the raincoats together through melting.

> This is plastic, so I inhale a lot of plastic smell, and then there are the recycled plastic products, that's even more dangerous. When we deal with the recycled products, we all have to wear mask or wear extra gears because some of us get allergies from these products, like they get rashes or itchy.

Other dangerous jobs included construction and industrial engineering. Bao, a 43-year-old brick-layer, shared that his job required him to climb and move around in high-rise buildings where one "*can have accident and die any time.*" Hoa, a 48-year-old industrial engineer also shared:

> When you weld, sometimes the fire is so hot that it burns your face; and then the smoke from welding and dust from rusted iron fly in the air, sometimes you inhale and feels like you can't breathe. I have back pain too, and I have to carry heavy stuff around, so when I get home in the evening, I am exhausted. I know it's hard work but I have to accept it."

Notably, even though migrant laborers endured considerable health risks, they were not provided with any health benefits or supplemental wages for hazardous job, even for those who were fully employed. If accidents happened to them, they had to pay out of pocket for all expenses. In addition, most migrant laborers had extremely limited access to information on public health and rarely buy health insurance. Often, propagandas on diseases and health care in the community are conducted by local authorities through different channels including public loudspeakers, neighborhood meetings, or door-to-door visits by community health workers. However, due to the temporary and isolating nature of migrant laborers' housing situation, they often have limited access to information provided through these channels. Ms. Hau, 35, a street vendor, said that she often went to work early in the morning and didn't return home until late in the evening, so she never received any health information that got distributed during the day. She revealed further that when community health workers came here, they only talked to the landlords and rarely approached the residents renting the rooms. In contrast, housemaids who lived full-time with their employers often received health information on behalf of the employers who went to work during the day.

> "The home-owner here go to work all day, they only come home in the evening, so I am often home alone. Sometimes, the local authorities will come to talk about health care, how to prevent certain diseases and give out free medicines too…" (Thanh, female, 53, housemaid)

The majority of participants in this study did not buy health insurance because they were self-employed and did not want to spend money on insurance.

> We're self-employed, how can we have health insurance? We are not like those who work for the government or big corporations. We are barely able to cover our daily expenses, how do we get money to pay for insurance? It's very difficult." (Thom, 30, female, vegetable seller)

Besides wanting to save money, another reason leading migrant laborers not to buy insurance was the complicating process of buying insurance and getting benefits if one needs to use it. The migrant laborers described this process as "*cumbersome*" and "*time-consuming.*" Toan, a 28-year old housemaid said that, "*If I want to buy health insurance, I would have to go back to my home village to get paperwork from the village clinic, then I have to get it certified at the local authorities, it's too complicated.*" Other people did not have health insurance because they thought that they were "still young and healthy," thus they would not need insurance. For the most part, they didn't seem to understand the meaning and benefits of health insurance.

Migrant Laborers' Mental Health

In Vietnamese culture, mental health was conceptualized broadly. This concept was not limited to clinical disorders but encompassed all elements of emotions, thoughts, self-regulation, relationships, spirituality, etc. Essentially, it encompassed all non-physical components of well-being. In this study, we focused on exploring whether or not migrant laborers experienced psychological issues such as stress, anxiety, loneliness, social isolation, difficulties in forming and maintaining relationships, etc. Since most migrant laborers were not familiar with clinical terminologies of mental health, we had to reframe these issues in simple language accessible to laborers. Overall, analysis of the interviews revealed three major issues in psychological well-being of migrant laborers: (1) low self-esteem due to internalized stigma and discrimination against migrants, (2) constant anxiety over contemporary working and living situation, and (3) social isolation and homesickness.

Low self-esteem due to internalized stigma and discrimination against migrants. The majority of participants in this study revealed that they felt they were discriminated and marginalized by "*city people*." Discrimination was expressed in many forms: open, verbal comments by random city-dwellers, distrust and unfair treatment by employers, negative attitudes by landlords and neighbors, or mistreatment by local authorities and policemen. Street vendors in particular experienced discrimination on a daily basis when they were regularly chased away if they attempted to stop in front of a restaurant, restaurants, store departments, or street corners to seek customers. On a daily basis, they faced yelling and name-calling by restaurant owners, security guys of upscale department stores, or residents for "*bringing bad luck*" to the restaurants or stores.

> "City people are different from us; they look down on us rural people. Once I went to apply for a job as a factory worker, but they refused. I went around collecting recycled trash, they laughed at my accent. I came into the houses of rich people, I saw so much left over from their meals, I felt hurt." (Nguyet, female, selling snack)

"Rural people" (nguoi nha que) or "city-outsiders" (*dan ngoai tinh*) became common labels used by city-dwellers to identify migrant laborers. The labels were used based on easy markers such as accents and dressing styles. Since most migrant laborers spoke with an accent, they became easy targets for humiliation by city-dwellers. The labels carried not only a sense of contempt but also an embedded social class structure and spatial segregation in which city people were placed above migrant laborers. Migrant laborers in this study were keenly aware of such structure and internalized it into their sense of self. This strong sense of being "outsiders" to the city prevented migrant laborers from going to public events, festivals, or celebrations even though they had been living in the city for a long time. For the most part, the city became a work place rather than a true habitat and migrant laborers would retreat to their room once their work day was over. Most expressed the belief that they were not only just "visitors" of the city but a burden, even parasite to the city.

The people in Hanoi, when they know I am from rural areas, they are very distant, reluctant to talk to me, or they show contempt when talking to me" (An, 35, female, selling vegetables at a corner market)

"They have money, of course they are different. Their life is so much better and they are more selfish too. Some are kind to us but some think we're nothing." (Son, male, factory worker)

Notably, discrimination happened at work places in rather obvious manner. Nam, a 27-year-old waiter at an inexpensive restaurant said that his boss frequently yelled at him and accused him of "*stealing*" because Nam was originally from Nghe An, a province believed by many Vietnamese people to raise "*cruel, calculated, and mean*" people. Since Nam spoke with a very strong Nghe An accent, his boss and co-workers often teased him and even called him "*wooden fish man*" (a label derived from folk story about Nghe An people's thrifty nature), making him withdrawn and reluctant to communicate. Worse, Nam's boss always showed distrust toward him and had several times accused of stealing money without evidence. Even though Nam felt sad and humiliated, he continued to work there because he needed money to support his father and younger sister at home. Each month, Nam was paid 3 million dong (US$150), of which he spent one million on all his expenses in the city (US$50) and sent 2 million (US$100) to his father. Since Nam did not want to spend money on himself, he did not buy new clothes, go out with friends, or have a girlfriend. "*I am too poor, who would love me?*" was his justification for not having friends or intimate relationships.

Social isolation. Most migrant laborers in this study revealed that they lived alone, had no or very few social relationships, and rarely participated in social activities in the city. A key reason leading to their social isolation was migrant laborers' lack of resources (money, time, and appropriate meeting places) to support maintaining a social life. Like Nam quoted above, many migrant laborers stated that it was "too expensive" to keep a social life in Hanoi because it would require going out and spending money on drinks, food, transportation, movie tickets, or some other expenses. Even for migrant laborers who are young adults and have needs, they sacrifice social life in order to save money to send home. Lam, a 26 year-old construction worker said that he wanted to find a girlfriend and get married but his current working life would not allow him. "*I am at work all day, when I get home, I am too tired, I only want to crash. I have no time for dating.*" Even if Lam had time for dating, he couldn't find any place in the city where "*I can meet and find a girl.*" Lam explained further that in his village, it would be easier for him since he was well-connected through his families and friends, plus there would be many village festivals and communal activities that would allow people to meet. But above all, Lam was keenly aware that he was probably "*too poor for a city girl.*" "*What girl would like to date a construction worker like me who is here one day but move to another city tomorrow; plus I am dirt poor.*"

Young women in this study also felt that they had limiting opportunities for making friends and dating because they worked hard and long hours. "*Exhausted,*" "*too tired,*" "*only wanted to sleep*" became salient expressions among migrant laborers, preventing them from after-work social activities. Hoa, a 26-year-old shop-keeper said:

"I am from a very poor village. I come here to make some money to escape poverty. I go to work all day long, then in the evening, I can only wash myself before climbing to bed and sleep until the next morning when I go to work again. I don't have much time to go anywhere. During weekends, I will oversleep to have some energy for the next week." (Hoa, 26, female, shop-keeper)

The sense of loneliness among young female migrant laborers was even more acute than the men and was intensified by their fear of "*becoming an old maid*." Gender norms in Vietnam dictate that young women should get married and start a family in their 20s while men had more time before they were expected to settle down. Van, a 25-year-old tailor in this study said that she was often too tired after a long working day, so she spent most evening in bed, listening to the radio instead of going out. She was very concerned that she would become "*an old maid*" if she continued living in the city with the current job. However, she also did not see a way out of this situation.

Though migrant laborers did not have much money or time to engage in social activities, what seemed to actually stop them from making an effort to engage was the thought that they were not *entitled* to such activities in the city. Many of them felt strongly that only city people could do "*city things*" and enjoy "*city life*." Even migrant laborers who brought their spouses or children to the city felt they were not rooted in the city and could not fully participate in city life. As such, they limited their interactions to only family members, roommates, neighbors, or co-workers who were primarily migrant laborers as well.

Social isolation made it more acute another issue of migrant laborers: the feeling of homesickness. Married women struggled the most with missing their children and husbands.

"Life in Hanoi is difficult, I can't get used to it. Sometimes I feel so lonely and sad, I always want to be with my family, I feel sorry for my kids without mother to take care of them, but I have to do it. Here in the city, nobody trust anybody, everybody to their own life, it's a rat race, I feel tired all the time. In the city, happiness is reserved only for people with power" (Ninh, female, 33, fruit vendor)

Constant anxiety and fear. A key theme about mental wellbeing of migrant laborers was that they constantly felt anxious about the temporary nature of their work and living arrangement. Most migrant laborers lived in poor neighborhoods, sometimes slums areas, where concentration of crime was also high, including drug use, prostitution, gambling, and gang activities. Robbery happened quite often, making laborers constantly alert and anxious. They felt they couldn't trust anyone – roommates, landlords, or neighbors since their neighborhoods were also least protected by law enforcement.

"A renting place like this one is very crowded, people come from everywhere, it's so complicated. There are drugs, prostitution, gambling, everything. And they just do it in broad daylight because there is no law enforcement around here. Especially petty thefts. Happens a lot. My stuff got stolen a few times. So now, I keep with me all my valuable stuff; otherwise I will lose them."

"This area is not very clean, often wet and has a lot of rats. But what concerns me the most is security. The burglars came a few times, I lost my phone and my roommate lost her laptop."

Female migrant laborers were particular concerned about their own security, to the extent that they dared not go out in the evening or return home from work too late. Van, a 25-year-old tailor, shared that she was very frightened anytime she had to stay late at work. She had to ask a co-worker to accompany home on those occasions. For laborers working as street vendors, coming home late at night was a regular reality because they often had to try to sell off the goods for the day. Fear became daily reality that they had to cope with. Hoa, a 55-year-old woman selling evening snacks said she constantly dealt with petty crimes in the evening.

> "I am scared when I have to work late. I am afraid of thefts, robbers, but then I have to get used to it. One time, two boys riding motorbikes stopped by, I thought they had money, so I sold them. But they ate, then got on their motorbike and just ran away."

In addition, street vendors had a constant particular and paralyzing fear: being seized by the police. In order to make Hanoi "safer, friendlier, and more organized," Hanoi City government had reinforced since 2009 a law forbidding street vendors on certain streets and neighborhoods, mostly in the downtown areas where offices, restaurants, department stores, and tourists concentrated. Local police and "market management officials" raided these streets on a daily basis, seizing all goods, vehicles, or equipment of street vendors. At first, street vendors complied with the law. However, since they found best customers in these areas, street vendors started to sneak back, fulling aware that they could be seized by the police because they would rather risk than not to make money. Their work days therefore became a constant hide-and-seek game with the police. They would stop whenever they saw a potential customer, appealed to the customer to buy their food, always watching out for police, and ran anytime they saw the police from afar. "*Heart-wrenching*," "*dangerous*," and "*walking on egg-shell*" were the terms street vendors used to describe their routines. Migrant laborers working on these areas then learned the schedules of the police, shared information and tactics with each other in order to cope with the fear. In one case, we were conducting the interview with Ms. Bac, a 33-year-old woman selling corn and sweet potato on the street when she suddenly screamed: "*Oh no, police, police, run, girl, carry the chair for me... Run! They always come between 8:30 and 9. I will lose everything if they catch me...*"

Coping Strategies and Help-Seeking Behaviors

Prevention is the best medicine. Facing health-challenging working and living conditions, a consistent approach among migrant laborers was to place great emphasis on prevention of illness and to "*go home*" to receive treatment if they did fall sick. Medical expenses were a great concern for all migrant laborers. Mr. Son, an electrical worker and fire worker for construction sites, said that he "*dared not get sick*," which echoed the mentality of most migrant laborers. They were exceptionally afraid of getting sick in the city because it would be too costly to get treatment and they would not have family members to take care of them. As the result, migrant laborers were very mindful about self-care in order not to get sick in the city. For most of them, self-care and prevention meant to eat three full home-cooked meals a day and avoid eating out to prevent food poisoning. It also meant to exercise and avoid activities if they took away resting time. Ms. Minh, for example, was 48 years old and migrated to Hanoi to sell sticky-rice balls in order to raise two children. She revealed that she got up very early in the morning to make the rice balls, then stayed at the market until the evening, when she returned to the room she rented. However, no matter how busy she was, she would make sure she did not miss breakfast, ate all three meals per day, and always cooked a full meal for dinner.

> "Whatever I do, I have to eat properly to stay healthy so that I can continue working. If I get sick, it would be very bad, where do I get the money to go to the hospital?"

The male migrant laborers also placed great emphasis on eating properly in order to have enough energy for the physically challenging jobs that most of them had. They also refrained themselves from health risky behaviors such as drinking or smoking, which contrast some literature suggesting that migrant laborers were more likely to involved in risky health behaviors since they lived far from home (Yang and Xia, 2006; UNAIDS, 2001; Yang, 2004). Mr. Son, the electrical worker mentioned before, therefore, made sure he ate three full home-cooked meals per day and limited his smoking and drinking to a minimal.

In addition to the standard preventive measures – eating properly and avoiding risky behaviors, we found that migrant laborers also came up with creative ways to protect their health within their limited resources. Ms. Thuy, 39, a sticky rice vendor, kept herself from mosquito bites while staying out on the streets by tying plastic bags around her feet instead of using mosquito spray. Most street vendors wore thick self-made mask and cloaks to protect themselves from dirt, exhausts on the street, and sunburn. They would wear raincoats on cold winter days even if it was not raining in order to keep warm. If they had to sit out on the streets for long hours, they would build a small "*fortress*" around them to keep from the sun and wind.

Self-treatment for minor health issues. If preventive measures didn't work and they did fall sick, most migrant laborers chose similar simple solutions. For simple problems such as a cold, headache, light fever, stomachache, they would rely on "*sleep it off,*" resting, eating well, rubbing balms, taking herbs, or some other traditional healing methods. They would also go to a pharmacist, described their symptoms, and bought whatever medicines the pharmacists recommended (note that Vietnam doesn't require doctor's prescriptions in order to buy medicines).

> "You need money for everything honey. So when I get sick, I only go to the pharmacy to get some pills. My kids get sick, I also take them to the pharmacy and ask them to give me a diagnosis, then I buy medicines. We are not going to the hospital or clinic." (Vui, female, cleaner)

It should be noted that since migrant laborers were in their working age and wanted to cut medical costs, they often disregarded serious health issues as "*minor*" and still relied on self-treatment. Mr. Hoa for example had been suffering from regular back pain for 5 years but he never went to a doctor to check; instead, he would buy pain relief patches once in a while to put on pain areas. On the days where the pain became unbearable, he would stay home to rest. For the most part, migrant laborers considered going to a doctor or hospital the absolute last resort.

> "Sometimes I want to go to the doctor but I heard it's very expensive to go to the hospital here; it's not like at home. Sometimes I get really sick, then I go around the corner to buy some medicines to take; I have never paid more than 20,000 VND. The other says, I had a motorbike accident, my arms and legs were hurt; so I had to borrow money from my friend to buy some medicines; I wouldn't have money for medicines on me (Son, male, electrical worker)

For some migrant laborers, the fear of hospital also rooted in another reason: they didn't want to know what other health issues they might be having due to their poor living and working conditions. "*If you go to check, they will find out a whole bunch of issues for you*" or "*You go in to check for one thing and you will come out with a few more*" were the fears of many migrant laborers. They would rather not know than to know and seek treatment. Accessing formal health care, therefore, was low among migrant laborers.

Going home for serious health issues. A notable trend in health behaviors of migrant laborers was to leave Hanoi to go home for diagnosis and treatment if they thought they had serious health issues, even though Hanoi had the most advanced facilities and resources in medical care. Once again, medical expenses were the main reason for their decision to go home.

> Everything in Hanoi is expensive, the pills are too expensive, so I often go home for treatment. Here, if you have to go to the hospital, it costs a lot of money." (Lan, female, street vendor)

> "If I need a check-up, I ask for a few days off to go home to do it; it's too expensive here, I dare not think about going to the hospital here." (Thuy, female, bread bakery)

This trend showed a "*reverse flow*" of health care for migrant laborers. Often, people from rural areas would go to Hanoi to seek treatment, especially for issues requiring advanced care. However, migrant laborers would go home first for initial diagnosis and treatment; they only returned to Hanoi for treatment as the last resort when local health system could not solve the problem.

For mental/psychological health issues. Dealing with social isolation, discrimination, loneliness, homesickness, and anxiety was more difficult for migrant laborers than dealing with physical health issues. However, the migrant laborers in this study did not seem to frame these issues as health issues, rather they assumed they were "*personal issues*" and a natural part of life as migrant laborers. As such, they just endured it and looked for support wherever possible without a clear strategies about maintaining their mental well-being. Overall, emotional support for migrant laborers was rare and came mostly from fellow migrant laborers or people with similarly "*outsiders*" or "*low*" status in the city.

> "My neighbors around here are mainly poor laborers from other provinces coming to Hanoi for jobs, so we are sympathetic of each other and we help each other out."

To cope with discrimination and social isolation, migrant laborers either chose to withdraw and band with fellow migrant laborers or blend in by adopting "*Hanoi norms*." Many laborers from provinces with strong accents chose to imitate Hanoi accents when they were in the city and then returned to their home-town accent once they went home or met with hometown fellows. Adopting "*Hanoi accent*" not only help them to avoid discrimination but also improve their chance to expand their social life. The switching between "identities" caused some to feel uncomfortable and stressed at the very least.

DISCUSSION AND CONCLUSION

This study asked three questions: (1) How do living and working conditions impact Vietnamese migrant laborer's physical health?; (2) How do living and working conditions impact Vietnamese migrant laborers' psychological/mental health?; and (3) What are migrant laborers' strategies in coping with health problems?

Based on in-depth interviews with 84 migrant laborers in Hanoi, the study found that migrant laborers consistently endured very poor working and living conditions that posed constant threats to their physical health. In particular, in order to minimize housing expenses, the majority of them chose to rent a small room or just a bed in shared rooms with up to 10 people in a room, mostly in poor neighborhoods or slums areas of the city. Migrant laborers constantly cohabitated with mosquitoes, rats, and other kinds of disease-transmitting insects and animals. Drug uses, prostitution, gambling, violence, and petty crimes happened regularly in their neighborhoods, with laborers in this study being direct victims multiple times, thus they had to keep any valuable possessions with them all the time. Most migrant laborers in this study had to work long and challenging hours, often getting up at or before dawn and returning from work late in the evening, without little or no break in between. Many of them had to work at physically challenging jobs, such as street vendors, waitresses/waiters, brick-layers, requiring them to carry heavy weight for long hours. The poor living and working conditions led migrant laborers to develop physical health issues, especially gynecological and contagious diseases, which easily spread when too many people shared small space. Migrant laborers in this study revealed that they developed back pain, migraine, sub-burn, and other health issues. Yet, most of them had no health insurance and did not seem to understand the significance of health insurance. Even for those who were employed long-term, they did not have any health benefits from employers. Migrant laborers also had very limiting access to free public health information. They had to develop their own tactics to protect their health and relied mostly on young age or health diet in order to prevent themselves from getting sick. Since most of them were in working age, they could "suffer through" minor issues such as temporary diarrhea, cold, allergies, rashes, itches or back pain; however, we did not know what would be the long-term impact of these poor living and working conditions on migrant laborers' health once they got old and had to "retire" to their hometown.

With regard to the second question, the study found that poor living and working conditions also created consistent issues for migrant laborers' mental wellbeing, most notably extended loneliness and anxiety, social isolation and discrimination. Even though participants in this study had been living for 5 years on average in Hanoi, they still considered themselves "outsiders" to the city, thinking that they were "rural people" compared to "city people." The sense of social exclusion was constantly reinforced by their employers, customers, landlords, neighbors, or general city people, who would ridicule and name-call migrant laborers based on their accents or dressing styles. This exclusion discouraged migrant laborers from going out, making friends, or joining diverse free public events available in the city. For the most part, migrant laborers did not have a social life in the city; instead they went to work and returned home to sleep, accepting that they were the low class, burden, even parasites to the city. A pervasive sense of anxiety regularly loomed over laborers due to their temporary living and working nature. The anxiety and social exclusion intensified their loneliness and homesickness, especially among females. Yet, they did not have much support or solutions to cope with the situation.

Facing many challenges in physical and mental health, yet, migrant laborers had simple coping strategies. Their main strategy could be summarized as: prevent sickness on your own when you can, and if you fall sick, then endure it or go home. Developing and maintaining personal healthy diet and sleep patterns (i.e., eating three full meals per day, sleep whenever they were not working to save energy) were the main method to keep themselves healthy to continue working. Depending on the nature of their work, migrant laborers also invented ways to protect their health in the lack of safety measures where they worked, including wearing masks and self-made gears. For minor physical health problems, such as cold, rashes, or diarrhea, they went to corner pharmacists to get over-the-counter medicines to treat themselves and just suffer through. For major issues, they would then return to their home towns to seek treatment and care from family members. High medical expenses in the city was the primary reason leading to migrant laborers' reluctance to engage with the healthcare system in the city.

Findings from this study were consistent with previous research on migrant laborers in Vietnam, pointing to the extremely unstable and difficult living and working conditions of migrant laborers in Vietnam (Nguyen, Hardesty, and Khuat, 2011, 2013). Nguyen and White (2007) pointed out that migrants' health deteriorated after migrating to the cities to work. Van Landingham (2003) suggested that rural-to-urban migrants faced mane challenges in maintaining physical, psychological, and emotional health. Kim, Pham, Vu and Schelling (2012) found that 25% of female migrant workers in industrial zones in Hanoi, Vietnam had reproductive tract infections (RTI) but only nearly 22% of those having RTI syndromes sought services due to long working hours, lack of information, and high cost of services. They also found a lack of health promotion programs suitable for migrants. With regard to mental/psychological health, findings from this study reinforced that most migrant laborers faced a pervasive feeling of social isolation and emotional swing created by longing for their "home" and the need to remain in the migrating location to make money. Single people were worried about their marriage and family prospect while married people felt torn and guilty about not providing enough care for their children, spouses, or parents left in the home towns (Locke, Hoa, and Tam, 2012; Nguyen, Hardesty, and Khuat, 2013). In this regard, the study was consistent with findings about physical and mental health of migrant laborers in other countries. For example, Webber and colleagues found that high work demands, fear of medical cost, and unfamiliarity with services prevented migrants working as beer promoters from accessing health care (Webber, Spitzer, Somrongthong, Truong, and Kounnavongsa, 2012).

However, findings of this study, particularly that migrants largely excluded themselves from social activities and risky behaviors in order to preserve health for their challenging work life, contradicted some previous studies where migrants were found to highly likely engage in risky sexual practices precisely to emotionally balance their hard working life. In a study with migrant coal miners in Vietnam, Ta Van Tuan (2010) found that migrant coal miners engaged in sex for relaxation and reward for their risky and hard work; they were also less inclined to worry about long-term risks of HIV infection because they faced accidents at work on a daily basis. The study did share that migrant coal miners were excluded from necessary health information, a salient theme found in most studies of migrants in Vietnam.

Overall, this study suggested that migrant laborers in Vietnam needed many support services in order to integrate into city life and live fully instead of using the city as a gigantic worksite without social life. Providing these support services are crucial in order to help migrant laborers function well in the receiving cities but also to maintain the functioning of migrants' families in the sending communities. Since migrants move between regions of the country, especially between rural and urban areas, they can potentially become agents of positive change, influencing good health practices in rural areas if they are provided with health information and support services in the cities. On the other hand, if they continue to feel excluded, isolated, and marginalized by the cities, they might involve in risky behaviors, which turn them into active transmitters of diseases. Moving foreword, the choice for Vietnam and developing countries with similar migration stories seems evident.

ACKNOWLEDGMENTS

The authors thank the National Foundation for Science and Technology (Nafosted) for funding the project "Social integration and inclusion of poor migrant laborers in urban Vietnam during industrialization and modernization period," of which this paper is based on. We thank Professor Pham Van Quyet of the University of Social Sciences and Humanities (Vietnam National University) and other members of the research team for their assistance in preparing this article.

REFERENCES

Bond, V., and Dover, P. (1997). Men, women and the trouble with condoms: Problems associated with condom use by migrant workers in rural Zambia. *Health Transition Review*, 7 Supplement, 377–91.

Brockerhoff, M., and Biddlecom, A. (1999). Migration, sexual behavior and the risk of HIV in Kenya. *International Migration Review*, *33*(4), 833–56.

Coast, E. (2006). Local understandings of, and responses to, HIV: Rural-urban migrants in Tanzania. *Social Science and Medicine*, 63(4), 1000–10.

Dang, N. A. and Nguyen, B. M. (1998). Guaranteeing to provide social services for migrant laborers in cities. *Journal of Sociology*, 4(64), 31-36.

Dang, N.A. (2008, September 9). Social protection and rural-to-urban labor migration. *Vietnam Development Forum*. Paper presentation at the Social Security in Vietnam: Preparation for Next Phase of Development Conference, Hanoi, Vietnam. Hanoi.

Institute for Social Development Studies (2011). *From rural areas to cities: Socio-economic influences of migration in Vietnam.* Hanoi, Hanoi: Publisher of Labor.

International Organization for Migration (2012). *Gender and saving money of migrant laborers.* Hanoi, Hanoi: Publisher of Science and Technology.

Kitchener, B. A., and Jorm, A. F. (2002). *Mental health first aid manual.* Centre for Mental Health Research, Canberra.

Ladinsky, J. L., Nguyen, H. T., and Nancy D. V. (2000). Changes in the health care system of Vietnam in response to the emerging market economy. *Journal of Public Health Policy*, 21(1), 82-98.

Landingham, V. (2003). Impacts of rural to urban migration on the health of working-age adult migrants in Ho Chi Minh city, Vietnam. Paper presented at: Conference on African Migration in Comparative Perspective. Johannesburg.

Le, K., Pham, L., Vu, L., and Schelling, E. (2012). Health services for reproductive tract infections among female migrant workers in industrial zones in Ha Noi, Viet Nam: An in-depth assessment. (2012). *Reproductive Health*, 9(1), 4-14.

Locke, C., Hoa, N. N., and Tam, N. T. (2012). Visiting marriages and remote parenting: Changing strategies of rural–urban migrants to Hanoi, Vietnam. *Journal Of Development Studies*, 48(1), 10-25.

Lurie, M. (2006). The epidemiology of migration and HIV/AIDS in South Africa. *Journal of Ethnic and Migration Studies*, 32(4), 946–66.

Ma, E., and Cheng, H. (2010). "Naked" bodies: Experimenting with intimate relations among migrant workers in South China. *International Journal of Cultural Studies*, 8, 307–328.

Nguyen, L.T., and White, M. J. (2007). Health status of temporary migrants in urban areas in Vietnam. *International Migration* 45(4), 102–34.

Nguyen, L. D., Raabe, K., and Grote, U. (2015). Rural–urban migration, household vulnerability, and welfare in Vietnam. *World Development*, 7179-93.

Nguyen, N. H., Hardesty, M. and Khuat, T. H. (2013). "I am tired but if I don't try to have sex, my wife will think I've been fooling around in the City": Work, migration, and sex among Vietnamese migrant laborers. *Journal of Sex Research*, 50(6), 548–559.

Nguyen, N. H., Hardesty, M., and Khuat, T. H. (2011). In full swing? How do pendulum migrant laborers in Vietnam adjust their sexual views to their rural–urban swinging lives? *Culture, Health and Sexuality*, 13, 1193–1207.

Vietnam Parliament (2012). *Law of labors.* 10/2012/QH13.

Rushing, R. (2006). Migration and sexual exploitation in Vietnam. *Asian and Pacific Migration Journal*, 15, 471–494.

Rydstrøm, H. (2006). Sexual desires and "social evils": Young women in rural Vietnam. *Gender, Place and Culture*, 13, 283–301.

Trinh, T. Q. (2004). Policy of migrant laborers and population allocation in the mountainous areas in Vietnam. *Journal of Sociology*, 2(86), 51-64.

UNAIDS (2001). *Population mobility and AIDS.* Geneva: UNAIDS.

United Nations Habitant (2007). *The challenge of slums: Global report on human settlements.* Retrieved from http://unhabitat.org/.

United Nations Population Fund (2008). *Productive health of migrant laborers.* Hanoi.

United Nations Population Fund (2010). *Internal migration: Opportunities and challenges for socio-economic development in Vietnam.* Hanoi.

United Nations Population Fund (2012). *Influence of cultural and social factors on productive health of female migrant laborers in Vietnam.* Hanoi.

United Nations Vietnam (2010). *Domestic migration: Opportunities and challenges to the socio-economic development in Vietnam.* Hanoi.

Van Tuan, T. (2010). Meanings of sex, concepts of risk and sexual practices among migrant coal miners in Quang Ninh, Vietnam. *Culture, Health and Sexuality*. 12(Suppl. 1), 31-40.

Weare, K. (2000). *Promoting mental, emotional and social health: A whole school approach.* London: Routledge Falmer.

Webber, G., Spitzer, D., Somrongthong, R., Truong Cong, D., and Kounnavongsa, S. (2012). Facilitators and barriers to accessing reproductive health care for migrant beer promoters in Cambodia, Laos, Thailand and Vietnam: A mixed methods study. *Globalization and Health*, 8(1), 21-38.

World Health Organization (2001). *Mental Health: New Understanding, New Hope.* Geneva: World Health Report.

World Health Organization (1951). *Mental health: report on the second session of the Expert Committee*. Geneva: World Health Organization.

Yang, X (2010). Migration, detachment and HIV risk among rural-urban migrants in China. In: F. Thomas, M. Haour-Knipe, and P. Aggleton (Eds.), *Mobility, sexuality, and AIDS*, (pp. 199–213). New York: Routledge.

Yang, X., and G. Xia (2006). Gender, migration, risky sex and HIV infection in China. *Studies in Family Planning*, 37(4), 241–50.

In: Migrant Workers
Editors: Qingwen Xu and Lucy P. Jordan
ISBN: 978-1-63485-272-2

Chapter 7

CHALLENGES AND SOLUTIONS OF FOOD SECURITY AMONG SEASONAL MIGRANTS: THE CASE OF SEASONAL MIGRATION IN INDIA

Anjali B. Borhade[1] and Mengxi Zhang[2,*]
[1]Disha Foundation, Nashik, India and Indian Institute of Public Health, Delhi, India
[2]Tulane University School of Public Health and Tropical Medicine, Louisiana, US

ABSTRACT

The chapter examines the link between seasonal migration and food security in developing countries. It aims to identify the implication of food security in urban destinations to strengthen policy-makers' understanding of this issue, as well as providing suggestions in various organizations to improve migrants' food security conditions. The case study in India provides positive evidence that the collaboration among the government, migrant community, and non-governmental organizations plays a significantly role in helping migrants to improve livelihood and secure right to food.

INTRODUCTION

The term temporary migrants is used interchangeably with seasonal, circular, short-term, and spontaneous migrants and refers to the people who temporarily live and work in a place other than their officially documented residences (Massey, 1985). In many developing Asian countries, such as Indonesia, Vietnam, China, Cambodia, and India, temporary migration is emerging as a dominant pattern of movement (Hugo, 2003; Zhao, 2003). In rural areas of India, people migrate to urban destinations, seeking employment opportunities to address

* Corresponding Author: Anjali B. Borhade, Indian Institute of Public Health Delhi, Plot No. 47, Sector 44/Institutional Area, Gurgaon, Haryana India-122002, Email: anjali.borhade@iiphd.org.

unexpected environmental and unfavorable economic conditions, especially during lean seasons (Keshri and Bhagat, 2011; Rogaly et al., 2002). Compared with long-term migrants, seasonal migrants are poor and illiterate (Keshri and Bhagat, 2011). In Bangladesh, research shows a similar migration pattern; the cause reported as famine, poverty, food insecurity, and unemployment (Afsar, 2003; Hossain, Kazal, and Ahmed, 2013). In Nepal, limited ownership of land is the motivating factor for temporary migration (Gartaula, Niehof, and Visser, 2012); families that do not have much land for cultivation often depend on remittance from the migrants at home (Gartaula et al., 2012). In China and Vietnam, temporary migrants working in urban areas are likely to retain their land in rural origins, which retains value due to tenuous land rights (de Brauw and Harigaya, 2007; Wong, Li, and Song, 2007). For temporary migrants moving from rural villages to urban cities for work and income, whole family migration is not common, and migrants in a family are usually those young, healthy, and more educated than others (de Brauw and Harigaya, 2007; Jacoby, Li, and Rozelle, 2002).

Although temporary migrants have contributed significantly to economic development and urban growth, they remain socially and economically marginalized in their urban destinations (Wong et al., 2007). Individually, separation from families, increased access to risky behaviors, discrimination, stresses from work, and risks associated with adjustment to a new and unfamiliar environment can have a negative impact upon migrants' life and health (Fu and Van Landingham, 2012; Lu, 2008; Van Landingham and Fu, 2012). Policy and regulation gaps put additional burden on migrants' urban life and health. Most Asian countries hold strict migration policies that reduce legal rights of migrants. In China and Vietnam, for example, the household registration systems classify residents geographically, which constrains migrants' employment, options for living and housing, access to healthcare and education for migrants' children, and their social participation in the urban destinations (de Brauw and Harigaya, 2007; Jacoby et al., 2002). The Chinese government offers temporary permits for migrant workers, but it does not provide equal access to welfare services for these 'permanent non-urban' dwellers (Wong et al., 2007). In Bangladesh, the government welfare entitlements do not apply to the seasonal migrants (Afsar, 2003). In India, temporary migrants who have not registered in urban areas cannot access the public distribution systems (PDS), the Indian national food security system that provides free and lower-price food for India's poor residents; some local governments provide temporary ration cards for migrants in urban destinations to access PDS; however, the process of receiving a temporary ration card is long and complicated (Deshingkar; and Akter, 2009).

In order to improve the conditions of seasonal migrants, various interventions were initiated and implemented at the policy and community levels. In China, for example, the government announced a public security reform plan in 2015 to replace all temporary permits for migrant workers with permanent residency, which comes with social security and the right to access education, healthcare, and public activities (Thomson Reuters, 2015). The Vietnamese government has also made progress, moving towards a better legal system through providing migrants resources, and the ability to access social services (Duong, Linh, and Thao, 2011). Parallel with government policy reforms, civil and social service organizations in some countries initiate and operate programs as well provide assistance at local level to promote migrants' social rights (Bryan, Chowdhury, and Mobarak, 2014; Deshingkar, 2006; Deshingkar and Akter, 2009). Nonetheless, despite the important roles served by non-governmental organizations and communities to protect and promote migrants' fundamental social and economic rights, these organizations' activities and programs are restricted by government policies; and unfortunately, most countries do not have plans or a specific timeframe for their policy reforms.

Migration can be a source of vulnerability for wellbeing and health. Among many challenges that seasonal migrants have experienced, the issue of food security is a comprehensive one that intersects with factors in different dimensions (Rai and Selvaraj, 2015; Uraguchi, 2012). On a national level, food security is used to measure and evaluate the domestic market to balance the food supply and demand (Pinstrup-Andersen, 2009). On a household level, it is defined as the interaction between household food access and food availability (Pinstrup-Andersen, 2009). Individual food security is associated with a set of non-food factors, including occupation, health conditions, and access to healthcare (Pinstrup-Andersen, 2009; Rai and Selvaraj, 2015). Due to the difficulties of accessing food and deficient food supply system, migrants in developing countries have distinct needs in food security. Among rural-to-urban migrants, sufficient food in markets, ability to access food, food safety, sanitation of living conditions are all challenged by limited income, insecure housing conditions, deficit policies, and insufficient local/community support. This chapter will explore the food security issues among seasonal migrants in developing countries and propose relevant solutions in different dimensions through a case study in India.

Seasonal Migrants and Food Security in Nashik, India

Economically and culturally, Maharashtra is one of the most advanced states in India. Nashik is a part of Golden Triangle of Mumbai-Pune-Nashik, which is the leading destination for rural-to-urban migrants in Maharashtra (Singh, 2015). Nashik is also one of the eleven fastest growing cities in the world (Census Organization of India, 2011), with a population growth rate of 22.30% (Census Organization of India, 2011). Nashik has a large number of seasonal workers; however, it is difficult to assess their numbers as they are a mobile and floating population.

Migrants to Nashik are both intra-and inter-state, coming from other drought-prone districts and regions of Maharashtra, such as Dhule, Jalgaon, Marathwada and Vidarbha, as well as lesser-developed states such as Bihar, Gujarat, Karnataka, Madhya Pradesh, and Uttar Pradesh. Most migrants belong to a large number of secular tribal groups, which are mainly *hindu koli* and *hindu konkana*. Seasonal migrants in Nashik typically seek work in the city for 8 to 10 months each year, usually from October to the following June. The pattern of migration corresponds with the agricultural seasons; they stay on the halt points during the lean season and return to their villages during the monsoon or other peak periods.

Seasonal migrants generally seek jobs at the locations called *nakas,* the word used to denote a road junction in Marathi, in local language (Naraparaju, 2015). *Nakas* are usually located at the boundary of the town, set on the main roads, and function as public labor markets as well as seasonal migrants' assembling areas (Deshingkar; and Akter, 2009; Naraparaju, 2015). There are also established *nakas* in the city often operated by contractors and others seeking to recruit daily wage workers. Nashik has nine *nakas,* which are located in vacant areas in parks and footpaths. The size and location of *nakas* vary depending on the number of accommodated migrants. *Nakas* are open, comprising no more than an open space in which the migrant family's belongings and cooking equipment are deposited and where the families cook, eat and sleep. These unauthorized 'dwelling' spaces are rarely covered by canvas, plastic, or tin sheets. The spaces also lack provisions for basic facilities, including water and sanitation.

Due to the unhygienic condition of the water supply, sanitation and drainage systems, and environmental pollution, migrants are vulnerable to nutritional deficiencies as well as respiratory and digestive system diseases (Dana, 2011; Ruel, Garrett, Morris, Maxwell, et al., 1998). In addition, living in these urban open spaces increases the struggles in physical safety and psychological health (Deshingkar and Akter, 2009; Swahn et al., 2012).

A Snapshot: Disha Foundation

Disha Foundation, a local non-governmental organization (NGO) based in Nashik, is dedicated to work for seasonal labour migration on health and development issues. Since 2004, Disha Foundation initiated the food security program targeting the populations of the six *nakas* in Nashik (Satpur, Peth Phata, Old/New Gangapur, Gangaghat, and Civil). Approximately 7,000 temporary migrants and their families settled at these *nakas*. Before and after the program, the Disha Foundation conducted assessments among migrants to obtain the experiences of migrant workers related to the issues of health and food security, to understand the situation and needs of the migrants, and to evaluate the program implementation. We summarize some observations here to demonstrate the migrants' desperate need for food security, the systematic barriers to protect their basic rights, and the improvement of their food security.

Access to food. Irregular employment and the nature of the work results in financial and food insecurity; economic exploitation is common as wages are unregulated, and promised wages are not always paid or paid on time, a situation fully being recognized in India (De Haan and Rogaly, 2015). Together with the lack of access to basic amenities in *nakas*, including water, toilet facilities, shelter and electricity creates challenges for migrants and their families. One of the migrant workers had this to say about their food crisis: "*It was very difficult for me to stay in the naka with two daughters; often, we don't get work for 15-20 days a month. Often we don't have food to eat.*" (Female, 34 years, Satpur *naka*). Another migrant said: "*I have not got work for the past 5 days. The food grain that I brought from my village is about to finish. I'm worried about my family; if I don't get work in the next few days, what we will eat, and how we will go back to our village?*" (Man, 32 years, migrated with family, Peth Phata *naka*).

Seasonal migrants in *nakas* have immense needs in food security. Some women and children must beg on the streets to supplement the family income. Anaemia and malnutrition were commonly observed among these migrant families. Tragically, women turn to sex exchange to survive the severe food crisis. Shah observed a similar association among poverty, migration, and gender oppression through a critical ethnographic study in India in her book *Street Corner Secrets* (Shah, 2014). The following is a story about a female migrant in Nashik:

> Savitri had initially migrated to Satpur *naka* with her husband and children. When her husband deserted her and her daughters got married and left home, she stayed alone in a *naka*. Savitri could not find work for two months so she started begging. She then kept a sexual relationsahip with a *Naka* contractor for food and a living space. She soon realised she was five months pregnant. Although she did not want the child, it was too late to have an abortion. Savitri gave birth to a baby boy. Considering her financial situation, she decided to sell her son to a couple in a *naka* for 5,000 rupees and 50 kg rice. (names have been changed).

Right to food. Access to subsidized food grain was identified as an immediate priority for migrants. The state government issues one ration card, also called the Household Consumer Card (HCC) per family. It is mainly used for purchasing subsidized food and fuel. The card is also serves as a proof of citizens' identification, which helped migrants seek jobs and access public services in urban destination. However, the portability of receiving a ration card is extremely low for seasonal migrants. Since the ration card is tied to a migrant's village of origin; the urban city government where migrants work and stay has no obligation to offer the card and provide services. According to India's national policy, migrants can receive a new ration card as long as they remove their names from their ration cards at home. However, this application needed documents to approve their fixed residential status which ignored the nature of seasonal migration. To fix this gap, Maharashtra became the first state to pass a Government Resolution in 2000 allowing seasonal migrants to obtain temporary ration cards in urban Maharashtra. The Government Resolution 1000/G.R. 399/2000/NP28 issued on the November 9th 2000 stated:

> ......as workers in the unorganised sector migrate in search of employment, do not reside in a fixed place and do not live in their native place, they do not have documentary proof, such as a birth registration certificate or a certificate for school enrolment for their children. It is also very difficult to get documentary proof on migration. Since these families are generally eligible for services under the Public Distribution System, the requirements of documentary proof are hereby relaxed. The normal procedure for getting a ration card - to complete an application form — should be observed on the basis of this information being given by the applicant, and the Supply Inspector should physically verify the living conditions of the family members and then the procedure to issue temporary ration cards for a certain period should be adopted. If the family wishes to reside at the same address for a longer period, the ration card should be renewed for such further period as necessary...... (Translated from Marathi, local official language of Maharashtra state of India).

However, it took several years of lobbying by local NGOs in Nashik after the implementation of this Government Resolution (Deshingkar; and Akter, 2009). The obstacles of the implementation suggest that the local government was, at best, not prepared for the policy change, and at worst, ignorant of the resolution. Similarly, when migrant workers are unaware of these policies, they are disempowered and unable to access the services to which they are entitled.

Disha Foundation. The Disha Foundation plays a mediating role between the state government authorities and the migrant communities. The foundation apprised the authorities about the government's plan to provide the temporary ration cards to migrants. Through consultations with the local Nashik division of PDS and the governmental authorities, an order was issued by the collectors of Fair Price Shops (FPSs). FPSs, also known as public distribution shops, are a part of the PDS that issues the ration cards. The order is to provide seasonal migrants with temporary ration cards for four months with the option to extend to 12 months against their existing ration cards. Migrants must have the temporary ration cards cancelled by FPSs before they return to their origin to be eligible to apply for subsidised food grain in their home villages. The temporary ration cards can be reactivated or renewed when migrants return to their urban destinations.

To facilitate the process of obtaining a temporary ration card, Disha helped identify certain barriers to receive PDS services, primarily migrants' inability to provide official documents such as residential proofs and income certificates. Given the unique situation of seasonal migrants, the PDS offered flexibilities of certain requirements, such as migrants can submit a letter from the contractor as income proof; a photo with family members standing in front of the luggage where migrants stay in *nakas* can be considered as a residential proof; a recommendation letter from neighbouring migrants or a membership card of Disha Foundation can be considered as proof of identification.

Given these flexibilities, in the first round in 2004, 55 temporary ration cards were issued to seasonal migrant families living in Civil *naka*. With the temporary ration cards, migrants can purchase food grain at a concessional rate from the FPSs close to their *nakas*. In addition, the Disha Foundation has conducted training programs for migrants to extend their ration cards on their own, prepare their own applications, and negotiate with ration office staff members independently. Many migrants expressed their gratitude and recognized the importance of the temporary ration card. A migrant woman said: "*Now we feel that we are citizens of Nashik. We can go and take food grain from nearest ration shop every month. We don't have to go back to our village just for getting our food grain, which was a very costly affair.*" Another migrant mentioned: "*Getting food grain from open market is very expensive, many times we do not get jobs almost for 15 days in a month, that time they face acute food crisis. In such situations, few parents ask their children to beg. This is most useful support for us.*" Until 2006, the PDS in Nashik has issued over 1,200 temporary ration cards to migrants, most of them from the tribes who are constantly moving back and forth seasonally for livelihood with their livestock. Following the successful practice in Nashik, the PDS in Trimbakeshwar Taluka, a sub-district of the Nashik district, piloted a practice and issued 50 cards to tribal members in their villages who routinely migrated to Nashik for temporary employment. The Nashik model has been further scaled up in few other districts of Maharashtra and Tamilnadu state in India. The Disha Foundation plans to upscale this model with PDS in other areas and cities by engaging in intra-state collaborations to comprehensively address seasonal migrants' needs in food and livelihood.

Lesson learned. Seasonal migrants in India are a highly vulnerable population and are subjected to a variety of degradations ranging from economic exploitation to social rights deprivation. Moreover, they are socially isolated in the urban destination and experience employment and financial uncertainties. Recognising their vulnerabilities, the Disha Foundation made the seasonal migrants aware of their rights and entitlements to government services. It also establishes links between migrant communities and the government authorities to facilitate migrants' access to the public services. Although the number of migrants receiving the ration cards is still small (11%of migrant families in the six *nakas*), the success demonstrates the siginifant impact of the support of non-governmental organizations on migrants' capacity to strive for the right of food security. Efforts are still needed to institutionalize the process so that policy implementation at the local level would become a routine process. To advocate for mainstreaming migrant populations and to enhance migrants' rights to access the basic services, NGOs can play a crucial role to facilitate the communication between migrants and governments and to monitor and enhance government administration.

CONCLUSION

Previous studies support the impact of income, food access, and living conditions on food security. In Asia, most seasonal migrants work in unskilled and irregular jobs in small-scale enterprises, where employees are paid less and seldom receive the employment benefits and legal protections (Ruel, et al., 1998). In southern African cities, migrants are more food insecure than long-term residents of the poorer areas. Unemployment rates were nearly half among migrants and they are less likely to find casual work (Crush, 2013). These negative factors set the seasonal migrants at high risk of poverty and food insecurity in diverse regions of the developing world.

Due to the multi-dimensional determinants, the issue of food security among seasonal migrants is complicated, and difficult to address. Additionally, the global food security agenda pays little attention to seasonal migration and urbanization. In developing countries, political power and bureaucracy always assume food security could be solved through increasing agricultural production instead of improving the rights of access to food among migrant workers (Gartaula, et al., 2012; Rai and Selvaraj, 2015). Although some countries have relevant revolutions, a lack of policy enforcement lags the policy implementation. In the emerging economies, changing dynamics within society can offer pathways for migrants to secure the right to live. The support from local and community level plays a significant role in protecting migrants' basic right. Consistent and further collaboration among the migrant community, local government, and NGOs is essential to improve migrants' livelihood and food security.

ACKNOWLEDGMENTS

Helpful advice from Ms. Erin Walker and Dr. Akhil Kshirsagar is gratefully acknowledged.

REFERENCES

Afsar, R. (2003). *Internal migration and the development nexus, the case of Bangladesh.* Paper presented at the Regional Conference on Migration, Development and Pro-poor Policy Choices in Asia, Dhaka.

Bryan, G., Chowdhury, S. and Mobarak, A. M. (2014). Underinvestment in a Profitable Technology: The Case of Seasonal Migration in Bangladesh. *Econometrica, 82*(5), 1671-1748.

Census Organization of India. (2011). Population Census.

Crush, J. (2013). Linking food security, migration and development. *International Migration, 51*(5), 61-75.

Dana, T. (2011). Unhygienic living conditions and health problems: a study in selected slums of Dhaka City. *OIDA International Journal of Sustainable Development, 2*(11), 27-34.

de Brauw, A. and Harigaya, T. (2007). Seasonal migration and improving living standards in Vietnam. *American Journal of Agricultural Economics, 89*(2), 430-447.

De Haan, A. and Rogaly, B. (2015). *Labour mobility and rural society*. Routledge.

Deshingkar, P. (2006). Internal migration, poverty and development in Asia: Including the excluded. *IDS Bulletin, 37*.

Deshingkar, P. and Akter, S. (2009). *Migration and human development in India*. Retrieved from https://ideas.repec.org/p/hdr/papers/hdrp-2009-13.html.

Duong, L. B., Linh, T. G. and Thao, N. T. P. (2011). *Social protection for rural-urban migrants in Vietnam: Current situation, challenges and opportunities*. CSP Research Report 08. Retrieved from http://www. ids.ac.uk/publication/social-protection-for-rural-urban-migrants-in-vietnam-current-situation-challenges-and-opportunities.

Fu, H. and VanLandingham, M. J. (2012). Mental health consequences of international migration for Vietnamese Americans and the mediating effects of physical health and social networks: results from a natural experiment approach. *Demography, 49*(2), 393-424.

Gartaula, H., Niehof, A. and Visser, L. (2012). Shifting perceptions of food security and land in the context of labour out-migration in rural Nepal. *Food Security, 4*(2), 181-194.

Hossain, M. Z., Kazal, M. M. H. and Ahmed, J. U. (2013). Rural-urban migration and its implications for food security in Bangladesh. *Shahjalal University of Science and Technology with the support of the National Food Policy Capacity Strengthening Programme*.

Hugo, G. (2003). Urbanisation in Asia: An overview. *Paper prepared for Conference on African Migration in Comparative Perspective, Johannesburg, South Africa*.

Jacoby, H. G., Li, G. and Rozelle, S. (2002). Hazards of expropriation: Tenure insecurity and investment in rural China. *American Economic Review, 92*(5), 1420-1447.

Keshri, K. and Bhagat, R. B. (2011). *Temporary and seasonal migration in India* (Vol. 66).

Lu, Y. (2008). Test of the 'healthy migrant hypothesis': A longitudinal analysis of health selectivity of internal migration in Indonesia. *Social Science Medicine 67*(8), 1331-1339.

Ruel, M. T., Garrett, J. L., Morris, S. S., Maxwell, D. G., Oshaug, A., Engle, P. L., Menon, P., Slack, A. and Haddad, L. J. (1998). Urban challenges to food and nutrition security. a review of food security, health, and caregiving in the cities. *FCND DISCUSSION PAPER*.

Massey, D. S. (1985). Migration surveys in low-income countries: Richard E. Bilsborrow, A. S. Oberai and Guy Standing. *Journal of Development Economics, 18*(2-3), 584-586.

Naraparaju, K. (2015). Impediments to contract enforcement in day labour markets: a perspective from India. *Journal of Institutional Economics, FirstView*, 1-26.

Pinstrup-Andersen, P. (2009). Food security: definition and measurement. *Food Security, 1*(1), 5-7.

Rai, R. K. and Selvaraj, P. (2015). Exploring realities of food security: Oral accounts of migrant workers in urban India. *Economic and Industrial Democracy, 36*(1), 147-171.

Rogaly, B., Coppard, D., Rafique, A., Rana, K., Sengupta, A. and Biswas, J. (2002). Seasonal migration and welfare/illfare in eastern India: A social analysis. *Journal of Development Studies, 38*(5), 89-114.

Shah, S. P. (2014). *Street corner secrets: sex, work, and migration in the city of Mumbai.* Duke University Press.

Singh, M. (2015). Internal migration in India. *Journal of Art and Science of Geography, 1*(1), 30-35.

Swahn, M. H., Gressard, L., Palmier, J. B., Kasirye, R., Lynch, C. and Yao, H. (2012). Serious violence victimization and perpetration among youth living in the slums of Kampala, Uganda. *Western Journal of Emergency Medicine, 13*(3), 253-259.

Thomson Reuters (Producer). (2015). China to scrap temporary residence permits: Xinhua.

Uraguchi, Z. B. (2012). Rural income transfer programs and rural household food security in Ethiopia. *Journal of Asian and African Studies, 47*(1), 33-51.

VanLandingham, M. and Fu, H. (2012). Migration and health in Southeast Asia. In Williams, L. and Guest, P. (ed.). *Demographic change in Southeast Asia: Recent histories and furture directions* (pp. 165-184). Southeast Asia Program Publications, Southeast Asia Program, Cornell University.

Wong, D. F. K., Li, C. Y. and Song, H. X. (2007). Rural migrant workers in urban China: Living a marginalised life. *International Journal of Social Welfare, 16*(1), 32-40.

Zhao, Z. (2003). *Rural-urban migration in China – What do we know and what do we need to know?* China Center for Economic Research, Peking University.

In: Migrant Workers
Editors: Qingwen Xu and Lucy P. Jordan
ISBN: 978-1-63485-272-2

Chapter 8

THE WELFARE BOUNDARY: A HIDDEN MECHANISM OF THE *HUKOU* REGULATION AND MIGRANT WORKERS' RIGHTS IN CHINA

Gaoming Ma * ***and Qiaobing Wu***
Department of Social Work, The Chinese University of Hong Kong

ABSTRACT

This chapter examines the relationship between the migration regulations and the social rights in the context of Chinese Household Registration System (*Hukou*). By analyzing the historical *Hukou* transformation, we find that the *Hukou* still affects the migrant workers' rights nowadays. We argue that such a problem is not merely caused by the *Hukou* itself, but is determined by the inherent mechanism of the social rights. The social rights have a natural characteristic of the spatial inequality so as to distinguish the insiders and the outsiders. It is the dynamics of the upward universalism of the social rights and the downward distribution of the social resources that finally forms the multi-layered welfare boundaries. Our analysis illuminates the future *Hukou* reform in China and may also help to improve the migration regulations in other countries.

The worldwide migrations grew tremendously in the past decades. The United Nations (2013) estimated that the amount of the international migrants increased from 154 million in 1990 to 232 million in 2013. Meanwhile, the number of internal migrants, those who move within the national border, also rocketed in the developing countries. Taking China as an example, statistics showed that there were 269 million migrant workers in 2013 (National Bureau of Statistics, 2014), 37 million more than the overall international migrants. However, compared with many studies on the international migration, less have focused on the internal

* Corresponding Author: Gaoming Ma, Department of Social Work, The Chinese University of Hong Kong, Shatin, NT, Hong Kong. Email: gmma@swk.cuhk.edu.hk.

migration (King, Skeldon, and Vullnetari, 2008; Ellis, 2012). Even the name of "migration" is directly equal to "international migration" in the western literature (King and Conti, 2013; Castles, Haas, and Miller, 2014).

The internal migration, though neglected to a large extent, is of great importance in the developing countries. The rural-to-urban migration, as the largest proportion of the internal migration, is not only the necessary stage of economic developments (Lewis, 1954), but also the vital sources of social problems. For instance, the migrant workers in China have been excluded from the urban welfare system by the Household Registration System (*Hukou*) since 1958 (Wu and Treiman, 2004; Wu, 2009). Meanwhile, the social exclusion of the internal migrants is not unique in China. Statistics showed that the population of slum dwellers in the developing countries increased from 767 million in 2000 to 828 million in 2010 (UNHABITAT, 2010). Those who were living in the slums were also excluded from the urban welfare like health, education, housing, etc. (UNHABITAT, 2010). Therefore, studies on the internal migration are extremely significant in the developing world.

Our research mainly focuses on the internal migration. The prominent question in this chapter is: Why are the migrant workers excluded from urban welfare system even if he/she has the same national citizenship? In other words, what on earth is the relationship between the migration regulations and the social rights? To address the question, we start from the *Hukou* system in China because *Hukou* can serve as an analytical context of the migration regulation. Then we will analyze the inherent mechanism of the social rights as well as its relationship with *Hukou*. And finally, we will discuss the contributions and the implications of our study.

Table 1. A Glance of the Historical Development of the *Hukou* System in China

Main Ages	Four Periods	Typical Regulations
Origin	1951-1963	1958 The Household Registration Ordinance *
	1964-1983	1964 Ministry of Public Security Regulation on *Hukou* migration (Draft) **
Reform	1984-2000	1985 Ministry of Public Security Interim Regulation on the Management of Urban Temporary Population ***
	2001-present	2014 The State Council Opinions on Further Promotion of the Reform of Household Registration System ****

Notes:

* The Standing Committee of the National People's Congress. (1958). *Zhonghua renmin gongheguo hukou dengji tiaoli.* [The Household Registration Ordinance of People's Republic of China]. Retrieved from http://www.npc.gov.cn/wxzl/gongbao/2000-12/10/content_5004332.htm.

** Ministry of Public Security. (1964). *Gonganbu guanyu chuli hukou qianyi de guiding (caoan).* [1964 Ministry of Public Security Regulation on Hukou migration (Draft)]. Retrieved from http://wuxizazhi.cnki.net/Search/SXBA196412002.html.

*** Ministry of Public Security. (1985). *Gonganbu guanyu chengzhen zanzhu renkou guanli de zanxing guiding.* [1985 Ministry of Public Security Interim Regulation on the Management of Urban Temporary Population]. Retrieved from http://www.rmlt.com.cn/2014/0731/300535.shtml.

**** The State Council. (2014). Guowuyuan guanyu jinyibu tuijin huji zhidu gaige de yijian. [2014 The State Council Opinions on Further Promotion of the Reform of Household Registration System]. Retrieved from http://www.gov.cn/zhengce/content/2014-07/30/content_8944.htm.

BACKGROUND: THE HUKOU SYSTEM AND ITS EVOLUTION

The original framework of the Hukou system. The *Hukou* system was stipulated in 1958, and had been strictly enforced since the early 1960s (Cheng and Selden, 1994). Such a stringent policy was first modified in 1984 in order to encourage the economic development in the urban areas. Two decades later, the State Council (2014) replaced the original agricultural and non-agricultural *Hukou* with the uniform residential registration. Table 1 is a glance of the historical periods and symbolic policies of the *Hukou* system. The original *Hukou* system had two prominent parts: the *Hukou Leibie* (Type of *Hukou*) and the *Hukou Suozaidi* (Place of *Hukou*) (Chan and Zhang, 1999). The *Hukou Leibie* was a label of either "the Agricultural *Hukou*" or "the Non-agricultural *Hukou*." Normally, those who had the Agricultural *Hukou* should live in the rural areas, while people who got the Non-agricultural *Hukou* could live in the urban areas. And the two types of *Hukou* cannot be interchanged automatically.

On the other hand, the *Hukou Suozaidi* referred to a spatial regulation that limited the citizens' ability to settle down in places different from where their *Hukou* is registered. Therefore, not only were the people with Agricultural *Hukou* forbidden to migrate to the urban areas, but also the urban residents with the Non-agricultural *Hukou* could not move to other cities (Ministry of Public Security, 1964). Only those with *Nongzhuanfei Zhibiao* (Quota to change the Type of *Hukou* and Place of *Hukou*) were permitted to migrate permanently (Chan and Zhang, 1999). However, the quota was very limited (Wu and Treiman, 2004). Table 2 shows the ten-level hierarchy of the *original* system based on the *Hukou Leibie* and *Hukou Suozaidi*.

Table 2. The Original Framework of the *Hukou* System in China*

Hukou Suozaidi (Place)	*Hukou Leibie* (Type)	
Beijing, Shanghai (Highest)	Non-agricultural Status	Agricultural Status
Big Cities (Second Highest)	Non-agricultural Status	Agricultural Status
Small Cities (Middle)	Non-agricultural Status	Agricultural Status
Towns (Second Lowest)	Non-agricultural Status	Agricultural Status
Villages (Lowest)	Non-agricultural Status	Agricultural Status

Note:

* Ministry of Public Security. (1964). *Gonganbu guanyu chuli hukou qianyi de guiding (caoan).* [1964 Ministry of Public Security Regulation on Hukou migration (Draft)]. Retrieved from http://wuxizazhi.cnki.net/Search/SXBA196412002.html.

The reform of the Hukou system and its problem. The strict *Hukou* segregation could not be maintained when the massive migration started along with the economic reform since 1978. The State Council (1984) began to admit the right of migration but refused to accommodate them in the urban areas permanently. Consequently, the migrant workers were labeled as "temporary residents" by the Ministry of Public Security (1985), which became a two-decade official stigma. Hence, the empirical evidence showed that migrant workers in this period were seriously excluded from urban social welfare system. For example, the proportion of migrant workers in the overall Shanghai population increased from nearly 0.5% in 1981 to 20% in 1997, while their eligibility to urban social welfare was totally suppressed

(Feng, Zuo, and Ruan, 2002). Many scholars have suggested that the *Hukou* segregation still exists (Lu, 2008; Chan and Buckingham, 2008; Wu, 2009). Even after the State Council changed the Agricultural and Non-agricultural *Hukou* into the uniform residential identity in 2014, the place of *Hukou* still served as a threshold. The migrant workers are permitted to settle down in the small cities, but not in the big cities. As shown in Table 3, there is still a five-level *Hukou* hierarchy after the *Hukou* reform in 2014.

Table 3. The New Hierarchy of the *Hukou* System in China

Spatial Ranks*	Identical Status**	*Hukou* conversion**
Megacity behemoths	Citizen *Hukou*	Strictly control
Megacities	Citizen *Hukou*	Strictly control
Large-sized cities	Citizen *Hukou*	Reasonably control
Medium-sized cities	Citizen *Hukou*	Gradually open
Small-sized cities	Citizen *Hukou*	Open

Notes:

* The State Council. (2014). *Guowuyuan guanyu tiaozheng chengshi guimo huafen biaozhun de tongzhi.* [the Announcement of the State Council on Adjusting the Criteria for the Classification of City Sizes]. Retrieved from http://www.gov.cn/zhengce/content/2014-11/20/content_9225.htm.

**The State Council. (2014). *Guowuyuan guanyu jinyibu tuijin huji zhidu gaige de yijian.* [2014 The State Council Opinions on Further Promotion of the Reform of Household Registration System]. Retrieved from http://www.gov.cn/zhengce/content/2014-07/30/content_8944.htm.

Our question here is: Why is the *Hukou* system so hard to abolish, as many scholars and official media oppose its existence? Up to now, the mainstream explanation is the dual function of the *Hukou* system (Peng, Zhao, and Guo, 2009; Wu and Zhang, 2010; Chan and Buckingham, 2008). Because *Hukou* is adhered closely to the urban social welfare, it is hard to reform the *Hukou* system while keeping social welfare system static. Therefore scholars suggest that *Hukou* should be separated from social welfare and only maintain the function of population management (Chan and Buckingham, 2008). Other scholars, however, suggest that social welfare system should be reformed first to achieve equal standards between the rural and urban areas (Peng, Zhao, and Guo, 2009). Both policy advocacies are intuitively understandable but may be unrealistic for the policy making. If the central government decides to disassociate *Hukou* and social welfare, at the same time another eligibility system must be established (Lu, 2008). Moreover, it is also impossible for China to provide the same welfare provisions for all the citizens. Therefore, it seems that the *Hukou* reform has stepped into a dilemma: Which one should be modified first, the *Hukou* system itself or the bounded welfare?

ANALYSIS: THE WELFARE BOUNDARY UNDERLYING THE HUKOU SYSTEM

From the problem of Hukou to the nature of rights. Instead of the *Hukou* itself, we argue that the five-level hierarchy and dual functions of the *Hukou* are determined by the welfare system, not vice versa. Because social welfare is the means to access resources, it is only available for members (often citizens) in a bounded territory (Lister and Dywer, 2012). People who have the membership will certainly have the social rights to access to the welfare resources. In other words, the inherent nature of the social rights requires certain membership registration system, like the *Hukou* in China. The problem is how to define the membership of the social rights. According to T. H. Marshall, social rights referred to "the whole range from the right to a modicum of economic welfare and security to the right to share to the full in the social heritage and to live the life of a civilized being" (Marshall and Bottomore, 1992, p. 8). More importantly, the social rights must achieve two main objectives: one was to abate the class inequality, and the other was to alleviate the spatial inequality (Marshall and Bottomore, 1992). While the class inequality was well studied and developed in the literature, the spatial inequality was almost neglected (Ferrera, 2005). The reason was clear, as Marshall argued, "the original source of social rights was membership of local communities and functional associations" (Marshall, 2014, p. 30), but "the citizenship whose history I wish to trace is, by definition, national" (Marshall, 1992, p. 9). Consequently, people who follow up with Marshall also accept the obvious hypothesis that the social rights are nationality-bounded.

The hypothesis of national social rights may be plausible in the postwar era; however, it can be problematic in the contemporary world where massive cross-border migration emerge. As Brubaker (1992) said, "although citizenship is internally inclusive, it is externally exclusive" (p. 21). Hence, the so-called universal concept of social rights is only at the national level; people without nationality will be directly excluded as outsiders (Benhabib, 2005). So even if the class-abating objective is achieved within the nation state, the spatial inequality will also cause social conflicts. For example, the Dutch government rejected to cover *Unger*'s medical expenses in Germany in 1964, while the court opposed to the authorities and ruled on the side of *Unger*. This 1964 famous *Unger* judgment case became the first signal to challenge the national social rights in the European Union (Ferrera, 2005).

From social rights to welfare boundary. Although the spatial inequality nature of social rights is pervasive in the modern era of migration, few studies have focused on the problem yet. As a preliminary trial, we describe the mechanism in the Figure 1. On the right side of the figure, there is a small and up-side-down triangle. It includes the right, the entitlement and the resources. In the welfare system, the social rights cannot be directly related with the resources; instead, it must be coordinated through the entitlement (Dwyer, 2010). Therefore, the right must associate with the entitlement first, and then indirectly to the resources. And the triangular relationship exists in every welfare program within a specific territory. For instance, in the British National Health Services, the right to health, the British citizenship, and the medical resources are the three elements of one triangle. Besides, the Chinese New Rural Cooperative Medical Scheme is a case of the county level. The three elements, which are the right to health, the county *Hukou*, and medical resources, become a triangle.

When there is massive cross-border migration, the territories will certainly be different from each other and thus will lead to the spatial inequality. As shown in the left side of Figure 1, the small triangles, representing the territories in reality, are not equal and sometimes conflict with each other. Owing to the universal value of social rights, the triangles in the bottom will move upward to the national level or even to the international level. Therefore, Marshall (1992) embraced national social rights because there was only local welfare at that time, while Dean (2013) conceptualized the social rights in an international level because the national welfare cannot solve the migration problems. The big triangle in the dotted line represents the upward direction of social rights, while the small triangle in the bold line is the downward direction of social resources. The different directions of the social rights and social resources will lead to different definitions of the membership. Unlike the upward direction of social rights, social resources are always restrained and distributed at the local level. And as we mentioned above, social rights must have an entitlement to social resources, so the entitlement becomes the symbol of the conflicts between social rights and social resources. In other words, the converse direction between the upward rights and the downward resources is always in conflict, so it must ultimately compromise at a certain level. Such a compromise, when it is relatively stable, is called "the welfare boundary." For instance, the Chinese New Rural Cooperative Medical Scheme is in the county level, so the county can be regarded as the welfare boundary. But in some provinces, the same insurance is organized by the city government, so the city can be regarded as the welfare boundary. Thus, we define the welfare boundary as the multilayered boundaries of the welfare system based on the upward universalism of the social rights and the downward distribution of the social resources.

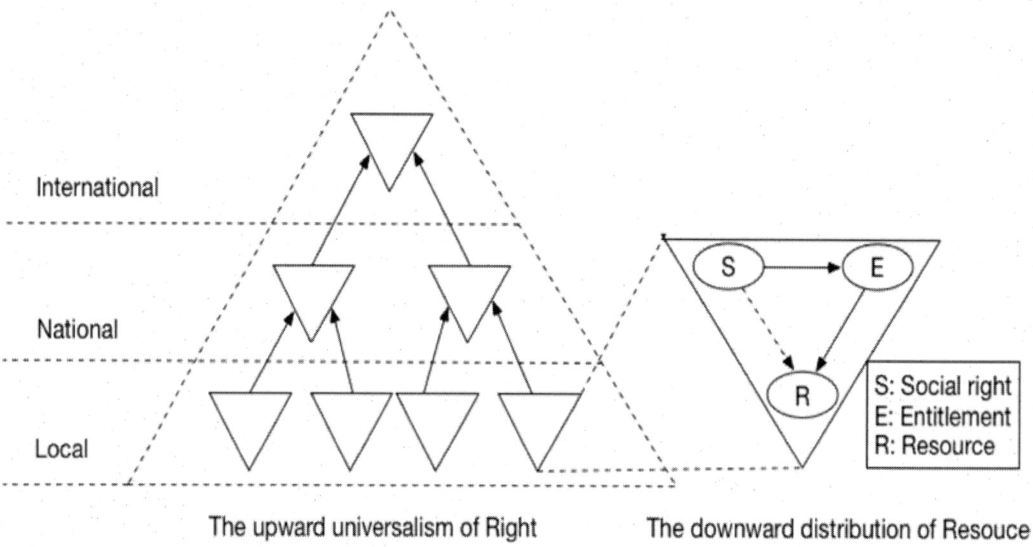

Figure 1. The Dynamics of the Welfare Boundary.

The welfare boundary hinders the Hukou reform. China's *Hukou* system is a vivid example of the welfare boundary. China has a five-level administrative hierarchy, which includes the central, the provincial, the municipal, the county, and the town level (Chan, 2010). Plenty of welfare provisions in China are financed and organized by the local governments. For example, the compulsory education is mainly funded by the county government, and the medical insurance is organized at the county or the city level. The migrant workers, though owing the national citizenship, may not be able to access to the city medical insurance if they do not have the local membership. And the migrant children may also not be able to enjoy the urban education because of their ineligible entitlement. Therefore, the conflicts between the universal social rights and localized social resources lead to various levels of the welfare boundaries. And these welfare boundaries in China are all institutionally represented by the *Hukou* status.

On the other hand, the welfare boundary is dynamic in the process of the *Hukou* reform. The original framework with ten categories (see Table 1) is more rigid than the recent policy with five divisions (see Table 3). And migrant workers have also been permitted to settle down in the small cities where population is less than 500,000. However, the strict control in the large cities and mega-cities shows that as long as the spatial inequality of the welfare provisions exists, *Hukou* will still exist. And it also explains why the *Hukou* system cannot be abolished easily.

DISCUSSION AND CONCLUSION

The controversial relationship between the migrant workers' rights and the migration regulations is one of the most important topics in the migration research. In order to reveal the hidden mechanism, we utilize the *Hukou* system in China as an analytical case. Based on the evolution of the *Hukou* system, we find that the spatial inequality is of great importance to understand the nature of *Hukou*. Unlike other researchers' focus on the *Hukou* itself, we argue that it is the inherent nature of the welfare rights that determines the dual functions of population management and welfare distribution of the *Hukou* system, not vice versa.

After a critical analysis of the social rights theory, we find that the classic narrative neglects the significant issue of the spatial inequality. Because of the spatial inequality, the rights and the resources will automatically conflict with each other and ultimately compromise at a certain level of the welfare boundary. Specifically, the welfare boundary refers to a multilayered boundary of the welfare system based on the upward universalism of the social rights and the downward distribution of social resources. Therefore, the *Hukou* system is a representative illustration of the welfare boundary, and it is certainly hard to be abolished.

The *Hukou* system in China is a good case of the welfare boundary at the local level; however, it is not the unique form. As long as there is the spatial inequality of the social welfare, there will be the welfare boundary. The *Propiska* system, established by the Soviet Union, is also a registration system of internal migration, and it still has influences in Russia and Kyrgyzstan (Buckley, 1995; Hatcher and Thieme, 2015; Kessler, 2001). The apartheid pass system in South Africa was also designed to constrain the free migration of Africans in the past centuries and its function to distinguish insiders and outsiders was thus similar to the *Hukou* system. (Alexander and Chan, 2004).

Moreover, many studies on the global citizenship, albeit not talking about the welfare boundary explicitly, were also one of the welfare boundary forms at the international level. For instance, people in the European Union have the European citizenship, but the immigrants from a third country could be totally excluded (Dean, 2013). Even the traditional immigration countries like Canada and the United States also have serious barriers that block the immigrants' welfare rights (Bohon, Macpherson, and Atiles, 2005; Koning and Banting, 2014).

Our study has significant implications for the migration policies. It demonstrates that the welfare boundary is dynamic and thus can be alleviated. Taking the *Hukou* system as an example, we could first decide the appropriate level of the welfare boundary, e.g., the county, the city, the province or the nation. Then we can either freeze the entitlement of the rights, or upgrade the resources to the right level in order to achieve the balance. The conflicts cannot be avoided, but the negotiation can end with a consensus.

Although we try to discover the underlying mechanism of the rights and the regulations, our theoretical analysis of the welfare boundary is only a preliminary trial. We also realize that our work still needs more support from empirical evidence. For example, although we argue that the welfare boundary has various forms in different nation states, the comparative characteristics need more examination. Moreover, in order to understand the dynamics of the welfare boundary, we need more data to test the interaction between the rights and the resources. And in terms of the policy implication, although we cannot provide specific suggestions right now, more research on the welfare boundary may help illuminate the solutions. We hope our study will spur more future research on the welfare boundary, and ultimately improve migrant workers' wellbeing.

REFERENCES

Alexander, P. and Chan, A. (2004). Does China have an apartheid pass system? *Journal of Ethnic and Migration Studies*, *30*(4), 609–629.

Benhabib, S. (2005). Borders, boundaries, and citizenship. *Political Science and Politics*, *38*(4), 673–677.

Bohon, S. A., Macpherson, H. and Atiles, J. H. (2005). Educational barriers for new Latinos in Georgia. *Journal of Latinos and Education*, *4*(1), 43–58.

Brubaker, R. (1992). *Citizenship and Nationhood in France and Germany*. Cambridge, MA, USA: Harvard University Press.

Buckley, C. J. (1995). The myth of managed migration: Migration control and market in the Soviet Period. *Slavic Review*, *54*(4), 896–916.

Castles, S., Haas, H. D. and Miller, M. J. (2014). *The age of migration: International population movements in the modern world* (5th.). New York: Guilford Press.

Chan, K. W. (2010). Fundamentals of China's urbanization and policy. *China Review*, 10 (1), 63-93.

Chan, K. W. and Buckingham, W. (2008). Is China Abolishing the Hukou System? *The China Quarterly*, *195*, 582–606.

Chan, K. W. and Zhang, L. (1999). The *hukou* system and rural-urban migration in China: processes and changes. *The China Quarterly*, *160*, 818–855.

Cheng, T. and Selden, M. (1994). The origins and social consequences of China's hukou System. *The China Quarterly*, *139*, 644.

Dean, H. (2013). The translation of needs into rights: Reconceptualising social citizenship as a global phenomenon. *International Journal of Social Welfare*, *22*, S32–S49.

Dwyer, P. (2010). *Understanding social citizenship (2nd ed.)*. Bristol: The Policy Press.

Ellis, M. (2012). Reinventing US internal migration studies in the age of international migration. *Population, space and place*, 18, 196-208

Feng, W., Zuo, X. and Ruan, D. (2002). Rural migrants in Shanghai: Living under the shadow of socialism. *International Migration Review*, *36*(2), 520–545.

Ferrera, M. (2005). *The boundaries of welfare: European integration and the new spatial politics of social protection*. OUP Catalogue.

Hatcher, C. and Thieme, S. (2015). Institutional transition: Internal migration, the propiska, and post-socialist urban change in Bishkek, Kyrgyzstan. *Urban Studies*, May, 1–17.

Kessler, G. (2001). The passport system and state control over population flows in the Soviet Union, 1932-1940. *Cahiers Du Monde Russe*, *42*(2-4), 477–503.

King, R. and Conti, F. (2013). Bridging the divide: The gap between the study of internal and international migration with an italian example. *Mah Se*, 13(1), 1-51.

King, R., Skeldon, R. and Vullnetari, J. (2008). *Internal and international migration: bridging the theoretical divide.* Sussex Centre for Migration Research Working Paper.

Koning, E. A. and Banting, K. G. (2014). Inequality below the surface: Reviewing immigrants' access to and utilization of five Canadian welfare programs. *Canadian Public Policy*, *39*(4), 581–601.

Lewis, W. A. (1954). Economic development with unlimited supplies of labour. *Manchester School*, 22(2), 139–191.

Lister, R. and Dywer, P. (2012). Citizenship and Access to Welfare. In P. Alcock, M. May, and S. Wright (Eds.). *The student's companion to social policy* (4th ed.) (pp. 255–261). Chichester, West Sussex; Hoboken, NJ: Wiley-Blackwell.

Lu Y. (2008). Hukou hai qi zuoyong ma - Huji zhidu yu shehui fenceng he liudong. [Does hukou still matter? The household registration system and its impact on social stratification and mobility in China]. *Sociological Studies*, 1, 149-162.

Marshall, T. H. and Bottomore, T. (1992). *Citizenship and social class*. London: Pluto Press.

Marshall, T. H. (2014). Citizenship and social class. In C. Pierson, F. G. Castles and I. K. Naumann (Eds.). *The welfare state: Reader (3rd ed.)* (pp. 28-37). Cambridge: Polity Press.

Ministry of Public Security. (1964). *Gonganbu guanyu chuli hukou qianyi de guiding (caoan).* [1964 Ministry of Public Security Regulation on Hukou migration (Draft)]. Retrieved from http://wuxizazhi.cnki.net/Search/SXBA196412002.html.

Ministry of Public Security. (1985). *Gonganbu guanyu chengzhen zanzhu renkou guanli de zanxing guiding.* [1985 Ministry of Public Security Interim Regulation on the Management of Urban Temporary Population]. Retrieved from http://www.rmlt.com.cn/2014/0731/300535.shtml

National Bureau of Statistics. (2014). *2013 nian quanguo nongmingong jiance diaocha baogao.* [Report on the 2013 national migrant workers monitoring survey]. Retrieved from http://www.stats.gov.cn/tjsj/zxfb/201405/t20140512_551585.html.

Peng, X., Zhao, D. and Guo, X. (2009). Huji zhidu gaige de zhengzhi jingjixue sikao. [The reform of China's household registration system: A political economics View]. *Fudan Journal (Social Science),* 3, 1-11.

The State Council. (1984). *Guowuyuan guanyu nongmin jinru jizhen luohu wenti de tongzhi.* [The announcement of the State Council on the entry of farmers into the towns and the *Hukou* conversion]. Retrieved from http://www.rmlt.com.cn/2014/0731/300534.shtml.

The State Council. (2014). *Guowuyuan guanyu jinyibu tuijin huji zhidu gaige de yijian.* [The State Council Opinions on Further Promotion of the Reform of Household Registration System]. Retrieved from http://www.gov.cn/zhengce/content/2014-07/30/content_8944.htm.

The United Nations. (2013). *International migration report 2013.* New York. Retrieved from http://www.un.org/en/development/desa/population/publications/migration/migration-report-2013.shtml.

UNHABITAT. (2010). *State of the world's cities 2010/2011.* London Sterling VA: Earthscan. Retrieved from http://mirror.unhabitat.org/pmss/listItemDetails.aspx?publicationID=2917&AspxAutoDetectCookieSupport=1.

Wu, K. and Zhang, L. (2010). Fazhan zhuyi zhengfu yu chengshi luohu menkan: Guanyu huji zhidu gaige de fansi. [Developmentalist government and urban Hukou threshold: Rethinking Hukou system reform]. *Sociological Studies*, 6, 58-85.

Wu, X. (2009). Household registration, social exclusion, and rural migrants in cities. In G. Wu and H. Lansdowne (Eds.), *Socialist China, Capitalist China: Social Tension and Political Transition Under Economic Globalisation* (pp. 29-54). New York: Routledge.

Wu, X. and Treiman, D. J. (2004). The household registration system and social stratification in China: 1955-1996. *Demography*, *41*(2), 363–384.

Part III: Workers on the Move and Social Identity

In: Migrant Workers
Editors: Qingwen Xu and Lucy P. Jordan
ISBN: 978-1-63485-272-2

Chapter 9

'Keeping Your Seat Warm': The Role of Seafarers' Wives in the Maintenance of Social Status and Societal Place

Helen Sampson * ***and Iris Acejo***
Seafarers International Research Centre,
School of Social Sciences, Cardiff University, UK

Abstract

This chapter considers the role of seafarers' wives in protecting the social identity of migrant seafarers within their home communities via the use of both 'kin work' and 'status work.' As a significant group of migrant workers who regularly return to the Philippines (usually annually) seafarers rely on their family members to maintain social relationships and social status in their absence. Communications between vessels and the shore are limited and whilst seafarers are at sea their wives, in particular, stand in for them in a variety of social roles. These range from making loans and charitable donations, to maintaining links with godchildren and extended family members. The chapter considers this under-explored aspect of migrant social identity drawing upon ethnographic fieldwork conducted in a town in the Philippines and on board a cargo vessel.

Introduction

Familial roles have long since been recognized as linked to occupational ones and as a result we have witnessed a complex interplay between gender norms, occupational obligations, and familial demands across different regions and cultures. As both societies and

* Corresponding Author: Seafarers International Research Centre, 52 Park Place, Cardiff University CF10 3AT, UK. Email: SampsonH@cardiff.ac.uk.

types of work change, so too are gender and familial roles affected and adjusted. The contemporary period has witnessed rapid transformations in employment patterns in relation to both gender and to the employment of migrant contract labour. Women now constitute a very significant proportion of the labor force and many migrants are engaged in relatively short-term periods of work abroad. In the period 2003-4, for example, some 496,037 foreigners were granted temporary residence with the right to work in Australia (Hugo, 2008). This latter phenomenon can be seen to frequently link to the progression of globalization and associated processes (Sampson, 2013).

While there is some evidence that in the traditional 'old industrial areas' of OECD nations gender roles are slow to adapt to new employment situations (as when male breadwinners are replaced by female ones within the household, see Morris, 1985; Harris, Lee and Morris, 1985), there has been less exploration of gender role adaptation in migrant communities when family members leave their communities for extended periods. Such work, as there has been in this area, has often related to the ways in which those who remain 'at home' may take on non-traditional roles within the family combining both male and female roles within traditional divisions of labor (e.g., Boehm, 2008; Trinidad Galván, 2015). In relation to seafarers such work has emphasized the ways in which seafarers' wives may become more independent and more competent in relation to tasks such as household maintenance, child discipline, and financial management, all of which have been identified as beyond the gender norms of the cultures concerned (McKay, 2015; Sampson, 2005; Thomas, Sampson and Zhao, 2003). However, in Sta Ana (a pseudonym for the community in the Philippines referred to in this chapter) we have found that not only do the wives of seafarers adopt such non-traditional roles when their partners are absent but they may also engage in activities which can be regarded as 'hyper extensions' of traditional gender roles in relation to the management of family and community relationships, which have been conceptualized as kin work (Rosenthal, 1985).

Kin work has frequently been found to be the domain of women in the community who play an important role in maintaining links between members of the extended family. Alicea (1997) describes how among Puerto Rican migrants to the United States such work can even extend beyond national boundaries in the establishment and maintenance of transnational family connections. Kin work may involve offering practical help, emotional support, financial support, or physical care. In a study of wives and widows comprising a diverse sample of women from Springfield Massachusetts (12% black, 88% white), Gallagher and Gerstel (1993) found that widows provided more time and practical help to both kin and friends than wives who focused more on material assistance as a result of their better financial position. In the Philippines, seafarers' wives may work and may have family responsibilities but it is conceivable that with an absent partner they may also have more available time to socialize with others and render support to those in need, of such, in the wider community beyond the immediate family (Waite and Harrison, 1992). This would resonate with the experiences of the wives of some Indian seafarers as described by Sampson (2013).

Seafarers and their wives constitute an appropriate area for the exploration of issues relating to migration and gender roles as the shipping industry has been significantly transformed by processes of globalization and it has come to exhibit what can perhaps be described as the most globalized labor market of any sector. Within this labor market there are a number of countries which are significant providers of seafarers to the global fleet, and seafarers from the Philippines constitute the largest segment of the labor force (Philippine

Overseas Employment Agency, 2013; Ellis and Sampson, 2008). As such Filipino seafarers spend an average of 8.5 months on board cargo vessels every year and an average of 88 days' vacation at home in the Philippines (Ellis, Sampson, Acejo, Tang, et al., 2012). Such long periods of absence, interspersed with relatively short periods of time at home, raise important questions relating to the maintenance of relationships between seafarers and community members in their hometowns as well as associated issues of social identity relating to seafarers' place within communities and their related status as community members.

Previous literature has indicated that having embarked upon a working life at sea, seafarers struggle to remain embedded in their home communities (Sampson 2005; Sampson 2013; Thomas, et al., 2003). Furthermore, it has been suggested that this is one of the main reasons that many seafarers give for terminating their maritime career at a relatively young age (Raunek, 2013). However, to date, there has been little written about the ways in which seafarers' families attempt to maintain their social relationships whilst they are out of reach and on board cargo vessels where communications are generally poor. In this chapter we therefore focus upon the ways in which many seafarers' partners (usually wives as there are few women seafarers in this sector) strive to maintain their 'place' in their home communities by undertaking a range of activities on seafarers' behalf and in their stead. These can be seen as broadly congruent with both 'kin work' (Rosenthal, 1985) and what we shall term 'status work,' a concept similar to Taylor and Hartley's (1975) term 'status maintenance' but intending to emphasize that status is being established — worked at — rather than simply being preserved. We are concerned with the ways in which seafarers' wives are associated with maintaining social relationships as well as keeping up appearances. In this way wives attempt to keep their husbands' 'seats warm' in their communities - an English expression which conveys the idea of keeping a comfortable place for somebody during a temporary absence.

The chapter is based upon fieldwork undertaken by one of the authors (Acejo) in a community which we refer to here as Sta. Ana. The town of Sta. Ana is a municipality of Iloilo province situated southwest of the capital city of Iloilo province in the Philippines. The town is ninety-five percent Roman Catholic and is steeped in religious traditions. Most of the town's events and activities reflect the historical influence of Spanish occupation (ending with the Spanish American war of 1898) and include cock fighting, fiestas, and other similar celebrations. The community's long-standing involvement in outward migration impacts on many aspects of Sta. Ana. However it is particularly manifest in relation to community attitudes towards migration and social ties. According to the municipal planning office in 2009, outward migration was associated with 17% of households and of around 2,494 migrants who left the area for work in 2006, 57% were seafarers. These established patterns of migration have influenced the outward-oriented outlook of residents, including their career choices making young people much more open to migration than might otherwise be expected. This is reflected in the international dispersal of migrants, which is quite widespread, testifying to the community's increasing global ties.

The fieldwork, that we discuss in this chapter, was undertaken over a period of three months and involved interviews with a total of 49 seafarers' partners (all of whom were wives as it is relatively rare for women to work as officers or ratings aboard non-passenger cargo ships) and 10 male working-age seafarers who were temporarily 'at home' on vacation. One of the authors lived in one of the communities where seafarers and their partners were based and visited common venues for socialization amongst seafarers including bars, sari-sari stores (stalls selling a variety of household items), cockpits (venues for cockfighting), restaurants, churches and the town's 'activity hall.' Interviews were conducted in Tagalog (the national language of the Philippines) and subsequently translated.

In the course of this research, a number of ways emerged in which seafarers' partners sought to make sure that their husbands were held in high esteem by both members of their families and the wider community. In doing this, partners protected both their husbands' status and also their own. The process can be seen to have involved wives in a certain amount of 'career support work' of the type described by Pavalko and Elder (1993) on behalf of their husbands in an effort to promote them as important and upstanding members of the local community who should be respected and welcomed upon their return. Thus we found examples of wives who were reluctant to talk (even in confidence to an interviewer from abroad) about their husband's involvement in less respectable activities in the town such as cockfighting and drinking. These endeavours resonate strongly with descriptions of the kinds of reputational work traditionally undertaken by middle-class women in affluent societies in support of their professional husbands' careers whether these be in religious service (Finch, 1980; Taylor and Hartley, 1975), the diplomatic service (Callan, 1975; Hochschild, 1969), or as doctors or academics (Fowlkes, 1980). However seafarers, and particularly ratings, do not have such 'professional' occupational status and in the context of their recurrent migration the work that their partners do on their behalf is related more to their community standing than their specific line of work. This chapter focuses on several features of this effort to maintain and protect seafarer-community relations and status namely: links with godchildren and extended family members; financially supporting parents and siblings; support for fiestas; making loans and charitable donations; and conspicuous consumption.

Women Supporting Male Careers and the Understanding of Kin Work

In the 1970s, 80s, and 90s, there were a number of studies that considered the role of wives in supporting the careers of their husbands (Pavalko and Elder, 1993; Finch, 1980; Fowlkes, 1980; Taylor and Hartley, 1975; Callan, 1975; Hochschild, 1969). More recent notable illustrations have focussed, in particular, on the ways in which the wives of high profile figures respond to public pressures to conform to certain behavioural expectations. We have seen, for example, how the wives of college and university presidents negotiate issues of identity and privacy in relation to community expectations with regard to the fulfilment of the traditional role of 'wife' (Trotman Reid, Cole and Kern, 2011) as well as how women married to sports personalities are required to maintain certain standards with regard to personal appearance and charitable acts (Gmelch and San Antonio, 2001). In recent decades, we have also seen an increased emphasis on the household division of labor with regard to 'emotion work' particularly with regard to the relationships between married couples (Minotte, Stevens and Minotte, 2007) which has some relevance here. Furthermore, work considering parenting and gender norms and roles is well-established (Seery and Crowley 2000).

Kin work became a focus for a group of scholars in OECD countries in the 1980s and 1990s who were interested in how women seemed to play a particular role in the community in supporting family members and friends. In operationalizing their research questions relating to kin work among older women in the US, Gallagher and Gerstel (1993) adapted a technique utilized by Fischer (1982) in undertaking network analysis and categorized help associated with kin work in three ways as: 'practical' assistance (such as meal preparation or carrying shopping); 'personal' assistance (such as advice about work opportunities); and 'material' assistance (such as gift-giving or loan making).

In this chapter we conceptualize the support provided to contemporary migrant Filipino seafarers, by their partners, as combining career-support and kin work. Throughout, there is a strong focus upon 'material' help which is of great significance in the context of the Philippines (Lamvik, 2002) and is particularly relevant in the case of seafarers as a result of their relatively affluent position in the community. Seafarers in the Philippines earn dollar salaries that are considerably in excess of the wages paid to local workers in Philippine pesos. For comparison purposes the average basic pay for officer grades paid in line with International Transport Workers' Federation (ITF) scales for open register vessels in 2013 was US$1,259 per month. This excludes paid overtime which is widely available on board, as well as leave pay, and other financial additions. By contrast the average income for a Filipino household according to the Family Income and Expenditure Survey (2012) was $415 per month. However, the discussion here is not limited to material assistance and does not discount the likelihood that some other aspects of support may simply be taken for granted in the accounts of participants.

Maintaining Links with Extended Family and the Community

While seafarers are away at sea they have very limited access to communications (Ellis, et al., 2012). Over time, increased access to email on board may come to transform relationships between those at sea and those on shore. However, for the moment, reliance on Short Message Service (SMS) and telephone calls has been reported by seafarers to limit the breadth of their contacts with people ashore to immediate kin (usually partners). Seafarers feel that it would be regarded as inappropriate for them to telephone friends whilst they are at sea, for example, and many also leave contact with their extended family to their wives. When asked if her husband communicated directly with his own family one woman explained how '*I do that [for him] ...say his brother will call me ...and then I will tell him*' (Adela). Another put it this way '*Whatever is the news with his Mom and siblings I relay the information to him*' (Czarina). This kind of practice is commonplace in Sta. Ana and seafarers' partners thereby play a key role in maintaining and protecting seafarers' social relationships. In some respects this may be seen as placing them in a position of considerable influence as they can manage other people's perceptions of their seafarer husbands whilst simultaneously managing their husbands' perceptions of other people. However, such management can be fraught with tension and seafarers' wives accounts often alluded to, or sometimes directly described, associated anxieties and tensions. At times therefore the adoption of the role of mediator was undertaken with reluctance.

Sometimes seafarers demanded more from their wives than the simple passing, to and fro, of information and news. We heard examples where seafarers put pressure on their wives to intercede with family members on their behalf in ways that they sometimes felt were inappropriate or likely to produce tension and conflict. One seafarer's partner for example suggested that her husband not only wanted her to keep him up to date with the things that were happening in the extended family but he also wanted her to act as an intermediary in relation to 'bones of contention.' She was (understandably) rather reluctant to take on this role but her husband would insist. She explained:

> He is updated (with the family situation) if I tell him. [...] I am very detailed in emailing. [...] He goes through me [to his parents]. If he is angry with something in their house — such as what his siblings are doing — I tell him that I can't reprimand them...he should be the one doing that. But he wants me to do it. (Lucille)

Seafarers relied on their wives to maintain relationships with their family and wider friendship networks but they also made it clear that they expected their wives to stand in their stead (to keep their seats warm) in a broader sense. As one seafarer put it:

> It is very hard for seafarers because they are in and out [of the community]. If there is an association, then the wife should continue [when the seafarer is at sea]. If he is on vacation, then he is the one who should participate. (Romeo)

Occasionally, alongside the efforts that they made with members of the extended family and the broader community, it was clear that seafarers' wives undertook kin work that was closer to home and some described the efforts that they would make to 'oil the wheels' of the relationships between frequently absent fathers and their children. When asked about seafarers' bonds with family members one seafarer's partner was quick to respond that '*I initiate that. I tell him that we should go to 'this place' and bring our daughters. We go malling [to the shopping mall] and then eat etc.*' (Candra). Such accounts resonate with the findings of other research which have indicated that even where fathers are regularly present women may take an active role in attempting to build the relationships between them and their children. This has been identified by Seery and Crowley (2000) as particularly relevant in situations where fathers are regarded as occupied with work for long periods of the day and mothers are full-time 'home makers'. While the parallels here are imperfect, Seery and Crowley (2000) hypothesize that in such households fathers take on the role of 'helper' rather than 'sharer' and this may produce the circumstances in which there is a need for mothers to play a more significant role in building relationships with fathers and children. They explain this hypothesis in connection to earlier work by LaRossa and LaRossa (1981) describing how:

> They noted that the extent to which women and men either embrace and/or disengage from the roles of parent and financial provider is central in shaping the degree to which each becomes involved in baby care. They suggested that women often are encouraged to embrace the parental role, given that society casts them as experts in caretaking, whereas men are socially encouraged to perceive themselves as mothers' helpers, as they disengage from parenting. Thus creating a differentiation between *helping* versus *sharing*. [...] We would hypothesise that among couples with sharing fathers, there would be less demand for mothers' father-child relationship management work ... (Seery and Crowley, 2000, p.118)

It is very easy to see how when seafarers, who have been absent for a long period of time, return home they are encouraged to adopt a 'helper' role and how seafarers' wives are inevitably cast as the 'experts in caretaking.' In these circumstances it is unsurprising that they too may require (and accept) more assistance in relationship building and management than other more present fathers who share more of the daily childrearing and domestic tasks.

Material (Financial) Support for Parents and Siblings

The financial arrangements in different families varied as would be expected. However, it is a requirement in the Philippines for all seafarers to remit 80% of their basic salary to a Philippines bank account; and in principle they can accept the remainder on board as a 'cash advance' or receive it at the end of the contract as a lump sum depending on the company rules. In most cases, seafarers' wives have access to such accounts and are in a position to spend and disburse the money they contain. In some families seafarers' wives also had an independent income as a result of their own employment and in many cases more than the basic remittance of 80% of basic salary was sent home.

Given the access to such funds, it was possible for wives to play an important role in protecting family members from financial hardship whilst at the same time taking steps to protect the relationships among family members. One seafarer's partner explained that in doing this she was protecting her own position in the family and investing in some ways in support that she herself might need to draw upon, at times, during her husband's absence whilst at sea. She suggested that to avoid making such financial assistance available would be undesirable and explained that she encouraged her husband to be quick with his generosity when he returned from a voyage. She described how to do otherwise would be:

> '[...] quite unacceptable. The impact would be on me. I control that, so I tell him 'go give it to them. It has been two weeks and you haven't given them some.' He says 'they should wait' but I insist that he gives them. [I tell him] 'They really expect something from you!' (Czarina).

Another seafarer's wife made it clear that to maintain social relationships it was imperative that she and her husband were seen to be generous. She felt that to maintain a social life, involving visitors coming to their home, that she and her husband had to spend money on gifts and on hospitality as well as helping out those who were in need with loans. She explained that:

> You know, last December he came back but he had just been on board for 3 months. He spent 500 USD for presents. [...] Here in our house, many people visited him. But he was happy with that because it suggests you have a good heart. People will not come to you if they know you will not help them. My relatives also come here.[...] Those who come sometimes ask for help others just visit us. (Ethel)

Wives would often mediate in family financial relationships when they felt called upon to do so. One woman who described her husband as rather irascible and hot-tempered described how his mother had come to learn that her best course of action, when in need, was to approach her son's wife. She explained that '*when his mother wants to ask him for something then she talks to me first. His mom also has problems...she cannot get through to her son*' (Grace).

Another example illustrated the extent to which wives sometimes seemed to have a more generous approach to their husband's families than they did themselves. One seafarer's wife said:

> Sometimes his siblings need money [...] but my husband tells me that we won't give money all the time [...] because we won't be able to save any money. Although, when it comes to his siblings you cannot help but lend money. (Elena)

Similarly she described how she insisted that her partner make direct regular payments to his mother after his reluctance to do so had led to some disagreements within the family. She explained that:

> I told him to give the money directly to his mother. I don't want the money to touch my hand before his mom's. I told him that his mother has more right to him because if not for his mom, he would not have been able to go to school...and he would not be where he is now. So he also needs to give money to his parents...in this way, there will be no trouble. (Elena)

In insisting upon her mother in law's 'right' to her husband's money, Elena (as the previous quote shows) was influenced by the local cultural norms which can be summed up in the term 'utang na loob' which roughly translates as 'debt of gratitude.' Seafarers, as well as their partners, were conscious of the need to 'repay' such debts of gratitude as were regarded as 'owing' to the members of seafarers' extended families who had made sacrifices in the past in order to allow them to study to become mariners.

Notwithstanding such prevalent cultural norms, in some cases there was disagreement between seafarers and their partners about the level of financial support that should be offered to family members. One woman suggested that this difference of view could be at the level of several thousand pesos when she described how:

> With my mom in law I give 5,000 php [Philippine pesos] a month. It depends on what she wants to buy with that. I give her medicines every first week of the month. I even buy her milk...groceries...Actually my husband just wants to give 2,000 but I told him that it seems like his mom is complaining. (Rana)

Although seafarers could be understanding about the need for partners to make decisions about who to lend, or give, money to in the extended family and what level of support to offer, there were occasions when decisions made 'on the ground' could anger seafarers who were away at sea. In one case, a woman reported that because of her sense of shame she loaned money to her husband's cousin which caused an argument between her and her husband. She told of how:

> There was a time his cousin borrowed money. I felt embarrassed in front of his Uncle so we lent the money to his cousin. Then my husband got mad because I lent the money out. Later on, this [argument between us] was patched up. (May)

Seafarers' partners felt that it was so essential to maintain harmonious family relationships in this way that some revealed that, if necessary, they would make such payments surreptitiously. Where they earned money themselves they might make payments directly from their accounts or in other circumstances they would find alternative ways of concealing such support or only revealing it once it had been given and was a 'done deal.' One who paid money to her husband's family from her salary recounted that:

> Family concerns, I deduct that from my money. His money I save that. Even the allowance for his mom, I take from my own earnings. (Grace)

Whilst another waited to tell her husband about financial support to relatives until after it had been paid, particularly in view of the fact that loans to his family often didn't get repaid in a timely fashion. She described how:

> When it comes to his siblings, I give money when I have money. Sometimes when we run short of money, we can't force them to pay it asap [as soon as possible]. Since they are siblings then you are ashamed to ask for the money. Sometimes I just inform my husband after I have lent the money. (Elena)

Despite such evidence of generosity and feelings of obligation it became apparent in the course of several interviews that the disparity between the earnings of seafarers and those of their wider kin could also lead seafarers and their partners to suspect family members of taking advantage of them and of not always being truthful about how money that was given to them was spent. This could cause friction in the family and to avoid such issues emerging seafarers partners reported being 'careful' about monitoring the expenditure of funds even when such scrutiny might be considered risky in relation to the maintenance of harmonious personal relationships. One explained:

> Before when they had a party, when I cannot give money, I ask my mother-in-law what is on the menu and then I buy the ingredients. If you give the money, you don't know if it is more or less. When it comes to my husband's siblings, I am strict when it comes to money…because I don't want the money to end in bad hands. So when they say, they will pay for the tuition fee, I will ask how much…and then ask for the receipt...I really check it. (Salve)

At the heart of almost all of these financial exchanges was a manifest tension between a need to be seen to be generous in the community (and often a genuine desire to be charitable) and limitations on resources. It seemed the expectations of the community could massively outweigh the resources of the seafarers and their families who felt under constant pressure not to be regarded as mean or lacking in community spirit. One seafarer's wife describe this tension as follows:

> Most people think that when you are a seaman then you have so much money so they ask for it. Also they expect you to give huge amount of money. But for me, it depends. […] I just participate with what I can give. I give in because that is my way of thanksgiving for the blessings. So it is hard if you are tight-fisted… (Ima)

A captain reinforced the extent to which seafarers were constantly attempting to balance the need to be generous, the need to protect their own self-interests, and the need to be pragmatic. In this they often understood that in order for their relatives to finally become less dependent upon them, and their dollar salaries, they (the seafarers) often needed to support them in medium term educational and business endeavours. The Captain explained it like this:

> Sometimes, you want to be practical. Sometimes you get irritated. You have goals in your life…you wish that you have this (money) for yourself. If you won't support your relatives, they will be like that (i.e., dependant) forever. So if you can support them and they can stand on their own then they won't depend on you anymore. For example, she (his wife) has a sister who is sending her kid to school. Now if you don't help them then they will be forever dependent on you. So if you help them, then they will be freed from that. (Joseph)

Decisions about offering material support to relatives were therefore complex and were associated with a sense of obligation, a need to maintain good social relations and sometimes an ambition to see members of the extended family achieving independence in order to free seafarers and their families from long-term continuous financial commitments.

Status Work

In some respects the wives of Filipino seafarers can be seen as occupying the same high visibility roles in their communities as the wives of politicians or celebrities in other cultures. Although there is less research than one might hope for in relation to the adoption of such supportive public roles there has been some interesting work published on groups as diverse as the wives of politicians in Israel and baseball players in the US. This work indicates that the wives of men with high status roles in the community may feel obliged to be particularly careful about their public persona (Simon, Zach, Oglesby and Bar-Eli, 2011) and their personal appearance (Gmelch and Antonio, 2001; Simon, et al., 2011). In relation to such concerns they may attempt to safeguard both their own reputations and relationships as well as those of their husbands. Seafarers' are not a part of a political or a celebrity class yet their economic achievements produce similar expectations with regard to some issues and these extend to their families and particularly their wives. In discussing visibility and status in their communities three main areas emerged where seafarers' wives reported a particular need to conform with social expectations that were felt to be specific to them: supporting fiestas; making loans and charitable donations; and conspicuous consumption.

Supporting Fiestas and Other Festivities

Fiestas play a very important part in the local culture and every village has at least one fiesta per year which is related to their saint's day with others occurring in conjunction with religious festivals such as Easter and Christmas. In addition there may be pageants and parades and a variety of community activities that require funds. These are occasions when the important and high-status members of the community are expected to contribute to the financing of events. This can be either by way of hosting large 'parties' with huge amounts of food and sometimes with waiters in attendance to serve the attendant delicacies, and/or sponsoring prizes and religious paraphernalia. One seafarer's partner described how extensive such affairs could be when she said '*with fiestas, we also prepare that. My siblings' visitors also come here. I pay for all that. So their co-teachers [their colleagues] will [all] come here*.' Another described in some detail the kinds of things that seafarers' wives were asked to contribute on such occasions:

> They ask for contributions. This is for mass, the menu, wine (for offering). During the municipal fiesta, they ask for sponsorship for trophies. I give them cash to buy trophies. Then those having a fiesta, will solicit money for the wall of the Church of the Miraculous Medal. [In December] All the carollers come here. Sometimes, I experience a shortage of cash because it becomes an extra expense for me. (May)

A seafarer made the links between social status, contributions to fiestas/local events, and conspicuous consumption, transparent when he explained how things worked in the community and how there was a certain pressure to 'keep up with the Joneses' which is an English expression (also known in the Philippines) which means match, or exceed, the conspicuous consumption of your social peers. He said:

> Here is how it works here in the pageants. It means there will be selling of tickets. 'Oh her father is a Captain,' this means that her father has to prove [demonstrate via largesse] that he is a Captain on the ship. The money they [Captains] can give can reach a million. You have to prove you are a Captain of the ship so that your daughter will be carried on that float. There are also solicitation letters where the norm is to outdo each other in donating big amount of money. You will also notice that their house has cars outside which they don't use that much. They are just there [for show]. (Arnel)

The evidence from the study of this community suggested that once again there was often a tension between more generously inclined seafarers' partners who were present in the community and working hard at kinship building and absent seafarers whose hard work was all directed towards earning dollars and whose main concern was the welfare of their immediate family. As one seafarer's wife explained:

> My husband will tell me not to spend much but when your child's classmates pay you a visit, your conscience gets pricked…so you spend. You prepare food. (Salve)

She continued highlighting the role of status and shame when she suggested that:

> When it comes to that gathering, it is embarrassing if you do not contribute. So even if my husband doesn't tell me to contribute then I do it on my own. (Salve)

While another seafarer's partner commented on the importance of not getting a bad name or being talked about critically in the community when she explained:

> We do... [throw big parties] because we have many relatives visiting us during fiesta. That will be his relatives…Even if there is gap [i.e., a social distance] and they are not close to us, we still invite them so they won't be able to say anything [negative]. (Judy)

The community expectations weighed heavily with seafarers' wives and some described how their contribution to fiestas and events never seemed to be regarded as sufficient and how there always seemed to be demands for more financial support from them as the households which were deemed to be affluent in the locality. One seafarer's partner described how:

> We have even [requests for funds] from the barrios…their centennial. You will also notice that if you give, they will [ask you to] give again next year. Sometimes it doubles… Not only religious, so there is the sports league and beauty pageant. We even receive solicitations even from barangay Manila, my husband's place of origin. (Grace)

However the expectation of parties and celebrations could also be closer to home and sometimes related to family events where seafarer households were expected to play a lead role in inviting family members to large celebrations. In practice this inevitably meant that it was seafarers' wives who organized such events and issued invitations because of the long absences of their migrant husbands. As such they also bore responsibility for getting things 'right' with respect to whom to invite and whom to omit in ways which resonated with the account given so many years earlier by Hochschild (1969) of the symbolic importance of decisions made by American Ambassadors' wives in relation to social occasions and activities. The following account is illustrative:

> If there are birthdays, you invite relatives and then neighbours. It is shameful not to invite the neighbours […] The same with relatives, if you don't invite them they will feel bad, so you have to invite them. […] The elders, you have to invite. If you don't they will really feel bad about it. You will also hear, a week afterwards, that this elder is mad at you because you did not invite him/her. […] (Ima)

Social occasions were therefore understood by seafarers' wives and community members to play a role in signifying and strengthening the bonds between individual family members as well as different family groups. To exclude individuals from such gatherings would be interpreted as a social slight and inclusion signified, by contrast, feelings of connection and affection between kin. Seafarers' wives paid close attention to such matters in planning social events and encouraged seafarers to be supportive of these attempts at kin work because they recognized the importance of maintaining the social glue that kept the family, including the often absent seafarers, embedded into the community.

Making Loans

Within their communities (and as has already been discussed) seafarers' partners generally made a regular allowance or a series of gifts to relatives and close kin who were in need. However, from time to time, they were also called upon to lend money to neighbours in the community and more distant relatives who lived on other islands. Such actions carried with them the risk that loans might not be repaid. Sometimes such acts were not revealed to seafarers and particularly when they were repaid over a relatively short duration as in the following case when a seafarer's wife described how:

> Yes they [neighbours] do [borrow money from me]. I also lend out money. They will borrow today and then return it the next day….I decide on my own. That is fine with him [seafarer husband]. He doesn't need to know. (Nina)

She added that in some cases she felt as though she were being 'tested' by friends and relatives and described how on one occasion:

> Before his aunt in Mindanao called long distance to borrow money. Maybe just to test me what kind of attitude that I have and whether I can be depended on in times of emergency. She borrowed 45,000 php. Maybe she was thinking that I will have to inform my husband first. But I just said, "Okay, when do you need? I can send it now." (Nina)

It was not always the case that seafarers' families felt that they were in a financial position to make such loans but they understood that the community perceived anyone whose husband earned a dollar salary to be very wealthy and they felt under quite strong social pressure to provide financial assistance to those who approached them. One seafarer's wife described how:

> Even if you don't have money. They will not believe that you don't have money. Not all seafarers have the same ranks. Some have small salaries. But because people expects that you are a seaman, so they are all the same. But for me, it differs. [...] Sometimes, I really feel pressured. Because it is different when your husband is just earning ordinary wages this is unlike other seafarers who earns higher wages. [...] If there is a tuition fee they have to pay [for example] I do [loan them money] because sometimes it is my parents asking for help. Sometimes, my co-teachers ask for financial help. (Mariel)

Thus loans were also a complex area which represented important material support but were also seen as more than this, constituting a mark of good 'citizenship.' Where such loans were difficult to make, seafarers' wives felt torn between the need to be seen to 'do the right thing' within thc community and within their families and the need to protect their own immediate financial interests.

Making Expensive Purchases (Status Related) and Keeping Up Appearances

A house in a migrant community may represent 'tangible evidence of [...] success' and may simultaneously symbolise 'owners' on-going connection to the place' (Thomas, 1998, p. 438). In Sta Ana, one of the most significant markers of status within the community was the house occupied by seafarers and their partners. The building of a house was frequently the first priority for many seafarers who were keen to establish their financial credentials with the display of a grandly designed residence with ample space. However the construction of a house takes a considerable amount of time and decisions about design, construction, and finance are frequently required at times when seafarers are remote and impossible to contact. In this case seafarers' partners were generally responsible for decision making and took on much of the responsibility for the construction of houses that not only 'spoke' of the financial status of the family but also served as a 'pronouncement' of the presence of the family in the community. In their accounts of the construction of houses and decisions about expensive purchases, in general, seafarers played a very minor role. One wife described how:

> I built this house on my own. I went to the city to buy the things needed for the house. I did it all. When we made the house plan, he was in the ship and I was here. (Czarina)

Another gave a very similar account and explained that she made all the decisions about house design and construction with the exception of those relating to technicalities such as the electrics. She said:

> Everything here in the house, I decided on that. This house, since he is far (10 months work with only 2 months vacation), I decided on everything about the house….Because he completely trusted me. In fact, in this house, when we constructed the house, I decided on everything. He doesn't want to meddle. I do the design with other technicalities, wiring, lights…then that is his part (Lilia)

And another emphasised her prioritisation of the house as the most important family investment and her husband's secondary role when arriving at decisions about expenditure when she said:

> If I decide on something, we buy it but he is consulted. This house I constructed this…he just sends money. The car, I bought that. But I still think whether he can afford it or not…our kids are from private school. Others who want to build a house will still wait for their husband because they want their husband to spend on it. For me, no. I use his allotment[‡] to build the house. (Ethel)

In a confirmatory account another woman suggested that in relation to all major items of expenditure she held the most sway. She explained that when buying a car:

> …both of us decided on it. But I had the last say…he asks, do you like this? Then I said, this the one I like. The others are suggesting but I tell him, not that. This is the one I like. (May)

Thus we can see that women played a very central role in deciding what major purchases to make and in this process they were very aware of the importance in the community of status. The importance of such conspicuous consumption in marking status was most eloquently expressed by one woman who was married to a Captain. Her husband was originally from a 'poor' family and she felt that as a result he had previously been overlooked by the community. She felt very conscious of the need to display their wealth to alter the way that he was regarded and treated as the following quote demonstrates:

> You have to show that you at least have some accomplishments [financial assets]. If they don't see that you have a house, they will say, "they don't have money." So on my part, I become challenged on how to see to it that in the situation of being a Captain, he have properties like a house etc. How I can do this and the like. So I plan this, I get this. […] My husband was very poor before. So was treated differently. He was not noticed. So I told him, your life before and your life now is different. He dresses ordinarily, you don't see him with big jewellery. But if there is an occasion which you know is attended by people who are doing well in life (naka-angat), then you also have to dress and fix yourself up so you can be on a par with them. He doesn't want that. But for me, I don't want them to say that, "now that you

[‡] This is the commonly used term for the monthly salary (or portion of the salary) that is paid by employers of seafarers directly into a Philippines bank account.

are a captain you are still the same (in appearance and maybe manner of dressing)." I told him we should also [be] level. (Aireen)

Being conscious of surveillance by the community and their associated expectations was a theme that was also highlighted by others who were aware that their own behaviour and appearance reflected upon their husbands and upon the status of the family. As one seafarer's wife explained the life she had was challenging because:

> You have to adhere to their expectations of you. They watch your every move. ...They challenge you. The way one dresses...seaman's wife? Why like that so shabby? Or if you have a new dress, they will say "that's natural!" Or they will say, how many years have you been married and you have no project? They always borrow money from you [...] there is a notion that you have money always. (Michelle)

Thus there was more to keeping up appearances than having a big house or making a lot of donations within the community. Seafarers and their families also had to make expansive gestures of hospitality, they needed to be willing to loan money to others and yet never request such loans for themselves, and they needed to attend to their personal appearance making sure that they looked the 'part' at all times and didn't 'let the family down.'

CONCLUSION

In this chapter we have considered the ways in which seafarers' wives respond to the need to maintain the position of their absent spouses within the community. In doing so we find resonances with past work on the public performance of the role of high status 'wife' (Gmelch and San Antonio, 2011; Hochschild, 1969) as well as that on emotion work (Jones, 2004). In this case seafarers' wives engage on both fronts, in establishing themselves and their absent husbands as respected members of the community as well as making an effort to emotionally (and financially) support family members, godchildren and friends, much in the spirit of the findings of di Leonardo (1987) with regard to the relationship building activities of Italian American women in the nineteen eighties. Notwithstanding the self-evident benefits of such efforts to the community, and the wellbeing of family members, such 'kin work' or 'kinkeeping' (Rosenthal, 1985) is not without its costs to seafarers' wives in terms of time, money, and emotion, particularly when effort is spread across a large number of family members (Gerstel and Gallagher, 1993) as is often the case with regard to the demands on seafarers' wives. It may also be experienced as particularly challenging when women are left to manage such 'work,' in relation to their husbands' connections. Thus seafarers' wives find themselves faced with a range of demands and expectations relating to the absence of their husbands as a direct result of their chosen occupation and migrant status. These demands may not always be anticipated by women when they choose to marry a seafarer. It seems that notwithstanding changes in gender roles in the Philippines (and elsewhere) certain types of work (in this case migrant contract employment) still demand a considerable degree of 'career support,' 'status work,' and 'kinkeeping' by partners, who are most commonly found to be wives.

Acknowledgments

We would like to thank all of the people who agreed to take part in this study. We are also grateful to The Nippon Foundation for the funding they provided to enable Dr. Acejo to undertake the fieldwork upon which this chapter is based.

References

Alicea, M. (1997). "A Chambered Nautilus" The contradictory nature of Puerto Rican women's role in the social Construction of a transnational community. *Gender and Society, 11* (5), 597-626.

Boehm, D. (2008). 'Now I am a man and a woman!': Gendered moves and migrations in a transnational Mexican community. *Latin American Perspectives, 35* (1), 16-30.

Callan, H. (1975). The premiss of dedication: Notes towards and ethnography of diplomats' wives,' in Ardener, S. (ed.), *Perceiving Women* (pp 87-104). London: Dent and Sons Ltd.

di Leonardo, M. (1987). The female world of cards and holidays: Women, families, and the work of kinship. *Signs, 12*, 440-453.

Ellis, N., Sampson, H., Acejo, I., Tang, L., Turgo, N. and Zhao, Z. (2012). *Seafarer accommodation on contemporary cargo ships.* Cardiff: SIRC.

Ellis, N. and Sampson, H. (2008). *The global labour market for seafarers: Working aboard merchant cargo ships 2003.* Cardiff: SIRC.

Fischer, C. (1982). *To dwell among friends: Personal networks in town and city.* Chicago: University of Chicago Press.

Fowlkes, M. (1980). *Behind every successful man: wives of medicine and academe.* New York: Colombia University Press.

Gallagher, S. and Gerstel, N. (1993). Kinkeeping and friend keeping among older women: The effect of marriage. *The Gerontologist, 33* (5), 675-681.

Gerstel, N. and Gallagher, S. (1993). Kinkeeping and distress: Gender, recipients of care, and work-family conflict. *Journal of Marriage and Family, 55* (3), 598-608.

Gmelch, G. and San Antonio, P. (2001). Baseball wives: Gender and the work of baseball. *Journal of Contemporary Ethnography, 30* (3), 335-356.

Family Income and Expenditure Survey (FIES). *2012 National Statistics Office Philippines.* Retrieved from http://nso-ncr.ph/special%20release/fies/2012%20Fies.pdf.

Finch, J. (1980). Devising conventional performances: The Case of clergymen's wives. *Sociological Review, 28* (4), 851-870.

Harris, C., Lee, R. and Morris, L. (1985). Redundancy in steel: labour market behaviour, local social networks and domestic organisation. In Roberts, B., Finnegan, R. and Gallie, D. (eds.), *Economic restructuring: unemployment and the social division of labour* (pp. 154-167). Manchester: Manchester University Press.

Hochschild, A. (1969). The role of the ambassador's wife: An exploratory study. *Journal of Marriage and Family, 31* (1), 73-87.

Hugo, G. (2008). Sydney: The globalisation of an established immigrant gateway. In Price, M. and Benton-Short, L. (eds.), *Migrants to the metropolis: The rise of immigrant gateway cities* (pp.68-96). Syracuse, NY: Syracuse University Press.

Jones, C. (2004). Whose stress? Emotion work in middle-class Javanese homes. *Ethnos, 69* (4), 509-528.

Lamvik, G. (2002). *The Filipino seafarer: A life between sacrifice and shopping*. Retrieved from http://www.diva-portal.org/smash/get/diva2 :122728/FULLTEXT01.pdf.

LaRossa, R. and LaRossa, M. (1981). *Transition to parenthood: How infants change families.* Beverly Hills, CA: Sage.

Mckay, S. (2015). So they remember me when I am gone: Remittances, fatherhood, and gender relations of Filipino migrant men. In Hoang, L. A. and Yeoh, B. (eds.), *Transnational labour migration remittances and the changing family in Asia.* Basingstoke: Palgrave Macmillan.

Minotte, K., Stevens, D., Minotte, M. and Kiger, G. (2007). Emotion-work performance among dual-earner couples: Testing four theoretical perspectives. *Journal of Family Issues, 28* (6), 773-793.

Morris, L. (1985). Renegotiation of the domestic division of labour in the context of male redundancy. In Roberts, B., Finnegan, R. and Gallie, D. (eds.), *Economic restructuring: unemployment and the social division of labour* (pp. 400-416). Manchester: Manchester University Press.

Philippine Overseas Employment Agency (2013). *Compendium of Overseas Filipino Workers Statistics.*

Raunek (March 11, 2013). 12 main reasons seafarers quit sea jobs. *Marine Insight*. Retrieved from http://www.marineinsight.com/marine/life-at-sea/12-main-reasons-seafarers-quit-sea-jobs/.

Rosenthal, C. (1985). Kinkeeping in the familial division of labor. *Journal of Marriage and Family, 47* (4), 965-974.

Sampson, H. (2005). Left high and dry? The lives of women married to seafarers in Goa and Mumbai. *Ethnography, 6* (1), 61-85.

Sampson, H. (2013). *International seafarers and transnationalism in the twenty-first century.* Manchester: Manchester University Press.

Seery, B. and Crowley, M. (2000). Women's emotion work in the family: Relationship management and the process of building father-child relationships. *Journal of Family Issues, 21* (1), 100-127.

Simon, S., Zach, S., Oglesby, C. and Bar-Eli, M. (2011). Role perceptions of senior politicians' wives in Israel. *Journal of Sociology, 48* (2), 187-205.

Taylor, M. G. and Hartley, S. F. (1975). The two-person career. *Sociology of Work and Occupations, 2*, 354-72.

Thomas, P. (1998). Conspicuous construction: Houses, consumption and 'relocalization' in Manambondro, Southeast Madagascar. *Journal of the Royal Anthropological Institute, 4* (3), 425-426.

Thomas, M., Sampson, H. and Zhao, M. (2003). Finding a balance: Companies, seafarers, and family life. *Maritime Policy and Management, 30* (1), 59-76.

Trinidad Galván, R. (2015). *Women who stay behind: Pedagogies of survival in rural transmigrant Mexico.* Tuscan, AZ: The University of Arizona Press.

Trotman Reid, P., Cole, E. and Kern, M. (2011). Wives of college and university presidents: Identity, privacy, and relationships. *Psychology of Women Quarterly, 35* (4), 547-557.

Waite, L. and Harrison, S. (1992). Keeping in touch: How women in mid-life allocate social contacts among kith and kin. *Social Forces, 70* (March), 637-654.

In: Migrant Workers
Editors: Qingwen Xu and Lucy P. Jordan

ISBN: 978-1-63485-272-2

Chapter 10

MIGRANT TRANSNATIONAL LABOR: WORK, IDENTITY, AND SOCIAL WELFARE OF SEAFARERS

David Jaffee*[*] and Suzie S. Weng
Department of Sociology, Anthropology and Social Work,
University of North Florida, US

ABSTRACT

As a result of globalization, the geographic reorganization and separation of commodity production and consumption, a complex chain of intermodal transportation and logistics has developed moving containerized goods to their final destination. The most widely used and significant transportation mode is the maritime container vessel. This chapter examines the migrant transnational labor force — known as "seafarers" — that work and live on these vessels. The chapter explains how seafarers are now part of a global labor market and constituting a migrant transnational labor force whose social identity is formed as a consequence of the nature and location of their work, and the multi-national composition of the seafarer community. The chapter also considers the conditions of work and associated occupational health and safety hazards, including the mental health impacts associated with long periods confined to a vessel, piracy, and separation from family, as well as how they have organized to address these terms and conditions of their labor. The chapter concludes with implications for policy and social service provision for seafarers, and the organizations, institutions, and agencies that have, and that could contribute further, to an improvement in their quality of work and life.

GLOBALIZATION AND THE SEAFARER LABOR MARKET

One of the central features of globalization has been the geographic reconfiguration of economic activities. Employing a 'spatial fix' strategy (Harvey, 1982), global capital has reorganized the production process geographically by relocating various aspects of the

[*] Corresponding Author: David Jaffee, Department of Sociology, Anthropology and Social Work, University of North Florida, 1 UNF Drive, Jacksonville, Florida 32224-2645, USA. E-mail: djaffee@unf.edu.

production process in economically and politically advantageous jurisdictions thus constructing what are variously labeled commodity chains, global production networks, and global value chains (Coe, Dicken and Hess, 2008). Enabling the efficiency of commodity flows are shipping containers, mega container vessels, and global and national intermodal transportation networks with the shipping container vessel representing the most significant mode of transportation getting the finished and semi-finished goods from points of production to consumption. The growing significance of logistics and supply chain management can be linked directly to the larger process of globalization (Coe, 2014). There is increasing and constant pressure to keep transportation costs as low as possible so that they do not nullify the labor cost advantage secured through the outsourcing/offshoring of production. One of the central strategies to achieve this objective is instituting low cost labor recruitment and flexible "just-in-time" labor deployment in transportation and distribution (e.g., Ciscel, Smith, and Mendoza, 2003). This has been facilitated by neo-liberal economic policies promoting deregulation and privatization which have weakened national labor and environmental standards (Bensman, 2008). The population that is the focus of this chapter — migrant seafarers working on merchant/container vessels — have been directly impacted by these globalization processes (Alderton and Winchester, 2002).

The seafarer labor force serving on board merchant/container vessels has evolved as the shipping industry has introduced new technologies and sought to reduce costs to remain competitive for the business of shippers and retailers. As with other forms of globalized production, shipping — already a globalized endeavor — has followed the broader pattern characteristic of global neoliberalism in offshoring and outsourcing (Alderton and Winchester, 2002; Liang, 2011). The purpose of offshoring is to derive cost advantages based on geographic variations in labor costs and regulatory environments. The purpose of outsourcing is to subject formerly in-house activities to market competition and eliminate the costs associated with managing that activity.

While a merchant vessel is, by definition, "off shore" it is still subject to the labor standards and regulations of the nation with which it is registered. At one point in time, merchant crews were recruited from national labor markets, largely European, and there were national and international standards of training and compensation (Lane, 1997). Under the "offshoring" strategy, shipping lines now use "open registries" allowing vessels to fly "flags of convenience" (FOC) that correspond not to the vessels' home nation but rather to countries (e.g., Panama, Liberia, Cyprus, Malta) with few or any labor regulations (Lillie, 2004). This has allowed ship owners to employ the cheapest labor possible from any country with minimal employment protections or benefits (Wu and Sampson, 2005). Additionally, the standardization of vessels, training, work roles, and shift patterns on board has made seafarers easily replaceable as vulnerable workers on temporary contracts who can be hired and fired at any time (Sampson, 2013b).

The outsourcing function is satisfied through third party global labor recruitment agencies (Liang, 2011) known as "crewing" or "manning" agencies which handle the recruitment and screening of workers in less developed countries thus forming a trilateral employment relationship between the seafarer, shipping line, and agency (Amante, 2004). Today the majority of seafarers come from Asia, with almost one in three from the Philippines (McKay, 2007), creating a highly racialized occupational system (Bonacich, Alimahomed, and Wilson, 2009). As the Organization for Economic Cooperation and Development (OECD) has abolished nationality crewing requirements, the shift to migrant labor has been completed. As an indication of this trend, the number of Filipino seafarers on European-owned ships in the 1980s increased from 2,900 to 17,057 (Alderton, 2004). By 2000, 40% of seafarers originated from Asia (BIMCO/ISF, 2010). Today, mixed nationality, or multinational, crews have become the norm (Alderton, 2004). The use of crewing agencies for labor recruitment in nations that have limited options for high-paying jobs has opened up the opportunity for easy exploitation and abuse by fake agents, agencies requiring unwarranted administrative fees, or agencies requiring upfront free labor services as necessary conditions for employment consideration (International Transport Workers Federation [ITF], 2006). Agencies can also blacklist seafarers who demand just treatment and equitable pay.

The globalization of the seafarer labor market, and the replacement of national with "migrant" labor, has occurred as the following factors have become solidified: 1) seafarers are recruited from any nation in the world; 2) shipping lines have established formal relations with manning agents located in national labor markets; 3) there are few if any formal barriers to seafarer employment beyond broad generalized international regulations/certifications; 4) multinational crewing is the norm; 5) employment security is precarious and contingent on the fluctuations in global trade; 6) there is virtually no relationship between the flag of the ship and the nationality of the crew, and 7) there is no globally enforced regulatory labor market infrastructure (Lane, 2000).

According to Sampson (2013b), one of the leading authorities on the labor market and working conditions of seafarers,

> ...the globalisation of the industry, while bringing opportunities to would-be seafarers in developing countries, has brought an overall deteriorization in the working and living conditions at sea. Seafarers are regarded somewhat, as 'commodities' rather than 'people.' There is often little concern for their welfare, little commitment to their long-term futures, and a very market-oriented approach to their recruitment, retention, and training...They are a highly exploited workforce with limited muscle in terms of industrial relations with their employers (p. 45).

This pattern is consistent with larger global trends that report the rise of "precarious work" (Kalleberg, 2011) and "fissured workplaces" (Weil, 2014) in almost all economic sectors generally, and in the logistics sector in particular (Jaffee and Bensman, 2015) where, as noted, downward pressures on costs are especially intense. In the case of the seafarer, they are hired on fixed term contracts of six to twelve months rather than as permanent fulltime employees (precarious), and the recruitment and employment contract is handled by a third party rather than the shipping lines thus establishing an arm's length relationship (fissured) (Sampson, 2013b).

While making up a very small percentage of the global migrant labor force (estimated at 1%), seafarers represent an interesting case due to their in-transit work site and the fact that the shipping industry was one of the first to establish a truly global labor market for the purpose of reducing labor costs (BIMCO/ISF, 2010). In 2010 it was estimated that the total size of the seafarer population was 1,371,000 with 47% coming from Asian nations (BIMCO/ISF, 2010) with about half of this total working on cargo ships, with container vessels accounting for 8.4% in 2000 (Alderton, 2004).

SEAFARER IDENTITY AND WORK LIFE

The seafarer as a member of the global labor force fits the description of the transnational migrant to the extent that while they are working as migrant labor they retain close ties, connections, and socio-economic relations with their nation and community of origin (Kearney, 1995). However, the definition and applicability of "transnational" to various populations is a source of considerable debate within the literature. In considering seafarers as transnational migrants, there are two populations of interest. The first are those who have left their home country and settled in other nations with maritime employment opportunities. The second are those who are on relatively short-term contracts and the time away from their home country is spent on a merchant vessel. The primary focus of this paper is on the latter, which makes up the growing proportion of this labor force. For this segment, the "receiving" location or destination is not a nation-state but rather a vessel. Sampson (2003) describes this as a "hyperspace":

> …without nationality and they move between, and operate beyond, national borders. They are truly 'hyperspaces' and the seafarers who occupy them form distinct, if miniature, 'global communities.' Such communities and hyperspaces are substantially different from transnational or diasporic spaces, networks and relationships (p. 276).

Thus the seafarers represent a unique category of transnational migrants by virtue of their workplace location (Borovnik, 2004). Further, because the hyperspace constitutes the vessel-as-workplace, the seafarers face the situation of never being able to leave the place of work, which takes on the character of a "total institution" (Acejo, 2012). There is no opportunity to spend time at the end of the workday with non-work family, friends, or in a transnational community defined by their nationality and culture, nor any basis for social integration or assimilation into a new national culture or society given the "deterritorialized" space aboard the vessel as well as the temporary contractual relationship. This basic fact of life shapes significantly both seafarer identity and work life.

Studies conducted on board the merchant vessels provide a better picture of the "structured space" that defines the conditions of work and seafarer identity (e.g., Acejo, 2012; Sampson, 2013b). Sampson (2013b) consistently emphasizes the fact that the space occupied by the seafarers on-board the vessel, which would constitute the other "nationality" to which they might be exposed, is structured and most of the experience is shaped by an occupational/contractual hierarchy. Most broadly, the on-board vertical division of labor is between officers and the "ratings." Among the officers, in addition to the captain are senior, junior, and petty officers. Within the ratings are able-bodied and ordinary seamen, along with motorman, cooks, and "messman" (Sampson, 2013b). Filipinos are most heavily concentrated among the ratings. The captain is referred to as the "master" to further reinforce the status hierarchy. Much of the work climate on board the vessel is determined by the personal management and interaction style of the captain (Kahveci, Lane and Sampson, 2002). The structural hierarchy is also emphasized in the assignment of on-board physical spaces with officers occupying the higher decks with more spacious and comfortable accommodations and ratings on the lower levels (Sampson, 2013b); often, messrooms and galleys are also divided according to hierarchy.

Forms of discrimination based on nationality, which are reinforced by the hierarchical division of labor, could potentially increase the salience of national identity. A 1996 poll conducted for the International Transport Workers' Federation (ITF) found that 25% of respondents experienced unfair treatment due to their race or nationality (Alderton, 2004). The multinational composition of the crew would seem to be a mediating factor. Where ships have fewer nationalities there can be a more colonial style division when officers come from one nation while ratings come from another. Discriminatory practices are likely to be more frequent under these conditions. Where the crew is mixed nationality, both between and within occupational categories, forms of discrimination, and the significance of national identity, are less common and occupational cultures prevail as most salient (Alderton, 2004; Kahveci, Lane and Sampson, 2002). On the other hand, discrimination is built into the global labor market apparatus to the extent that compensation levels for equal work are based on the nationality of the seafarer and/or the manning agencies that operate within their country (ITF, 2006).

Given that Filipinos represent the largest proportion of merchant seafarers, the existing understanding of identity construction has focused heavily on this group. McKay's (2007) field research of Philippine manning agents, ship management firms, and seafarers highlights the two worlds that the seafarers navigate — one at home between voyages, and the other on-board the vessel. In the former, seafarers are awarded high prestige for their material resources gained at work and the cosmopolitan adventure associated with the seafaring life; in the latter, the Filipino seafarer largely occupies a subordinate and racialized occupational position within the hierarchical structure onboard the vessel. McKay (2007) documents the role of the Philippine state, through the Philippine Overseas Employment Administration (POEA), in promoting a particular characterization of the Filipino as somehow naturally suited for work aboard a vessel as "the most dependable shipmate" who is "adaptable and hard-working," possessing "charm and friendliness" which "makes for a harmonious relationship essential to the working situation on board" and "he keeps within set rules and regulations" (p. 624). Acejo (2012) describes this as adhering to the Filipino value of *pakikisama* (getting along) as a cultural form of conformity. This potentially emasculating portrait of the deferent Filipino seafarer is countered with the national narrative of heroic adventurism, providers of financial security, and global representatives of the Philippine nation thus, according to McKay (2007), constructing a "double masculine consciousness" that is sustained through the physically separated and segregated two worlds they inhabit. These "habitats of meaning" (Hannerz, 1996) are a significant aspect of the transnational identity(ies) shaping process.

Those who have studied the onboard experiences of seafarers conclude that the transnational label may be a misnomer as Sampson (2013b) writes that:

> … the degree of embeddedness aboard may be seen to be insufficient to characterize the experience of being a seafarer as a transnational one…True transnationality might be said to occur where individuals feel that they have two homes of similar significance to them. In many cases seafarers do not experience the ship as a home and do not feel integrated into the "community" of seafarers aboard to a significant extent (p. 122).

On board the vessel national identity is far less important (Dimayuga, 2008) than "contractual engagement and occupational culture" (Alderton, 2004) where "seafarers' belongingness when on board is primarily coursed through their membership in a community of practice" (Acejo, 2012). This pertains to that social identity that has the greatest salience and meaning for seafarers at the place of work.

Seafarer Working Conditions

Working conditions vary dramatically from ship to ship (Sampson, 2013b). Studies aboard the vessels have provided some general observations about the working conditions faced by seafarers. Much is focused on the formal and informal hierarchical nature of work relationship and the use of social space, as well as the intensification of labor as a result of merging the place of work and residence (Acejo, 2012; Sampson, 2013b). Broader studies of the industry document some of the occupational safety and health issues faced by seafarers. The 2000 study by the International Commission on Shipping titled "Ships, Slaves, and Competition" identifies the core issue and challenge (2000):

> The underlying cause of sub-standard shipping is the commercial advantage that a ship owner can gain through avoiding international standards for safety, environment protection or labour conditions… The elimination of sub-standard shipping requires a sustained attack on this fiscal advantage, using commercial and regulatory mechanisms (p. 8).

The OECD (2001) defined "sub-standard shipping" using the following criteria: 1) technically unsound; 2) fails to comply with mandatory international conventions; 3) irregularly maintained; 4) insufficiently trained and qualified crew; 5) poor employment conditions for crew; and 6) poor shore-based management.

Seafaring generally, in sub-standard shipping in particular, has been and remains a high risk occupation. Compared to other occupations, seafarers have high fatal injuries and risks to mortality from suicide, homicide, disappearances at sea, and undetermined causes (Alderton, 2004; Bloor, Thomas and Lane, 2000; Roberts, 2008). There is a wide range of industry practices when it comes to seafarers' health and safety (Bloor, et al., 2000). There is no regular published analysis of industry deaths as a whole. A method for analyzing casualties was finally set up in 2000 but the reports are dependent on casualty investigators by the flag State, all of which range in terms of their capacity and willingness to conduct investigations in a thorough and professional manner (Alderton, 2004). The fragmented evidence that does exist indicates that, generally, the work-related fatalities and non-fatal injuries of seafarers are significantly higher among workers from the developing world compared to the developed world (Alderton, 2004). Additionally, compared to the general workforce, Danish seafarers, for example, have 11.5 times higher fatal injuries and drownings than the Danish male workforce on shore (Hansen, 1996). Among seafarers employed in British shipping, there has been a large decrease in fatal accident rates in the 20th century (Roberts, 2008). Much of the reduction is attributed to ship design improvements, safety equipment, rescue services, and less hazardous working practices (Roberts, 2008). Despite the large reduction in fatal accident rates, the rate in British merchant shipping from 2003 to 2012 was still 21 times that of the general British workforce during the same time period (Roberts, Nielsen, Kotłowski and Jaremin, 2014). The fatal accident rate from 1996 to 2002 was 16 times (Roberts and Marlow, 2005).

The deck department seems to have the highest risk exposure which consist of cargo-related duties on deck in bad weather, mooring and towing operations, and asphyxiation in enclosed spaces that include cargo tanks and holds (Roberts, et al., 2014). Internationally, mooring and towing that include ropes breaking or ropes striking seafarers, has been found to consistently associate with fatal injuries (Hansen, 1996; Roberts and Marlow, 2005). Roberts and colleagues (2014) attributed most of fatal accidents to human factors, not mechanical. While some fatalities may be due to human error, it should be noted that human error can be a consequence of inadequate training, lower crewing levels, commercial pressures, quick turnaround times, long working hours, and many other factors that can contribute to seafarers' fatigue (Bloor, et al, 2000). Poor working conditions that include excessive noise, vibration, and heat contribute to higher levels of fatigue (Alderton, 2004) that can then impact mental health (Iversen, 2012). Generally, there is a deterioration of the practice of safety across shipping (Sampson, 2013a) which corresponds to the foreign flagging and global labor market trends in the industry (Couper, 2000).

Crewing practices are a major factor impacting the working conditions of seafarers. This can pertain to both the quantity and quality of vessel crews. Despite the decline in crew labor costs as a result of the global labor market, it remains one of the first targets when shipping lines are seeking to reduce costs (Alderton, 2004). While some crew reductions are due to technological advances and automation, other reductions have simply shifted a larger workload to a smaller number of seafarers (Bloor, et al., 2000). According to Silos and colleagues (2012), the average crewing level of a general cargo vessel was 60% smaller in 2002 compared to 1970. This leads to injuries and fatalities as seafarers carry out tasks that should be completed by more individuals. Further, fewer people assigned to complete onboard tasks results in longer work hours, inadequate and interrupted sleep patterns, and increased fatigue (Bloor, et al., 2000).

The quality of the crew and the training requirements has also been impacted by the desire to reduce labor costs through global labor market and foreign flagging practices. According to Sampson (2013b), the priority of cutting labor costs raises concerns for the competence of seafarers and the retention of competent crew members aboard vessels. As a consequence, there have been growing concerns regarding training, education, and certification of seafarers. An International Maritime Organization (IMO, 2001) study found 17% of survey respondents stated that they sailed with someone who had a fraudulently obtained certificate and of this group, 90% held fraudulent certificates themselves (Alderton, 2004). The same report identified the increase in private training programs that led to difficulty in maintaining standards. Another report in 1998 commissioned by the European Union found that in general, training schools, particularly in poor countries, are not adequately funded to provide the training necessary, particularly on sophisticated equipment, for people to work in offshore labor markets (Alderton, 2004).

With heavy workloads that leave little time for anything else (Sampson, 2013b), the lifestyles associated with the seafarer workplace can also contribute to a higher health-related risks. Seafarers are more likely to engage in unhealthy behaviors than the general population (Alderton, 2004). These behaviors include greater tobacco and alcohol use, less exercise, and greater consumption of sugar and fat that can lead to obesity. All the behaviors can have severe health consequences, including increase risk of lung cancer and heart disease. With an occupational problem involving a lack of activity within confined spaces, poor diet, and sedentary work duties, a significant number of ships do not provide the basic standards of recreational accommodation (Alderton, 2004). From shore and ship exposure, seafarers are susceptible to infectious diseases, including high rates of sexually transmitted diseases (Alderton, 2004). Compared to other occupational groups, seafarers have higher prevalence of infectious diseases in developed countries (Hansen, 1996).

Given the high risk nature of the seafaring occupation, mental health of seafarers has not received much attention. According to Stevenson (2009), lack of attention to mental health care may be due to its absence addressed by maritime law or labor organizations, and the stigma associated with mental health. Seafarers themselves may not seek mental health services in fear of not being able to obtain employment. In addition to fatigue mentioned earlier, other contributory factors that impact the mental health of seafarers due to the nature of their work include piracy, loneliness, and leave from family (Iversen, 2012). Piracy is an occupational health and safety risk experienced by seafarers. According to Abila and Tang (2014), seafarer hostages are mostly from non-OECD countries where the social welfare system is not well developed. As of 2011, 3,863 seafarers reported having experienced assault and abuse from pirates, with 31% having been captured (Abila and Tang, 2014). In a study of four Italian seafarers five months after they were released, victims showed anxiety, social adjustment disorder, emotional instability, somatic disorders, depression, phobic problems, and post-traumatic stress disorder (Ziello, Angioll, Fasanaro and Amenta, 2013). Among Filipino seafarers who were taken hostage by Somali pirates and experienced physical and psychological abuse, support was limited to material losses and physical treatment (Abila and Tang, 2014). Despite traumatic mental health issues that include post-traumatic stress disorder and depression, seafarers reported no systematic attention or treatment (Abila and Tang, 2014).

Transnational crews often consist of strangers who become temporary shipmates. For some, the familiarity of similar ships, work, places visited, and experience with fellow crew members provides the support for a viable occupational culture. Seafarers also share experiences on the basis of similar employment conditions (Borovni, 2007). Despite the commonalities, social isolation is a persistent aspect of seafarers' lives, particularly due to hierarchies between officers and ratings that greatly influence professional and social relationships. To maintain respect and authority, officers are hesitant to befriend junior colleagues. Women seafarers on gender imbalance vessels are often socially isolated. Working conditions such as reduced crew levels, rigid work schedules, and single-person tasks also minimizes social contact (Acejo, 2012). Separate leisure and dining areas for different crew members based on the hierarchical structure of vessels only further isolates members. Communication with family in general, and during deep-sea periods, is difficult with mail service being slow, email only available to certain ranks or nationalities aboard, and telephone via satellite prohibitively expensive (Sampson, 2013b). Changes associated with containerization and container terminal location, as well as national security after 9/11 terrorist attack in New York that has limited sale of mobile phones during port, has limited seafarers ability to connect with family members. Lack of shore leaves, little port time with fast turnaround, and ports located in isolated places further minimize seafarers' social contacts. In an environment of social isolation, higher addictive behavioral patterns, stress, depression, and suicide can be found among seafarers.

Seafarers are separated from their families and friends months at a time while they are at sea that can range from six months (Alderton, 2004) to two years (Borovni, 2007). This work pattern not only impacts friendships, family life, and relationships, but also the mental health of seafarers, particularly since seafarers are forming fewer friendships onboard. With limited time and opportunity as well as the high cost to stay in contact, seafarers are unlikely to keep up with friendships ashore. For those with no shore-based support, the anxiety is particularly harmful and can lead to suicide at sea (Alderton, 2004). Being away from family contributes to stress and anxiety about loved ones, including their partners' ability to take care of the household, partners' sexual fidelity, and children's behavior. The stress is heightened when there is a family crisis and the seafarer is not able to assist being so far away. If seafarers are worried about the family, stress can induce health consequences (Borovni, 2007). Worries about family members are enhanced if there are restrictions with ship-shore communication. Homesickness and loneliness may affect behaviors and work performance. Distracted or poor work performance can impact safety at work or job security.

Efforts to Address Migrant Seafarer Working Conditions

Regulation. The shipping industry is regulated by International Maritime Organization (IMO) in regards to ship standards and the International Labor Organization (ILO) for health, labor, and welfare standards (Bloor, Datta, Gilinskiy and Horlick-Jones, 2006). Rather than relying on flag states, port states have formed regional alliances all over the world to enforce standards due to highly publicized maritime disasters (Bloor, et al., 2006). Following the Maritime Labour Convention of 2006, inspectors follow a common inspection manual and practice with the power to inspect the ships in compliance with ILO and IMO conventions that include conditions of employment. If deficiencies are found, inspectors also have the power to detain the ships until the issues are resolved. There are some shortcomings to the port state enforcement, however, that include port states only committing to inspect a portion of foreign-flagged ships at their ports due to the resources required, poor records of effective enforcement, and port state control subject to bribes.

In an effort to bring some semblance of a labor market institutional structure to what is a largely an unregulated global labor market for seafarers, the ILO established the Maritime Labor Convention in 2006 that has been ratified by 67 nations. The Convention represents a bill of rights for seafarers that is designed to address abuses and protect seafarers from sub-standard working conditions. These include the right to safe working conditions, fair terms of employment, decent living and recreational facilities, access to health protection and medical care, welfare, and social security. The Convention includes formal complaint procedures to ensure compliance and enforcement along with maritime labor certification awarded to vessels that have established verifiable labor standards.

As the nation supplying the largest percentage of seafarers and depending heavily upon their remittances, the Philippines has established various labor market institutions designed to regulate work in the shipping industry. The government run Philippine Overseas Employment Administration (POEA) is charged with accrediting and regulating the crewing agencies and enforcing various legal statutes regarding seafarer employment and working conditions. This includes the Migrant Workers Act of 1995 and the Standard Employment Contract (SEC) based on conventions established by the ILO. There are also several seafarer labor unions in the Philippines. Together, these national organizations mediate the tripartite relationship that exists among the seafarer, shipping line, and crewing agency (Amante, 2004).

Unionization. The ILO and the International Transport Workers' Federation (ITF) have documented the range of labor abuses and made recommendations for improving the working and living conditions of seafarers (Lillie, 2004). While at one time seafarer unionism ensured a modicum of workplace protection, this is no longer the case given the globalization of the labor market and the use of flags of convenience (FOC). Today it is the ITF that has assumed the leading collective bargaining role in representing and protecting seafarers globally with the primary focus on establishing standards for wages and working conditions aboard FOC vessels (Koch-Baumgarten, 1998; Lillie, 2004). The ITF is an international association of individual unions with developed countries making up the majority of its membership and decision making (Koch-Baumgarten, 1998). At the broader global level, the ITF represents a unique case of establishing a trade union regime in the face of the forces of globalization that militate against collective action and enforcement (Koch-Baumgarten, 1998). In an attempt to impose a uniform labor cost scale, ITF has forced a centralized wage bargaining system with employers (Lillie, 2004). Under ITF contracts, seafarers can earn higher wages, sometimes several times higher for seafarers from developing countries (Lillie, 2004). Because of ITF's influence, some ship owners who are not under ITF contracts are voluntarily paying wages close to ITF standards as a way to avoid dealing with ITF (Lillie, 2004).

Welfare. For the most part, seafarers' entitlement and access to benefits and welfare services varies significantly across flag states, port countries, seafarers' home country, and employers with no particular entity having the duty to offer such services. Vessels that fly "flags of convenience" often treat welfare in its strictest form and limit it to disability payments and repatriation. The Norwegian Government Seamen's Service, an agency of the government of Norway, has been highlighted as a model that provides cultural and recreational activities, language courses, and social services to Norwegian seamen and all seamen on Norwegian ships at home, in local ports, in ports around the world, and through their shipping companies (Alderton, 2004). Providers work closely with other welfare groups such as the International Seafarers' Clubs. Another government entity that is well-known to provide welfare services is the United Kingdom's Merchant Navy Welfare Board that consists of ship owners, seafarers' trade unions, and national charities (Alderton, 2004). The board's main objective is to assess the welfare needs of the seafarers and their dependents in British ports and then coordinate with charities to provide services. Because seafarers are temporarily employed, many do not have long-term benefits like employer-based pensions and health care (Sampson, 2013a). For some, like German-flagged vessels, seafarers are entitled to make social security payments that allows them to access state-based social benefits such as health care, pensions, and unemployment (Sampson, 2013a). Panama's regulation pays wages to seafarers if they are disabled. The amount and length of payment is based on degree of disability and service (Alderton, 2004). Cyprus includes rehabilitation and repatriation for seafarers in their annual budget with no specificity of contributions (Alderton, 2004). But the seafarer labor market has become globalized, access to national social welfare systems as a right of citizenship has diminished. To help fulfill gaps left by government entities, global non-governmental organizations such as Missions to Seafarers are available at some ports to provide welfare and emergency services (Alderton, 2004). Another NGO, the International Seafarers' Welfare and Assistance Network is a membership organization to promote seafarers' welfare through direct services as well as support other entities, including ships, to provide services to seafarers in the implementation of the Maritime Labor Convention 2006. The ITF's Seafarer Trust provides union-funded services directly and through unions, missions, and welfare agencies at port locations across the globe (Kahveci, 2007). Specifically with regards to mental health, social welfare organizations have recently tried to raise awareness and improve seafarers' mental health (Stevenson, 2009). Maritime health professionals and scholars have also increased attention on mental health (Jezewska, Iversen and Leszczynska, 2013).

Support. While seafarers are at sea, families provide the important connection to life back home and support needed for seafarers to do their work. Families also provide the practical support of managing the household and childcare (Fidler, 2015). Many seafarers' wives and families do not have support services, particularly those in countries that have few seafarers and/or are geographically dispersed. Their only support usually comes from family and friends. Several factors have been found to be significant in the well-functioning of the household when seafarers are away that include the number of people in the household, the amount of financial contributions, the time abroad, and the frequency of contact (De Haan, Brock and Coulibaly, 2002). For family members who were left behind, partners may experience stress in the form of mental health issues, children may perform at a lower level in school or have social and psychological development issues, and older adults may feel a sense of abandonment (Yeoh, Graham and Boyle, 2002). For some partners, they have more formalized means of support such as the Seafarers' Wives Associations for Filipino seafarer wives and families (Alderton, 2004). For some seafarers, social welfare is usually dependent on informal support from family members. In the Republic of Kiribati, for example, family members are obligated to assist one another in times of need as the system of social welfare (Borovni, 2007). While at sea, seafarers have increasing used visiting chaplains as a form of support (Alderton, 2004).

DISCUSSION AND IMPLICATIONS

Because seafaring is globalized and many are on temporary contracts, it is extremely difficult to address all seafarers' needs in personal and family wellbeing. One way to address social welfare needs is to collaborate with existing unions, government entities, and associations that already work with seafarers and their families to increase their knowledge and voice. Given the global nature of seafaring, collaborations must be developed between social welfare institutions and seafarer organizations to evaluate and provide social services, particularly related to mental health (Ziello, et al., 2013). To improve on the working conditions of migrant seafarers, areas that must be addressed include safety, physical health, mental health, and labor market standards.

Safety. Occupational health and safety largely depend upon the owners, agents, and masters of ships. Owners need to be held responsible for their ships to comply with good standards of safety and working conditions. Some fatalities are preventable and prevention measures can take place. Roberts and colleagues (2014) recommend increased safety training as well as pairing new crew members to those who are more experienced. Mooring and towing ropes can be inspected and maintained with replacement of worn ropes (Roberts, et al., 2014). Asphyxiation in enclosed spaces can also be prevented by following procedures and checklists when entering enclosed spaces. Life vests and safety harnesses should be worn in potentially hazardous operations that are along the sides of ships or at great heights

(Roberts, et al., 2014). Related to food, catering, and accommodation, port state control inspectors are increasingly becoming important enforcement agencies (Bloor, et al., 2006) and should conduct frequent inspections and target ships that are recurring offenders.

Physical Health. With safety as a continuing concern for seafarers, crew members, including ratings, should have access to the ship's medical professionals. To treat common life-threatening emergencies related to the profession, vessels must have medical supplies and basic equipment on board. Because seafarers are at high risks for sexually transmitted diseases (STDs), sexual health and sexual risks for crews should be part of their training. Medical professionals on board should be trained on how to diagnose and treat STDs. Medical professionals should view the crew member as the client and treat all patients in a confidential manner in order to gain the trust of patients. Predictable shift schedules can be used as a way to avoid crew member sleep disturbances. The attitude of the captain has been found to be influential in crew members' engagement in recreational activities (Alderton, 2004). To avoid social isolation and seafarers remaining in their cabins when not on duty, captains can encourage seafarers to be more active as a way to maintain good physical health.

Mental Health. To decrease isolation, shared meal times provide an important opportunity for seafarers to socialize with others while at sea. It allows seafarers to spend time together to develop and nurture social relationships that is crucial for their emotional well-being. Ways to maximize casual interactions can also help to decrease isolation and loneliness. When seafarers experience trauma at sea that range from acts of piracy to casualties, mental health services should be readily for available access. While ships are unlikely to employ professional mental health practitioners onboard, innovative ways to address acute trauma and on-site interventions should be explored before victims seek help from professionals in port cities.

According to Borovni (2007), seafarers' complain most about the lack of communication with their partners while they are away. Regular contact with family and friends back home is crucial for seafarers to maintain emotional and psychological wellbeing. These relationships provide the support needed for seafarers to work away from home for months at a time. Contact is particularly crucial during crises at home. All forms of communication should be made available to seafarers at all times to connect them to their loved ones. The cost should not be prohibitive but viewed as a necessity that will contribute to better work performance. Ships should adopt advancements in technology allowing seafarers to stay in contact with their family and friends back home on a regular basis. Keeping up with those back home can provide a sense of participating in home life that will decrease stress and worry.

Other ways to strengthen family relation is to have members move closer to the seafarers' work. One strategy is to allow members to migrate with the seafarers, including families of ratings (Borovni, 2007). Travelling together allows family members to have a better understanding of life and work at sea. It would shorten family separation time and allow the maintenance of family bonds. For wives who have travelled with seafarers, it has improved the quality of their relationship (Borovni, 2007). To have the option of family members travel, more facilities on ships are needed for accommodations. Another option for families to spend time together is having family members join seafarers at port during longer turnaround times.

Labor Market Standards and Institutions. Finally, and most generally, it is vital that this globalized migrant labor market have institutions supporting and enforcing the established comprehensive conventions and standards outlined by international organizations and agencies such as the IMO and ILO. There have been several treaties, codes and conventions but responsibility for monitoring and enforcement is lacking (International Commission on Shipping, 2000). The primary source of the problem lies in abdication of responsibility by the flag state and thus the flag of convenience system that, to a large extent, has as its purpose the circumnavigation of more stringent labor regulations. The unilateral governance units that have stepped in to fill the gap are state, regional and port entities concerned with the impact of vessel practices on their shores. Thus, much of the emphasis has been on environmental impacts and on vessel practices and procedures that would also pertain in some cases to health and safety such as crewing.

The now established practice of recruiting seafarers from South East Asian countries, where the labor force is most vulnerable to exploitative employment practices, may be best addressed through government regulations, by the labor supplying nations, of all aspects of the employment relationship from the operation of manning agencies to the labor contracts to the levels of compensation to repatriation. Ideally, these institutional mechanisms can be established with direct labor union participation that would enhance the ability of seafarers to grieve and seek adjudication of unethical and illegal practices. More specifically, the International Commission on Shipping (2000) has recommended that "the ITF, national maritime unions and relevant governments of flag and labor supplying States work cooperatively to implement appropriate working conditions for seafarers based on international conventions" (p. 174).

The ITF (2006) issued its own report on the working conditions and human rights of seafarers. Among the recommendations are the need to establish an authentic legal and regulatory connection between the flag nation and the vessel owners, that procedures relating to national security should not limit the freedom of movement of seafarers nor their access to social welfare and/or labor organizations, and the need to research and document the prevalence of blacklisting of seafarers by manning agencies. The world's global economy and dependence on seafarers to work on shipping containers as a way to control costs is unlikely to decrease. As such, the rights and welfare of seafarers and their families must be at the forefront of the industry.

REFERENCES

Abila, S. S. and Tang, L. (2014). Trauma, post-trauma, and support in the shipping industry: The experience of Filipino seafarers after pirate attacks. *Marine Policy*, *46*, 132–136.

Acejo, I. (2012). Seafarers and transnationalism: Ways of belongingness ashore and aboard. *Journal of Intercultural Studies*, *33*(1), 69–84.

Alderton, T. (2004). *The global seafarer: Living and working conditions in a globalized industry*. International Labour Organization.

Alderton, T. and Winchester, N. (2002). Globalisation and de-regulation in the maritime industry. *Marine Policy, 26*(1), 35-43.

Amante, M. S. V. (2004). Industrial democracy in the rough seas: The case of Philippine seafarers. *The Industrial Relations Research Association, Proceedings of the 56 The Annual Meeting, January,* 3-5.

Bensman, D. (2008). Globalization and the labor markets of the logistics industry. *Industry Studies Conference Paper.*

BIMCO/ISF. (2010). Manpower update 2010: The worldwide demand for and supply of seafarers. Dalian Maritime University and Warwick Institute for Employment Research.

Bloor, M., Datta, R., Gilinskiy, Y. and Horlick-Jones, T. (2006). Unicorn among the cedars: On the possibility of effective "smart regulation" of the globalized shipping industry. *Social and Legal Studies*, *15*(4), 534–551.

Bloor, M. and Sampson, H. (2009). Regulatory enforcement of labour standards in an outsourcing globalized industry the case of the shipping industry. *Work, Employment and Society*, *23*(4), 711–726.

Bloor, M., Thomas, M. and Lane, T. (2000). Health risks in the global shipping industry: an overview. *Health, Risk and Society*, *2*(3), 329–340.

Bonacich, E., Alimahomed, S. and Wilson, J. B. (2008). The racialization of global labor. *American Behavioral Scientist, 52*(3), 342.

Borovnik, M. (2004). Are seafarers migrants?-Situating seafarers in the framework of mobility and transnationalism. *New Zealand Geographer*, *60*(1), 36-43.

Borovni, M. (2007). Labor circulation and changes among seafarers' families and communities in Kiribati. *Asian and Pacific Migration Journal (Scalabrini Migration Center)*, *16*(2), 225–249.

Ciscel, D. H., Smith, B. E. and Mendoza, M. (2003). Ghosts in the machine: new immigrants and the redefinition of work. *Journal of Economic Issues, 37* (2), 333-341.

Coe, N. M. (2014). Missing links: Logistics, governance and upgrading in a shifting global economy. *Review of International Political Economy, 21*(1), 224-256.

Coe, N. M., Dicken, P. and Hess, M. (2008). Global production networks: Realizing the potential. *Journal of Economic Geography, 8(3),* 271-295.

Couper, A. (2000) Implications of maritime globalization for the crews of merchant ships. *Journal for Maritime Research, 2*(1), 1-8,

De Haan, A., Brock, K. and Coulibaly, N. (2002). Migration, livelihoods and institutions: Contrasting patterns of migration in Mali. *Journal of Development Studies*, *38*(5), 37.

Dimayuga, R. (2008). The social identities of Filipino seafarers. *Asian and Pacific Migration Journal*, *17*(1), 79-90.

Fidler, C.-A. (2015). The impact of migration upon family life and gender relations: The case of South Asian seafarers, c. 1900–50. *Women's History Review*, *24*(3), 410–428.

Hannerz, U. (1996). *Transnational connections: Culture, people, places*. Taylor and Francis US.

Hansen, H. L. (1996). Surveillance of deaths on board Danish merchant ships, 1986-93: Implications for prevention. *Occupational and Environmental Medicine*, *53*(4), 269–275.

Harvey, D. (1982). *The limits to capital*. Blackwell.

International Commission on Shipping (2000). *Ships, slaves, and competition*. Australia.

International Transport Workers Federation (2006). *Out of sight, out of mind: seafarers, fishers, and human rights*.

Iversen, R. (2012). The mental health of seafarers. *International Maritime Health*, *63*, 78–79.

Jaffee, D. and Bensman, D. (2015). Draying and picking: Precarious work and labor action in the logistics sector. Unpublished manuscript.

Jezewska, M., Iversen, R. and Leszczynska, I. (2013). MENHOB – mental health on board. *International Maritime Health*, *64*, 168–174.

Kahveci, E. (2007). *Port-based welfare services for seafarers*. International Research Centre, Cardiff University.

Kahveci, E., Lane, T. and Sampson, H. (2002). *Transnational seafarer communities*. Seafarers International Research Centre, Cardiff University.

Kearney, M. (1995). The local and the global: the anthropology of globalization and transnationalism. *Annual Review of Anthropology*, *24*, 547-65.

Kalleberg, A. L. (2011). *Good jobs, bad jobs: The rise of polarized and precarious employment systems in the United States, 1970s-2000s*. American Sociological Association, Russell Sage Publishers.

Koch-Baumgarten, S. (1998). Trade union regime formation under the conditions of globalization in the transport sector: Attempts at transnational trade union regulation of flag-of-convenience shipping. *International Review of Social History, 43*(03), 369-402.

Lane, T. (1997). Globalization, deregulation and crew competence in world shipping. *Transport Regulation Matters,* 98.

Lane T. (2000). The global seafarers' labour market: problems and solutions. Retrieved from http://www.icons.org.au/images/93SIRC.pdf.

Liang, A. W. (2011). Sailing on a neoliberal sea: Multinational seafarers on container ships. *Hong Kong Anthropologist*, (5), 1-20.

Lillie, N. (2004). Global collective bargaining on flag of convenience shipping. *British Journal of Industrial Relations*, *42*(1), 47–67.

McKay, S. C. (2007). Filipino sea men: Constructing masculinities in an ethnic labour niche. *Journal of Ethnic and Migration Studies*, *33*(4), 617-633.

Molloy, D. J. (2010). Social work at sea. *Reflections: Narratives of Professional Helping*, *16*(2), 94–108.

Organization for Economic Cooperation and Development (2001). *The cost to users of substandard shipping*. Organization for Economic Cooperation and Development. Geneva.

Roberts, S. E. (2008). Fatal work-related accidents in UK merchant shipping from 1919 to 2005. *Occupational Medicine*, *58*(2), 129–129.

Roberts, S. E. and Marlow, P. B. (2005). Traumatic work related mortality among seafarers employed in British merchant shipping, 1976-2002. *Occupational and Environmental Medicine*, *62*(3), 172–180.

Roberts, S. E., Nielsen, D., Kotłowski, A. and Jaremin, B. (2014). Fatal accidents and injuries among merchant seafarers worldwide. *Occupational Medicine*, *64*(4), 259–266.

Sampson, H. (2013a). Globalisation, labour market transformation and migrant marginalisation: The example of transmigrant seafarers in Germany. *Journal of International Migration and Integration*, *14*(4), 751–765.

Sampson, H. (2013b). *International seafarers and transnationalism in the twenty-first century*. Manchester, UK: Manchester University Press.

Sampson, H. (2003). Transnational drifters or hyperspace dwellers: an exploration of the lives of Filipino seafarers aboard and ashore. *Ethnic and Racial Studies*, *26*(2), 253-277.

Silos, J. M., Piniella, F., Monedero, J. and Walliser, J. (2012). Trends in the global market for crews: A case study. *Marine Policy*, *36*(4), 845-858.

Stevenson, D. B. (2009). Seafarers' rights to mental health care. Retrieved from http://seamenschurch.org/article/seafarers-rights-mental-health-care.

Weil, D. (2014). *The fissured workplace: why work became so bad for so many and what can be done to improve it.* Harvard University Press.

Wu, B. and Sampson, H. (2005). Reconsidering the cargo sector's seafarer labour market: A 21st century profile of global seafarers. *Ocean Yearbook, 19*, 357–380.

Yeoh, B. S., Graham, E. and Boyle, P. J. (2002). Migrations and family relations in the Asia Pacific region. *Asian and Pacific Migration Journal, 11*(1), 1–12.

Ziello, A. R., Angioll, R. D., Fasanaro, A. M. and Amenta, F. (2013). Psychological consequences in victims of maritime piracy. *International Maritime Health*, *64*, 136–141.

In: Migrant Workers
Editors: Qingwen Xu and Lucy P. Jordan
ISBN: 978-1-63485-272-2

Chapter 11

OPPORTUNITIES AND CHALLENGES OF RETURN MIGRATION

Uma A. Segal[*]
School of Social Work, University of Missouri, St. Louis, US

ABSTRACT

Much literature explores the reasons for immigration, but data on the return of expatriates, particularly those in their pre-retirement years, it is still lacking. Census figures in the Global North reveal consistently dropping birth rates and increasing longevity, resulting in gaps in the labor force and concerns about perpetuation of society and culture. While the Global South has a burgeoning population, its "Brain Drain" is particularly troubling as countries lose several from their skilled workforce with a resulting mentorship gap for the next generation. The return of emigres can help alleviate significant issues facing several nations and can be beneficial to some emigres who are unable to find positions commensurate with their qualifications which is known as a "Brain Waste." An increasing pool of working-age migrants return to their countries of origin, and "circular migration" is rising with the ease of transportation and globalization. Some, among these migrants choose to return "home" permanently, and while the home country may greatly benefit from the return of these expatriates, their return is not always smooth. The skills learned abroad may be inapplicable in the homeland, returnees may have difficulty reintegrating, and their offspring may struggle with adaptation and acculturation. This chapter explores this relatively new phenomenon of return migration and suggests that "home" nations must recognize returnees as a potential asset and develop effective policies, programs, and services to assist this unique group of migrant workers reestablish themselves, allowing maximal use of their human capital.

[*] Corresponding Author: Uma A. Segal, School of Social Work, University of Missouri–St. Louis, 1 University Blvd. 121 Bellerive Hall, St. Louis, MO 63121-4400, USA. Email: umasegal@umsl.edu.

INTRODUCTION

Several extant theories aim to explain the phenomenon of international migration, and despite their significance in helping understandings of the process, increasing globalization, growing interdependence, evolving perceptions, and acceptance of ethnic communities suggest that existing theories may now be lacking. It is clear migrants leave their homelands for another in the face of at least one, if not all, of the following reasons: (1) in search of better living conditions, (2) to escape political or ethnic conflict, and (3) to avail themselves of opportunities in new free trade areas (Castles and Miller, 2009); but transnationalism, and preference for movement between countries as work and other opportunities become available, is on the rise. Regardless of theoretical perspectives and the myriad reasons provided for emigration, at the human level, the overarching cause for international migration is the strong belief that life in the new country will offer greater benefits, at least in the long run, than will life in the homeland.

Data on human migration indicate that movements from the Global South to the Global North, and between countries of the Global South are substantial, while migration from North to South is limited (International Organization for Migration [IOM], 2015). Census figures in several countries of the Global North continue to reveal dropping birth rates and increasing longevity, resulting in gaps in the labor force and concerns about perpetuation of society and culture. Numerous countries of the Global South indicate concerns about the "brain drain" they experience as talent (i.e., skilled workers) moves to more developed countries to maximize personal opportunities for growth and success. The flight of talent frequently includes the exit of several people who could potentially train subsequent generations; the brain drain has an even longer lasting effect on the sending nation with the loss of mentors.

The most immediate and practical resolution to address labor force gaps in the North and talent loss in the South is through increased and targeted immigration, nevertheless, most nations have long been wary of foreigners, and particularly those from societies socially, economically, and culturally different from them. This is particularly evident currently, in April 2016, as thousands of Syrian refugees and many other Middle Eastern migrants and refugees continue to attempt entry into the European Union (EU) raising issues about implications for EU countries as well as for immigrants. Migration to developing countries from the North is not generally regarded as an opportunity by those who live in the latter, and talent flows less frequently in this direction. Concerns of cultural contamination, changing social identities, and resource allocations are shaking the very foundations of several EU countries with the arrival of Middle Easterners, however, developing nations are also highly suspicious of Western influences and the "Americanization" of the world.

A large proportion of emigrants expect that, eventually, when they have achieved their goals, whether these are educational, economic or otherwise, they will return to their homelands and all they left with emigration (Segal and Heck, 2012). However, it is evident that the longer these individuals remain in the host country, the more acclimatized they become to its culture and lifestyle, and the more distant becomes the reality of returning to the place of nativity. The desire, though still mentioned by migrants, is rarely followed by action, and what remains is the "return illusion" (Hoffmann-Nowtny, 1978). This is believed to be a common and inevitable part of the migration process, as indicated in a seminal collection of essays on return migration (King, 1986). Hugo (2003) penned the oft repeated truism that, "there is nothing so permanent as a temporary migrant" (p. 22), yet it is also evident that some migrants do return home, but few countries recognize that reintegration can be difficult or have programs to address related issues (International Labour Organization [ILO], 2010).

Return migration is defined by the IOM (2015) as "The movement of a person returning to his/her country of origin or habitual residence, usually after at least one year in another country. The return may or may not be voluntary" (p. 199). Much literature explores the reasons why people emigrate, but limited empirical research focus has been placed on the return of these expatriates (ILO, 2010), particularly those in their working pre-retirement years. Although literature suggests that a large proportion of labor migrants, both skilled and unskilled, anticipate returning home after a period of time or when goals have been attained (Klinthäll, 2006), the vast majority of migrants gradually establishes roots and return migration is continuously postponed. Expatriates may provide a viable pool of individuals who can fill labor or talent shortages and may have a fundamental interest to return to the land of their birth. International migrants tend to maintain cultural, economic, and emotional ties to their homelands (ILO, 2010) and increasing globalization and social media permit strong connections with international networks. Since identity is often linked with phenotype and when there is a marked visible difference between immigrant and host, affiliation with parental culture may be especially strong. Identity into successive generations is shaped by an emotional allegiance to the ancestral country of origin, and with increasing ease in transnational travel "ethnic homecomings" of later generations are not uncommon (Markowitz and Stefansson, 2004; Münz and Ohliger, 2003).

As migrants return to their homelands, it is just as essential that they be prepared to return as it was for them to be prepared to emigrate. The ability to mobilize both human and social resources once they have returned to the homeland is a major ingredient in their reintegration (Cassarino, 2004). This chapter discusses migration among working-age individuals who return to their countries of origin, their experience of reintegrating after several years or decades of absence, and the implications for the labor force and communities in their homelands. The chapter also attempts to assess whether there exist any policies, programs, and services to assist this unique group of migrant workers as they reestablish themselves in their ancestral homelands.

Return Migration

The implications of migration are substantial for migrants and their families as well as for sending, transit, and receiving countries. Most literature on migration has focused on the experience of the entering immigrant and/or refugee, the process of adaptation in the host country, and social and economic implications for both the migrant and the receiving nation. Generally adults who migrate are of working age, and their entry into a new country has been found to meet unmet labor force needs. Further, it is clear that, overall, even if in the initial years some are a drain on governmental, educational, health and other resources, over time, they contribute substantially to the economy of the country to which they migrate. Most migrants move to better their opportunities and lives, not to be dependent. Even if they gain financially with the move, they give up too much, personally, socially, culturally and in a number of other ways, to make the transition to another land only to rely on governmental handouts. Contrary to Emma Lazarus' famous poem on the Statue of Liberty, those who are the most tired, hungry, and poor among the teaming masses do not have the personal strength and resilience and are intrinsically too needy to have the courage to migrate.

Not all who migrate, even in search of better opportunities, stay permanently outside their birthplace, but few researchers have sought to study their experiences. Data on the return of migrants to their homelands, continues to be sparse (ILO, 2010), although there is a growing body of theoretical and conceptual knowledge about the subject. Indicators are that with transnational movements, some migrants do choose to return "home" permanently and include those who (1) find that they prefer to raise children in the homeland with their own ancestral values and culture, (2) return because the homelands are now more economically and politically stable, (3) have fulfilled their several-year contracts in host nations, and (4) must return because there are no longer available jobs in the host country. Others are returned involuntarily, as deported individuals unauthorized to remain in the host country, or as repatriated refugees, who are returned to the native places that are no longer deemed dangerous. While the home country may greatly benefit from the return of these expatriates, their return is not always smooth. The skills learned abroad may be inapplicable in the homeland, individuals may no longer be socially and politically aligned with their ancestral nation and find it difficult to reintegrate, and their offspring may have issues of adaptation and acculturation.

The contribution that return migrants make to their home country depends much on the circumstances under which they return and the resources with which they return. Larger scale return migration only occurs when the economic and political conditions in the homeland become attractive, or are more attractive than those in the destination country. The ILO (2010) reports that this occurred in the latter part of the 20th Century and first decade of the 21st Century, for example, when ethnic Russians who had been forced out of the former Soviet Union returned to the Russian Federation; Italians returned to Northern Italy from Germany; and Ireland was able to attract back its skilled expatriates. When there were expectations of the economic boom in the BRIC (Brazil, Russia, India, and China) countries, their respective *Diasporas* returned and also made substantial investments. In recent years, the flow from the U.S. to Mexico has been larger than the flow into the U.S. A recent Pew Research Center report on indicates that between 2009 and 2014, in the U.S., there was a net loss of 140,000 Mexican migrants, and the primary reason given was for family reunification (Gonzalez-Barrera, 2015).

In their theoretical and empirical analysis of the behavior of returning migrants, Borjas and Bratsberg (1996) indicated that people tend to return to rich, rather than poor, countries, and they are more likely to return to countries that are in close proximity. Hence, of the Mexicans and Chinese in the U.S., the former are more likely to return to Mexico than are the latter to China. However, with changes in transnational travel and communications, perhaps proximity will no longer be as significant a factor as it has been heretofore. Borjas and Bratsberg (1996) develop a "Skill Sorting" model that proposes that people move because of their skills and return because they either have achieved their goals or failed to appropriately predict the likelihood of success. This model, they believe, predicts population flow in terms of size and skill level. Thus, if the migrants selected to leave a country are highly skilled, those who will return will be those who are less skilled; when less skilled migrants leave because they have better opportunities abroad, it is more likely that the returnees will be those who are the more skilled and they will utilize their accumulated resources and skills in the homeland. This model received empirical support by Rooth and Saarela (2007), but Bijwaard and Wahba (2014), who also sought to test this perspective, found that the migration pattern is U-shaped as did Nekby (2006). Those who have the lowest incomes are the most likely to return, but those with the highest will also return more frequently than will those at middle income levels. The tendency to return, however, declines after about six years (Bijwaard and Wahba, 2014). Assets in the home country also influence return, and those with significant assets, even if they have good host country incomes, are more likely to return than are those without assets in the homeland. Dustmann (2003) suggests that there are some correlations between duration of the migration and the desire to return and that migrants select to return when their income levels get high, while Constant and Massey (2006) found no correlation between earnings and return, although individuals who were unemployed were more likely to return. Although most studies tend to look at economic reasons for movement, there are several others, such as family relationships, interests, and other non-monetary/financial considerations that underlie people's decisions to return. These are more difficult to measure. Qualitative research on migrant intention to return reveals that responses will change depending on when the study is conducted as circumstances in a migrant's life change over time and so do their intentions (Klinthäll, 2006).

In addition, the timing of return is crucial, as this has implications for the resources an individual may have accumulated in the host country (King, 2000, Vertovec, 2007). If migrants have been in the host country long enough to accumulate the competencies and skills as well as build social and professional networks, they are able to carry significant resources to the homeland that will stand them in good stead as they reestablish themselves and reintegrate. If they do not spend a sufficient length of time abroad and are not able to augment their professional and personal resources, they have little to offer the home country. To be a "sustainable return," migrants should be away long enough to acquire these resources and return to the homeland before their retirement years so that they are able to optimize the use of their human, social, and economic capital in their home countries (ILO 2010).

HOME COUNTRY'S RESPONSIBILITY

If sustainable return is of benefit to the home country, it is surprising that nations have not developed policies and programs to recruit their expatriates. The globalization of several professional and social opportunities has seen the increase in mobility of technological, research, and scientific skill; however, the recruitment of the *Diasporas* has received minimal attention. The return of migrants can be essential for a country's balanced growth and development for skill transfer as well as access to international professional networks for research and education in the home country (Gill, 2005). Once expatriate researchers and scientists become ensconced in the host country, they can unconsciously alienate themselves from their own lands and the opportunities they can provide in moving those countries forward (Gill, 2005), hence home countries may need to develop opportunities to attract them back. Likewise, given the literature that indicates that among the returnees are several who are not able to accumulate resources or establish themselves in the destination country, their native countries should be prepared to receive them and help them reintegrate. This may require the development of policies and social service and health care programs to increase employment, address health needs, and assist in cultural and social adaptation. It may also require reinstituting access to the services they were once entitled. For example, the return of the Irish has been fairly dramatic, even in the face of Ireland's economic downturn (McGreevy, 2013), yet several do not have access to governmental services, although they have retained their Irish citizenship. They have also had to take the "habitual residency test" to indicate that they are back permanently and should be allowed to vote and access services (IrishEcho, 2015), but the government is now taking this into consideration to ensure their reintegration (Deenihan, 2014).

Several theories of return migration have gradually emerged, although empirical data on the phenomenon is sparse. Among those is Cerase's (1974) article that assesses Italian returnees from the U.S. He categorized four types of return: (1) return of failure (those who fail to integrate), (2) return of conservatism (those who plan on returning with the resources to purchase land and maintain the existing culture of their homelands), (2) return of retirement (those who select to spend their old age in their native land), and (4) return of innovation (those who plan on using all the tangible and intangible resources they have accumulated to enhance personal, social, and community experiences at home). Regardless of reasons for return, migrants must navigate certain domains. This is necessary, in fact, whether individuals are emigrating or returning, although the process and trajectory may differ. Among these are the establishment of their identities, addressing economic or occupational issues, and assessing health and health care access. Although in instances of repatriation and deportation, the state has a hand, overall, return migration is a phenomenon that is initiated by the migrant, without the involvement of macro level decision makers.

Social Identity of Returned Migrants

As emigrants plan for their return to their origins, they frequently fail to realize that they have been inexorably changed by the immigrant experience. They may retain several of the norms of their own cultures, yet they have acquired new perceptions and realities from the host country, and have woven these separate realities into a workable whole. Hence, frequently the culture with which they are most comfortable is a one of "fusion" that integrates their bicultural, or multicultural, experiences. Although they may feel they do not truly belong to the host culture, even if they may have spent several decades living in it, they find that when they return to the homeland with sufficient resources, the culture they left at emigration no longer exists. For them, their native culture has been truncated to the time when they emigrated, and the country to which they return may be substantially different, having evolved and changed economically, socially, politically, and culturally in the years in between.

Flores (2009) presents a thoughtful view of the return of these migrants, recognizing that they carry with them "cultural remittances" that may or may not be welcomed by those who did not leave. Studies show that while the return of emigres is welcomed when they bring their resource capital and put it to good use in the homeland, their foreign ways of living are less than acceptable, and their home country behaviors are antiquated. They challenge norms and create tensions, having created a new identity. Eventually the two groups usually come to an understanding and appreciation of differing social identities; nevertheless, of those who return, not all are able to adjust, and several plan, or do, return to the host country (Maron and Connell, 2008). In essence, since globalization has now made commonplace the process of cross national movement and the relative cost of travel has declined, migration is no longer a completed journey.

Although migration has occurred since time immemorial, migrations and extensive border crossings have been regulated for only about two and a half centuries. Circular migration and the migration of second and subsequent generations is a more recent phenomenon, perhaps also a result of increasing globalization. The return of migrants' descendants to their ancestral homes is another, new and more recent form of migration. For example, as India's economy improved, and as the government established internship programs to attract expatriates, professional second generation Indian Americans have found employment opportunities in major cities of India (Jain, 2010). The intension of this group is not to migrate permanently, but its members establish homes and families in India, and the final outcome has yet to be written. A 2009 publication by Conway and Potter focuses specifically on the return of the second generation from around the world to diverse countries and the struggles it faces in establishing an identity in its ancestral homeland.

When they return to their ancestors' homelands, returnees may be marginalized as cultural foreigners (Tsuda, 2009), and this rather extreme experience has been common particularly for Japanese descendants from Brazil. An edited publication (Lesser, 2003) skillfully pools the insights of nine researchers who focused on the *Nikkeijin* (or *Nikkei*) foreign nationals of Japanese heritage, who migrated to Brazil at the beginning of the 20th Century. The story of this population is particularly unique in that it has been marked by significant transnational movements not seen in other migration groups and evidence

> "...a rarely studied but extraordinary case of transnational homemaking, breaking, and transforming: the migration of hundreds of thousands of Japanese to Brazil in the first half of the twentieth century, followed by the migration of hundreds of thousands of Brazilians to Japan in the last decades of the same century." (Lesser, 2003, p. 1)

This may well be a pattern to be found in the future with other returnees and their descendants. In the latter part of the 19th Century, an informal agreement between Brazil (that desperately needed agricultural laborers) and Japan (that was industrializing and displacing its agricultural workers) resulted in a migration stream from Japan to Brazil. Between 1908 and 1941 about 189,000 Japanese had made Brazil their home; another 50,000 arrived after World War II (Lesser, 2003), and all came with expectations of an improved quality of life. In the 1930's Brazilian thrust toward assimilation, "ethnic cysts" were seen as dangerous, and nationalistic measures discriminated against and monitored those who were different (de Brito Fabri Demartini, 2010). This is not dissimilar to what may be currently unfolding the Europe, and particularly in France and Belgium, following the five coordinated terror attacks in Paris on November 13, 2015.

We do not know yet what will occur with the Europe-born descendants of the Middle East conflicts, but the response of the *Nikkei* in the middle of the 20th Century was to purposefully establish a Japanese Brazilian identity. Although there were substantial internal disagreements about what that identity would be, it did, nevertheless, carve a distinct cultural, economic, and social niche for the Japanese Brazilian community (Lesser, 2003). The outcome, however, was a "racialization" of this population, both by the majority population and the Japanese Brazilians, themselves, who sought to preserve their identities (Tsuda, 2007). Perhaps history is repeating itself in Europe at the end of 2015 and into 2016.

The size of the current Japanese Brazilian population, at 1.7 million, is substantial. In the 1980s, the profound economic crisis in Brazil, the sense of "otherness" experienced by Japanese Brazilians, and glorification of the ancestral homeland made these *Nikkeijin* look to Japan which was experiencing an economic boom in the 1980s. With the declining numbers of working age Japanese and Japan's preference for cultural homogeneity, the country especially welcomed the decedents of its emigrants who had settled in Brazil. In 1985, there were 1,955 Brazilians of Japanese origin in Japan, but by the end of 2008, this number had burgeoned to 312,582 (*Statistical Handbook of Japan*, 2011), and they currently compose the second largest foreign population in Japan, after the Chinese.

Despite the anticipated mutual attraction between Japan and the Japanese Brazilians, the return migration of the *Nikkeijin* has had mixed results for both the immigrants and Japan. The financial gains to the Brazilian Japanese are substantial and were reflected in the remittances they sent back to Brazil from Japan in the last decade in the amount of $2.5 billion annually (Bendixen, 2006; Tsuda, 2003). The benefit to Japan was the presence of a large contingency of "Japanese" workers. However, it became increasingly clear to both the Japanese and the *Nikkeijin* that there are significant cultural and social differences between the two – most of the latter speak Portuguese and do not understand Japanese, their mannerisms and modes of interaction reflect Latin American patterns, their attire is inconsistent with that of the Japanese, and barring their physical characteristics and names, they are not really Japanese (Personal meeting with teachers, Brazilian School, Tsukuba, Japan, June 15, 2012). Thus, the Brazilian Japanese population is in an oddly unique position. It is "racialized" in both Brazil and Japan. It is a group that does not look Brazilian, yet, since it is primarily composed of the second and third generation children of Japanese immigrants, it is culturally more akin to the Brazilians than to the Japanese.

With its economic downturn, in 2009, Japan began sending back to Brazil large numbers of *Nikkeijin* workers whose jobs were eliminated or were replaced by Japanese workers. In several instances, Japan paid for their trip back, with the stipulation that they agree to never return (Tabuchi, 2009). Brazil was the only Latin American nation, which in 2011, evidenced a drop in remittances to $2.0 billion (Multilateral Investment Fund, 2011) suggesting that there were fewer *Nikkeijin* to send money back from Japan. In an interesting twist of fate, several Japanese Brazilians, since 2011, returned to Brazil on their own volition as the economic deterioration of Japan was been replaced by the growth of the Brazilian economy (Inter-American Development Bank [IDP], 2012) when Brazil was poised to fend off the effects of the global crisis (Biller, 2012).

It is true that often the experience of emigrants' descendants is not as smooth as they anticipate, having integrated into the lifestyle of the host country. It is also erroneous to suppose that returnees, either the emigrant generation or their offspring, sever ties to their host countries as is abundantly evident by responses of migrants moving recently from the U.S. to Mexico, who gave family reunification as their primary reason for return, but indicated that they have strong relationships and family members still in the U.S. and anticipate maintaining those connections (Gonzales-Barrera, 2015). Return migration may include circular migration, but even if it does not, it always retains elements of transnationalism, since social capital and networks persist across borders (Carling and Erdal, 2014) and mobility options in both directions are persistent.

Occuptional Challenges

Much is written about the migration-development nexus, indicating that the connections between the two enhance both, however, with transnationalism, they may pose additional difficulties. Overall, as suggested by Cervase (1974), when return migration is voluntary and individuals are in their working years, they may return as investors and as innovators, enhancing the development of the country to which they return, and perhaps, to some extent, depleting the one they leave. Entrepreneurial activities of returnees are found to be successful when they apply their technological and scientific knowledge, as well as the business skills and cultural norms acquired abroad. Even when returnees' return is based on reasons of family reunification or lack of significant achievements abroad, they are able to engage in innovative activities in the homeland with relative success (Marchetta, 2012).

Remittances to the homeland run in billions of dollars worldwide each year, and in 2013 totaled $583 billion, with projections of $610 billion by 2016 (World Bank, 2015). In addition to adding to the economy, these serve several purposes: support of family in the homeland as well as support of community and services. Expatriates usually see remittances as contributing to the support of their families and communities at home as well as a monetary and social investment for their return. Financial investments in the home community improve one's social stature and standing, ensuring a higher position in the society upon return (Mahmud, 2014). This differs from the position of the innovators or the entrepreneurs who utilize networks and human, social, and monetary capital to develop opportunities for themselves that will, in the long run, benefit the country.

Several Burmese workers are currently residing in Thailand, and the opportunity for returning is imminent as change is expected in the nation's political structure with the November 2015 election of Nobel Peace Laureate Aung San Suu Kyi. These migrants were poised to return, even before the election, as Myanmar's development became evident. The majority of these migrants are agricultural low wage workers who, nevertheless, had better earning opportunities and feared less persecution in the nearby Thailand (Thet and Pholphirul, 2015). With improved public services and more foreign direct investment opportunities as well as deregulation, these migrant workers would highly likely return. If investment opportunities are paired with, or are followed by the development of jobs with appropriate wages, along with political stability, Burmese workers report that they will return (Thet and Pholphirul, 2015).

Conversely, when the "brightest and best" decide to return to the homeland, it is usually for reasons other than to maximize their income. While investment and innovation opportunities may be draws, the final decision regarding return, according to a study of high performing international students from Pacific countries is that it is strongly related to lifestyle preferences and family associated reasons (Gibson and McKenzie, 2011). A very large proportion of top performing students did emigrate, but between one-third and one-quarter of these students had either returned or indicated that they planned to return, and while income was not the overriding or only motivator, migrating in either direction was associated with expectations of salary gains. Return migration, however, can mitigate brain drain, particularly for developing nations, and may even aid in progress resulting in a brain gain by returning augmented talent to the home country (Dustmann, Fadlon and Weiss, 2011). Brain gain has generally been associated with receiving countries in the developed world, but returnees with increased human and social capital may enhance home society opportunities upon their return.

Migration may lead to economic success and it may also result in failure; likewise, the presence of immigrants may improve conditions in a nation, or they may be a drain on its resources. It is evident that if there is a match between the needs of the country and the human capital entering it, there will be fewer occupational challenges, even in the presence of cultural variations. Returning migrants who are in their working years may be faced with occupational challenges, or they may bring to their homeland experience and capabilities that are much needed to improve the economy. Included in the occupational challenges is the intersectionality of social and political conditions, the socio-economic background of the returnee, and gender and gender role expectations.

As aforementioned theory has indicated, those with substantial human and social capital and those with very little capital are the most likely to return to their homelands; the former so that they may innovate or invest, and the latter so that they may find employment. However, human experience rarely lacks complexity. Men may find it relatively easy to utilize the resources and skills acquired in the host country and reintegrate effectively into the homeland, however, women may find it difficult to acquire employment, may find little left of their remittances and may not be able to adjust to life with their native families (Segal and Heck, 2012). They may find it more difficult to navigate the differences between changed and traditional gender roles and may be more likely to retain stronger transnational bonds, distancing themselves from reintegration in the homeland (Vlase, 2013).

The return of migrants to Kerala, India, provides an interesting case study, particularly related to gender issues. While the U.S. recruits large numbers of Keralite nurses because of their training and English language facility, a large number of both female and male Keralites who are less educated go to the Gulf countries. Aware of possibilities of human exploitation, the Indian government has imposed restrictions on the movement of women under the age of 30 seeking domestic work. Males are legally recruited by Gulf state employers for manual labor; however, frequently women are smuggled in to fill domestic labor needs in those countries. These are usually women who are destitute or who have been abandoned or abused by their spouses (Vandsemb, 2014).

Keralite family men usually send substantial remittances, which allow their wives at home to improve their quality of life. In addition, in their absence, the women assume status and decision making power that they may not have had earlier. With the return of their husbands, most retain much of the status and decision making rights they held in their absence. Women who leave their families and children to assume positions as nannies are also able to send remittances, but several experience conflicting emotions regarding leaving children with extended family members. Both men and women return home with accumulated finances and skills, and many are able to maintain a better quality of life. Several males, however, engage in circular labor migration to ensure a steady flow of income. The interesting outcome of these migrations appears to be the ability to raise children out of poverty and to put them on a path toward more stable occupations (Vandsemb, 2014).

The Philippines did attempt to develop policies for return migration, although, like other countries, it does not keep a close count on numbers returning. Since it is a major temporary labor exporting country (with migrant absences for several years), it is cognizant of the need to assist them in reintegrating. Economic reintegration is the most concerning to the government as some studies indicated that only 44% of the returnees sought wage employment upon their return, and of these, only about 50% actually found jobs after returning. A full 39% did not seek employment because they felt the wages offered were too low (Battisteller, 2004). The government did attempt to develop policies to mandate remittances by residents working abroad in order to fund reintegration, but this was not successful.

Labor shortage is evident in several countries and the ability to attract and keep immigrants is low. These countries may turn to the expatriates and develop an active program to attract them. Some countries with declining populations with low birth rates, high levels of emigration, loss of labor and talent, and the inability to replace the "brain drain" may need to take more proactive measures to make the country more attractive to its expatriates. Concerns regarding population loss are evidenced by several countries and researchers indicate return migration as an option. They suggest that migrants with cultural connections to their homelands will find it easier to integrate (Georgiev, 2008; Triandafyllidou, 2010; Iontsev et al, 2010), and others discuss the costs and benefits of the return and reintegration of expatriates to these countries (Heleniak, 2002; Klinthäll, 2006; Shima, 2010; Tsuda, 2003). In the early 2009s, Russia established its 2006-2012 State Program on Providing Support for Voluntary Re-settlement of Compatriots to the Russian Federation, extending financial incentives for people of Russian origin to encourage return to the country. However, this has not been effective in drawing back expatriates in large numbers.

HEALTH AND HEALTHY BEHAVIORS

Although there is some literature on economic and cultural issues facing return migrants, data on their health and mental health is virtually non-existent. Some limited research focuses on the illness and disease, such as HIV infections (Urmi et al, 2015), and a few on the mental health of repatriated refugees (Fu and Vanlandingham, 2010; von Lersner et al, 2008); however, these are insufficient to provide a clear picture of the health of returning migrants. Davies and colleagues (2011) postulate that the health of returnees is just as variable as other factors related to migrants. A great deal is dependent on the lifestyle in the destination country, including their financial status, access to health care, general health norms of the society in which they were living, etc. Some returning migrants are extremely healthy, while others may be frail and with chronic disease, and this reflects health consequences of many aspects of the migration process. Thus, social determinants and risk factors intersect with immigrant and labor policies that allow, or disallow, access to health care services (Davies, et al, 2011). Those with resources may return healthy, others may choose to return to the destination country for treatment when they become ill (Razum, Sahin-Hodoglugil, and Polit, 2005), yet others may have to return because of poor health, lack of access to health care, and consequent unemployment (Clark, et al, 2007). In some instances, men in poor health are less likely to return to their homeland, while women of the same background and culture are more likely to return if their health is failing (Sander, 2007), suggesting different levels of cultural and social support.

There is literature about the "healthy immigrant effect," or findings that immigrants are generally healthier than the native population, perhaps because of the self-selection process. However, over time, this positive differential seems to disappear with acculturation. Hameed and colleagues (2013) found that both female and male returnees to Kerala had a higher rate of chronic disease than did those who had never migrated, and the longer they were away, the higher was the prevalence rate. It is known that Kerala is enigmatic; because in India, where infant mortality is high and longevity is low, the state boasts a mortality rate of 12 per 1,000 and a 74 year life expectancy (Government of India, 2011), not dissimilar to that of most developed nations. Chronic disease (diabetes, cardiac concerns, and hypertension) which is low among the non-immigrants, is surpassed among the returnees by over 50%, risk factors of cigarette and alcohol use are higher among returnees even though education levels for those who did not emigrate is lower. The incidence of chronic disease is found to be even higher and surpasses that found in industrialized countries (Hameed, et al., 2013).

Once again, while literature on the mental health of immigrants, and particularly refugees, is growing exponentially, systematic data collection and analysis on returnees is sparse. Nevertheless, the few studies that do exist reveal that findings provide inconsistent and conflicting information, suggesting that this, too, is much dependent on the interplay of human and social capital. Some found that repatriated refugees evidenced trauma in the reintegration process, which may lead to substantial mental health concerns (Fu and Vanlandingham, 2010; von Lersner et al., 2008), while others suggest that the resilience factor may help reacclimatize people upon their return, but mental health receives little attention (Siriwardhana et al, 2013; Siriwardhana, 2015), so there is little data to support either position.

CONCLUSION

The research of return migration is, in some ways, in its infancy. There have been lone voices calling for evidence based literature to address the experience of this population, the resources it brings, and the issues it faces. Countries of origin appear to be generally unaware of this growing phenomenon, and most have paid minimal attention to the impact of these returnees on their economy, governmental programs, social services, and health care systems. Only purposeful scouring of the extant literature reveals that the size of this movement is growing in several countries, and people are returning not only because of the reasons proposed by theorists in the late 20th Century, but also for other reasons, including family reunification, “homesickness” and the desire to be on familiar territory, and perhaps for other reasons that have not yet been identified or voiced.

It is clear that with the ease of travel and increasing globalization migration becomes attractive and attainable by more people in more countries and in a variety of circumstances. The very opportunities that afford emigration and immigration also give rise to the possibility of return migration, when expatriates of a country return to their homeland. While return migration has not received the concerted attention of researchers, policy makers, and program planners, this growing phenomenon will have considerable impact on countries of origin, destination, and migrants. These will, in turn affect development, trade, human rights, and a variety of other aspects of society, because returnees are migrants who have the largest networks with the greatest interconnections (IOM, nd). It is essential that countries of origin encourage the return of their emigres by establishing policies that facilitate the transfer of capital and technology and that assist them in reintegration (ILO, 2010). The IOM (nd) suggests a comprehensive approach to understanding return migration and ensuring that policies and programs maximize reintegration to enhance development of the home country, ensure health and health care needs are addressed, human rights are not violated, and national security measures are in place.

The process of "Assisted Voluntary Return" is outside the scope of this chapter, but is the assistance that is provided by the IOM to help in the reintegration of certain vulnerable groups who return to their homelands. Assisted Voluntary Return is defined as "the administrative, logistical, financial and reintegration support to rejected asylum-seekers, victims of human trafficking in human beings, stranded migrants, qualified nationals and other migrants unable or unwilling to remain in the host country who volunteer to return to their countries of origin" (IOM Glossary, 2011). This assistance is based on the contributions of donors and may include cash for immediate use or may involve more sustainable reintegration efforts such as help with small business development, employment placement and health, education, and training (IOM, 2011). Receiving governments should turn to the IOM for assistance in developing their own programs. In 2011, the IOM assisted in the movement of 31,134 migrants from 40 host countries with reception and reintegration in 166 countries of origin; another 23,900 received assistance after arrival in their ancestral lands (IOM, 2011).

Researchers de Haas, Fokkema and Fihri (2014), through their large sample analysis of survey data on 2,832 returnees to Morocco, challenge earlier theories about return migration, at both the micro and macro levels. Much of the literature on return migration has looked at the contributions of returnees to the home country and there has been less focus on individuals' decisions for returning. The failure to understand these decisions at a micro level can well be the reason for the failure of governmental policies to attract and retain returnees. In most parts of the world, migration is not an individual decision, nor is return; it is a tool that is utilized by families to distribute risk and, likewise, accumulated assets (de Haas et al., 2014). Hence, the commitment to returning is often high, as the decision is taken collectively for the well-being of the family. This may mean that individual family members or sub-groups of the family return, while others remain in the destination country. The research world is not oblivious to the realization that migration, particularly temporary labor migration, which may last several years, is an outcome of family decision making and influence in migration patterns (Segal, 2008).

Although both developed and developing countries are aware that they may benefit from immigrant human and social capital, and although several have indicated interest in attracting their expatriates, few have made concerted efforts to develop the infrastructure to make the return attractive. In addition to providing economic opportunities and access to health, education, and welfare programs, the returnees' social and psychological needs may also need attention for smooth integration. Literature on the Japanese Brazilians and the returning Irish reveal that governmental policies may not only be lacking in their ability to reintegrate, they may, in fact, be alienating. Just as several migrants decide early that they do not belong in the destination country, returnees often do not wait several years to acclimatize themselves to the country they once left but that differs so greatly from the one they remember. Returnees may well decide they do not belong in their "homelands" and return to the destination country where they lived for several years and in which they may have become increasingly comfortable.

Despite there is a fair amount of information on Brazilians of Japanese ancestry, relatively little attention has be directed to the return of the second and subsequent generations of offsprings of the emigres. These groups are also making the migration back to the ancestral homeland, and many come with significant human capital and large international networks. Countries of origin may see fit to develop immigration and economic policies that will ease their integration and develop training programs that will prepare them to function effectively at both professional and personal levels in their ancestral culture.

The Organization for Economic Cooperation and Development (OECD) (2008) reported that although information on returnees is not closely monitored, departures from OECD countries can be anywhere between 20% and 75% of entrants in that year. This does not indicate whether people move to a third country or return home. There may be instances of secondary migration, when they leave for a country other than the one of origin or they engage in the process of circular migration, returning several times to the destination country, however, about 20% to 50% leave within five years of their first migration. Overall, the return rate does not vary by gender, but there is greater likelihood that mobility is greater when the level of development between the sending and receiving country is similar (OECD, 2008). Clearly, this is a sizable group. Some may require reintegration policies and programs, although several can probably adapt with little difficulty. However, if they are perceived, or perceive themselves, as failures, there may be longer term issues with which the individual, family, and community may have to address.

Davies and colleagues (2011) raise some important points in their summary indicating that that the issue of return migration needs attention, and that the experience and health of returnees, including access to healthcare, may be different among different groups but also different from those of either the native populations or the emigrants. They and Siriwardhana (2015) call for the countries of origin to recognize the unique health and mental health needs of these populations, and suggest that to “maintain and improve the health of returning migrants, multi-sectoral policies at global and national levels should facilitate access to appropriate and equitable health services, social services, and continuity of care across and within borders” (Davies, et al., 2011, p.1). In other words, there is a significant gap in recognizing the needs of this large, and growing migrant group; the world as a whole, and nations individually, need to join hands in addressing their health needs, and other needs, many of which are a reflection of individuals’ human capital and have implications for the nation’s social capital.

The IOM (nd) proposes that three players must prepare for (and are affected by) return: the migrant, the returning government, and the country of origin. When the migrant is prepared for the return, the reintegration process is smoother and avoids the stigma of failure. Countries of origin may establish programs for reintegration with financial assistance, cultural brokering, and counseling. The governments that are losing the migrants may be able to open dialogue, partnerships, and trade agreements with countries of origin, using the returnees’ network of resources. Countries may consider adopting policies that will encourage the return of their emigres or encourage circular migration, recognizing that this may be beneficial for the global economy, for the country of origin, and for the migrant. The ILO (2010) proposes the establishment of visas that promote circular migration for temporary work, with programs for reintegration. In some sectors, there is a growing recognition in the economic, political and social arenas, that the return migration of emigres is a phenomenon which significantly impacts local, national, and international communities and has implications for the movement of people globally. Nations may need to join hands in facilitating the process of return and reintegration so that benefits of networks, acquired knowledge and skills, and life changing experiences can be maximized for the country of origin, the sending nation, and the global community.

REFERENCES

Baba, Y. (2009). Pattern of return migration among Japanese-Brazilians: Who returns to Brazil and why? Paper presented at the 28th International Congress of the Latin American Studies Association, in Rio de Janeiro, Brazil (June 10 – 14).

Bakke, P-J. (2014). *Sharp identities, leaving traces drawing back home: An exploratory qualitative study on the individual choice of return migration.* Thesis study at the Norwegian University of Science and Technology, Faculty of Social Sciences and Technology Management, Department of Adult Learning and Counselling.

Battistella, G. (2004). Return migration in the Philippines: Issues and policies. In Massey, D. S. and Taylor, J. E. (eds). *International migration: Prospects and policies in a global market* (pp.212 – 225). Oxford, UK: Oxford University Press.

Bendixen, S. (2006). The remittance process in Brazil and Latin America. Presented at the 2006 Annual Meeting of the IDB.IIC, March 3 – 5, 2006. Retrieved from http://www.iadb.org/am/2006/doc/SergioBendixeneng.ppt.

Biller, D. (2012, August 31). Brazil economy emerges from slowdown as stimulus takes hold. *Bloomberg News*. Retrieved from http://www. bloomberg.com/news/2012-08-31/brazil-s-economy-emerging-from-slowdown-as-stimulus-takes-hold.html.

Borjas, G. J. and Bratsberg, B. (1996). Who leaves? The outmigration of the foreign-born. *The Review of Economics and Statistics, 78* (1), 165-176.

Bovenkerk, F. (1974). *The sociology of return migration: A bibliographic essay*. The Hague: Martinus NijHoff.

Carling, J. and Erdal, M. B. (2014). Return migration and transnationalism: How are the two connected? *The Authors International Migration, 52* (6), 1 – 12.

Cassarino, J. P. (2004). Theorizing return migration: The conceptual approach to return migrants revisited. *International Journal on Multicultural Societies, 6* (2), 253 – 279.

Castles, S. and Miller, M. J. (2009). *The age of migration: International population movements in the modern world (*4th Edition). New York, NY: The Guildford Press.

Cerase, F. P. (1974). Expectations and reality: a case study of return migration from the United States to Southern Italy. *International Migration Review, 8* (2), 245–62.

Clark, S. J., Collinson, M. A., Kahn, K. and Tollman, S. M. (2007). Returning home to die: circular labour migrants and mortality in rural South Africa. *Scandinavian Journal of Public Health, 35*, 35–44.

Constant, A. and Massey, D. S. (2003). Self-selection, earnings and out-migration: a longitudinal study of immigrants to Germany. *Journal of Population Economics, 16*, 631–653.

Conway, D. and Potter, R. B. (eds.) (2009). *Return migration of the next generations: 21st Century transnational mobility.* London, UK: Ashgate.

Davies, A. A., Borland, R. M., Blake, C. and West, H. E. (2011). The dynamics of health and return migration. *PLoS Med,* 8(6), 1-4.

de Brito Fabri Demartini, Z. (2010). Immigration in Brazil. In Segal, U., Elliott, D. and Mayadas, N. S. (eds). *Immigration Worldwide*. New York, NY: Oxford University Press.

de Haas, H., Fokkema, T. and Fihri, M. F. (2014). Return migration as failure or success? The determinants of return migration intentions among Moroccan migrants in Europe. *Journal of International Migration and Integration, 16* (2), 415–429.

Deenihan, J. (2014). Returned to Ireland? Some emigrants feel out of the loop when they come home. *The Journal. ie*. Retrieved from http://www. thejournal.ie/young-immigrants-conferance-1673340-Sep2014/.

Dustmann, C. (2003). Return migration, wage differentials, and the optimal migration duration. *European Economic Review*, *47*, 353–369.

Dustmann, C., Fadlon, I. and Weiss, Y. (2011). Return migration, human capital accumulation and the brain drain. *Journal of Developmental Economic*, *95* (1), 58 – 67.

Flores, J. (2009). *The Diaspora strikes back*, New York, NY: Routledge.

Fu, H. and Vanlandingham, M. J. (2010). Mental and physical health consequences of repatriation for Vietnamese returnees: A natural experiment approach. *Journal of Refugee Studies*, *23* (2), 160 – 182.

Gibson, J. and McKenzie, D. (2011). The microeconomic determinants of emigration and return migration of the best and brightest: Evidence from the Pacific. *Journal of Development Economics, 95* (1), 18 – 29.

Gill, B. (2007). Homeward bound? The experience of return mobility for Italian scientists. *The European Journal of Social Science Research, 18* (3), 319 – 341.

Government of India (2011). *Annual report to the people on health*. Ministry of Health and Family Welfare. Retrieved from http://www.mohfw.nic.in/showfile.php?lid=1049.

Govert E. B. and Wahba, J. (2014). Do high-income or low-income immigrants leave faster? *Journal of Development Economics, 108* (2014) 54–68.

Gmelch, G. (1980). Return migration. *Annual Review of Anthropology*, *9*, 135 – 159.

Gmelch, G. (1983). Who returns and why: Return migration behavior in two North Atlantic Societies. *Human Organization*, *42*, 46 – 54.

Gonzalez-Barrera, A. (2015). *More Mexicans leaving than coming to the U.S.*. Pew Research Center: Hispanic Trends. Retrieved from http://www. pewhispanic.org/2015/11/19/more-mexicans-leaving-than-coming-to-the-u-s/.

Hameed, S.S., Kutty, V. R., Vijayakumar, K. and Kamalasanan, A. (2013). Migration status and prevalence of chronic diseases in Kerala state, India. *International Journal of Chronic Diseases, 2013*, Article ID 431818, 6 pages.

Hoffmann-Nowotny, J-J. (1978). European migration after World War II. In McNeill, W. H. and Adams, R. S. (eds). *Human migration: patterns and policies (pp.* 85-105). Bloomington, Indiana: Indiana University Press.

Hugo, G. (2003). *Migrants and their integration: Contemporary issues and implications.* Adelaide, Australia: University of Adelaide. Retrieved from http://portal.unesco.org/shs/en/files/3426/10704409801Graeme_Hugo.pdf/Graeme+Hugo.pdf.

Inter-American Development Bank (March 8, 2012). *Report: remittances to Latin America and the Caribbean rose to $61 billion in 2011*. Retrieved from http://www.iadb.org/en/news/news-releases/2012-03-08/report-remittances-to-latin-america-rose-in-2011,9899.html.

International Labour Organization (2010). *International labour migration: A rights-based approach.* Retrieved from http://www.ilo.org/wcmsp5/groups/public/---ed_protect/---protrav/---migrant/documents/publication/wcms_208594.pdf.

International Organization for Migration. (2011). *Assisted voluntary return and reintegration: Annual report of activities, 2011*, Geneva, Switzerland: IOM.

International Organization for Migration (2015). *World migration report*, Geneva, Switzerland: IOM.

International Organization for Migration (nd). *International dialogue on migration: Managing return migration.* Retrieved from https://www.iom. int/jahia/webdav/shared/shared/mainsite/microsites/IDM/workshops/managing_return_migration_042108/presentations_speeches/managing_return_migration.pdf.

IrishEcho (2015). *Returning emigrants face obstacles, forum hears.* Irish Australia online. Retrieved from http://www.irishecho.com.au/2015/07/06/returning-emigrants-face-obstacles-forum-hears/35132.

Jain, S. (2010). *For love and money: Second-generation Indian Americans 'return' to India.* Migration Policy Institute. Retrieved from http://www. migrationpolicy.org/article/love-and-money-second-generation-indian-americans-return-india.

King, R. (1986). *Return migration and regional economic problems*, London, UK: Croom Helm.

King, R. (2000). Generalizations from the history of return migration. In Ghosh, B. (ed.): *Return migration: Journey of hope or despair?* Geneva: International Organization for Migration.

Klinthäll, M. (2006). *Immigration, integration and return migration.* Presented at the International Symposium on International Migration and Development, Population Division, Department of Economic and Social Affairs, United Nations Secretariat, Turin, Italy.

Lesser, J. (2003). *Searching for home abroad.* Durhan, NC: Duke University Press.

Markowitz, F. and Stefansson, A. (eds.) (2004). *Homecomings: Unsettling paths of return.* Lanham, MD: Lexington Books.

Mahmud, H. (2014). "It's my money": Social class and the perception of remittances among Bangladeshi migrants in Japan. *Current Sociology, 62* (3), 412-430.

Marchetta, F. (2012). Return migration and the survival of entrepreneurial activities in Egypt. *World Development*, *40* (10), 1999 – 2013.

Maron, N. and Connell, J. (2008). Back to Nukunuku: Employment, identity and return migration in Tonga, *Asia Pacific Viewpoint*, *49* (2), 168–184.

McGreevy, R. (March 9, 2013). Coming home: The big decision for emigrants. *The Irish Times*, Retrieved from http://www.irishtimes.com/blogs/generationemigration/2013/03/29/coming-home-the-big-decision-for-emigrants/.

Multilateral Investment Fund (2011). *Remittances to Latin America and the Caribbean in 2011: Regaining growth.* Retrieved from http://idbdocs.iadb. org/wsdocs/getDocument.aspx?DOCNUM=36723460.

Münz, R. and Ohliger, R. (eds.) (2003). *Diasporas and Ethnic Migrants: Germany, Israel, and Post-Soviet Successor States in Comparative Perspective.* London: Frank Cass.

Nekby, L. (2006). The emigration of immigrants, return, vs onward migration: evidence from Sweden. *Journal of Population Economics*, *19*, 197–226.

Organization for Economic Cooperation and Development (2008). *International Migration Outlook 2008*. Paris: OECD Publishing. Retrieved from http://www.oecd.org/migration/mig/43999382.pdf.

Razum, O., Sahin-Hodoglugil, N. and Polit, K. (2005). Health, wealth, or family ties? Why Turkish work migrants return from Germany. Qualitative studies with re-migrants in Turkey. *Journal of Ethnic and Migration Studies, 31*, 719–739.

Rooth, D-O. and Saarela, J. (2007). Selection in migration and return migration: Evidence from micro data. *Economics Letters, 94*, 90–95.

Sander, M. (2007). *Return migration and the healthy immigrant effect*. DIW SOE Papers on Multidisciplinary Panel Data Research 60. Retrieved from http://www.diw.de/documents/publikationen/73/74655/diw_sp0060.pdf.

Segal, U. A. (2008), Mexican Migration to the United States: A Focus on Missouri. *Journal of Immigrant and Refugee Studies, 6* (3), 451-462.

Segal, U. A. and Heck, G. (2012). Migration, minorities and citizenship. In Lyons, K., Hokenstad, T., Pawar, M. and Huegler, N. (eds). *SAGE handbook of international social work (pp.* 100 -115). London, UK: Sage.

Siriwardhana, C. (2015). Mental health of displaced and returnee populations: Insight from the Sri Lankan post-conflict experience. *Conflict and Health, 9*, 22-24.

Siriwardhana, C., Adikari, A., Pannala, G., Siribaddana, S., Abas, M., Sumathipala, A. and Stwart, R. (2013). Prolonged internal displacement and common mental disorders in Sri Lanka: The COMRAID Study. *PLoS ONE, 8* (5), e64742.

Statistical Handbook of Japan (2011). Retrieved from http://www.stat.go.jp/data/nenkan/pdf/yhyou02.pdf.

Tabuchi, H. (April 22, 2009). Japan pays foreign workers to go home, *New York Times.* Retrieved from http://www.nytimes.com/2009/04/23/business/global/23immigrant.html?pagewanted=all&_moc.semityn.www.

Thet, M. M. and Pholphirul, P. (2015). The perception of Myanmar development on its return migrants: Implications for Burmese migrants in Thailand. *International Migration and Integration.* First online June 26, 2015.

Tsuda, T. (2003). *Strangers in the ethnic homeland.* New York, NY: Columbia University Press.

Tsuda, T. (2007). When minorities migrate: The racialization of the Japanese Brazilians in Brazil and Japan. In Parreñas, R. S. and Siu, L. C. D. (eds.), *Asian diasporas: New formations, new conceptions (pp.*225-251). Stanford, CA: Stanford University Press.

Tsuda, T. (2009). *Diasporic homecomings: Ethnic return migration in comparative perspective*. Stanford, CA: Stanford University Press.

Urmi, A. Z., Leung, D. T., Wilkinson, V., Miah, M. A. A., Rahman, M. and Azim, T. (2015). Profile of an HIV testing and counseling unit in Bangladesh: Majority of new diagnoses among returning migrant workers and spouses. *PLoS ONE 10* (10), e0141483.

Vertovec, S. (2007). *Circular migration: The way forward in global policy*. Working Paper No. 4. Oxford, UK: IMI.

Vandsemb, B. H. (2014). Gender, work, and social change: Return migration to Kerala. In Nielsen, K. B. and Waldrop. A. (eds). *Women, gender and everyday transformation in India (pp.* 75 – 88), New York, NY: Anthem Press.

Vlase, I. (2013). 'My husband is a patriot!': Gender and Romanian family return migration from Italy. *Ethnic and Migration Studies, 39* (5), 741 – 758.

von Lersner, U., Elbert, T. and Neuner, F. (2008). Mental health of refugees following state-sponsored repatriation from Germany. *BMC Psychiatry, 8* (88), 1-16.

World Bank (2015). *Remittances growth to slow sharply in 2015, as Europe and Russia stay weak; pick up expected next year.* Retrieved from http://www.worldbank.org/en/news/press-release/2015/04/13/remittances-growth-to-slow-sharply-in-2015-as-europe-and-russia-stay-weak-pick-up-expected-next-year.

Zolberg, A. (2006). *A nation by design: Immigration policy in the fashioning of America.* Cambridge, MA: Harvard University Press.

In: Migrant Workers
Editors: Qingwen Xu and Lucy P. Jordan
ISBN: 978-1-63485-272-2

Chapter 12

THE HIGHLY-SKILLED IN HONG KONG 'ASIA'S WORLD CITY'

Narine N. Kerelian and Lucy P. Jordan *
Department of Social Work and Social Administration, University of Hong Kong

ABSTRACT

Highly-skilled migration is a growing phenomenon with young transmigrant professionals (YTP) taking the lead in mobility for work. The Asia-Pacific is a particularly significant talent-attracting region with its global cities vying for talent. This chapter focuses on the territory of Hong Kong, where declining birthrates, talent shortages, and the desire for becoming "Asia's World City" appear to influence policies receptive to this cadre of (preferred) migrants. This chapter continues to highlight highly-skilled migrant attracting policies as a trend within the Asia-Pacific, through the examples of Tokyo and Singapore, which are also looking to gain a competitive advantage and realize world city aspirations. A pilot study on understanding the meaning of place conducted in Hong Kong with British and American YTP is used to reveal the micro-layers of everyday life — the human dimension — providing a glimpse into opportunities and challenges of highly-skilled migration. Changing demography raises critical questions on how Asian global cities, such as Hong Kong, envisage their societies, which may require more holistic policy approaches to address evolving diversities.

INTRODUCTION

Highly-skilled migration is a growing phenomenon with young transmigrant professionals taking the lead in mobility for work. One of the most significant locations for this category of talent is situated within the economically vibrant Asia-Pacific (Matthewman, 2011). This chapter focuses on Hong Kong, where a trend of declining birthrates (Hong Kong

* Corresponding Author: Lucy P. Jordan, Department of Social Work and Social Administration, University of Hong Kong, Pokfulam Road, Hong Kong. Email: jordanlp@hku.hk.

Census and Statistics Department, 2013), talent shortages (Manpower Group, 2015), and a desire for becoming "Asia's World City" (Chu, 2010; Shen, 2010; Law and Lee, 2012) appear to influence policies receptive to this cadre of (preferred) migrants. Twenty years on from Findlay's notion of "skilled transients" as an invisible phenomenon (Findlay, 1995, p. 515), highly-skilled migration, talent attraction and retention have become key and visible initiatives for many governments and multinational corporations in the race for talent. However, what remains relatively invisible are the micro-layers that constitute the everyday lives of highly-skilled migrants in their situated locales as their talents, skills and financial contributions often take primacy in societies that view them as (foreign) workers first. Highly-skilled migrants are "broadly defined by occupation as business professionals, high-tech workers and engineers, medical workers, students and scholars, NGO workers and entrepreneurs" (Ewers, 2007, p. 121) though migration policies often categorize students separately. According to Shachar (2011, p. 415), "The rise and spread of the global race for talent is one of the most significant developments in international labor migration in the past few decades. Yet, it has received only scant attention in academic circles despite its growing prominence in the real world of law and policymaking." Early on, Sassen's (1995 and 2001) work revealed social polarization in the form of a low-skilled vs. highly-skilled migrant inflow binary shaped by world/global city labor demands. Research on highly-skilled migrants, in particular on multinational employees, has been conducted by multinational firms and global consultancies (e.g., HSBC Expat Explorer, A. T. Kearney's Global Cities Index), yet much of these studies have taken a business-centered perspective of talent retention, focusing on employee satisfaction and adaptation to quality of life reports that measure the attractiveness of global cities. Although states/territories may view highly-skilled migrants through a functional lens as human capital supply to address labor shortage demand, highly-skilled migrants are not a-cultural sojourners — they arrive with "embodied cultural capital" (Nohl, Schittenhelm, Schmidtke and Weiss, 2014), dreams, and desires as they interact with local contexts. To view highly-skilled migrants as purely labor-supply may overlook broader motivations of highly-skilled migrants in their mobility and settlement choices. Along with their labor are the everyday human dimensions where work is but one aspect within a wider rationale for situating themselves in the societies where they temporarily 'settle.'

This chapter begins with a policy profile of highly-skilled migrants in Hong Kong. Next, we will explore how young transmigrant professionals are positioned in Hong Kong's (particularistic) world city aspirations. Immigration policy schemes favorable to highly-skilled migrants guide the exploration of global city trends, including other major cities in the Asia-Pacific. To contextualize these macro-level phenomena, we explore the micro-level lived experiences of young transmigrant professionals through their accounts of working, living, and recreating in Hong Kong. British and American 'White' professionals constitute the largest group of highly-skilled migrants in the territory, and data from a pilot study conducted in 2014 in Hong Kong with five British and American young transmigrant professionals will provide discovery on how highly-skilled migrants within the study experience a sense of place in Hong Kong through their residence, workplace, and leisure place(s) where temporal conditions of employment migration and broader aspects of migrants' daily lives reveal opportunities and challenges of being highly-skilled in Hong Kong.

TALENT ATTRACTION: HONG KONG POLICY PROFILE

According to the Hong Kong Immigration Department, the Hong Kong Special Administrative Region has "autonomy over its immigration policy" (Hong Kong Yearbook, 2014). The Basic Law of Hong Kong, a remnant from the days of British colonial rule informs the "entry, stay, and departure" of people from "foreign states and regions" (Hong Kong Yearbook, 2014). Mainland China is increasingly becoming a key source of migration into Hong Kong and in addition to highly-skilled migrant schemes; the One-Way Permit scheme allows a daily quota of 150 Mainland Chinese, generally for family reunification, into Hong Kong. The Hong Kong Census of 2001, 2006, and 2011 illustrates that over 90% of Hong Kong's population is ethnically Chinese.

Table 1. Population by Ethnicity, 2001, 2006 and 2011 (A104)

Ethnicity	2001		2006		2011	
	Number	%	Number	%	Number	%
Chinese	6 364 439	94.9	6 522 148	95.0	6 620 393	93.6
Indonesian	50 494	0.8	87 840	1.3	133 377	1.9
Filipino	142 556	2.1	112 453	1.6	133 018	1.9
White	46 584	0.7	36 384	0.5	55 236	0.8
Indian	18 543	0.3	20 444	0.3	28 616	0.4
Pakistani	11 017	0.2	11 111	0.2	18 042	0.3
Nepalese	12 564	0.2	15 950	0.2	16 518	0.2
Japanese	14 180	0.2	13 189	0.2	12 580	0.2
Thai	14 342	0.2	11 900	0.2	11 213	0.2
Other Asian	12 835	0.2	12 663	0.2	12 247	0.2
Others(1)	20 835	0.3	20 264	0.3	30 336	0.4
Total	6 708 389	100.0	6 864 346	100.0	7 071 576	100.0

Despite sharing the same ethnicity, tensions between Mainland Chinese and Hong Kong Chinese take place in the territory, with the former experiencing social exclusion (Lee and Law, 2013). As the Hong Kong government grapples with this issue, in 2015, measures for attracting a new type of co-ethnic migrant have been introduced. "With their knowledge of foreign languages and culture, the *second generation of Hong Kong emigrants* with a good education background" are seen to be a "valuable source of vibrant workforce" for their parental home-territory (Hong Kong Immigration Department [ImmD], 2012). Injecting the city with this new form of Chinese human capital, the second generation of Hong Kong Chinese emigrants, appears less contentious to a territory with a strongly localized identity as this category of migrants may be deemed as carrying Hong Kong Cantonese cultural capital transferred from their parents as well as espousing knowledge from overseas. Strategies to fill present and projected labor shortages may be hedged through these diversified policies for non-local talent attraction, to "complement" (ImmD, 2015) Hong Kong's shrinking local workforce.

Hong Kong, the Highly-skilled and World City Aspirations

In addition to mobilizing its efforts for attracting Chinese talent to the territory, Hong Kong is seeking professionals from other nationalities to contribute to its workforce. Highly-skilled migrants are woven into the 'Asia's World City' branding strategy, marketing Hong Kong as a "pluralistic and inclusive society" (Brand Hong Kong, 2015). British and American White highly-skilled migrants contribute to this branding endeavor by adding to Hong Kong's population diversity. Despite clustering Caucasian nationalities under one uniform 'White' designation in its 2011 Hong Kong Thematic Report on Ethnic Minorities, the territory maintains a claim to cosmopolitanism and plurality (Brand Hong Kong, 2015). In the Thematic Household Survey Report 39 on Racial Acceptance in Hong Kong with one thousand Hong Kong Chinese persons as respondents, Caucasians were at the top of the hierarchy of racial acceptance after Chinese in a range of indicators, including but not limited to, living next door to a person of a different ethnic group to having family members or employers from a different ethnic group (Hong Kong Census and Statistics Department, 2009). Thus, in addition to government measures for talent attraction, which appear to intake a large number of White highly-skilled professionals, the social climate appears to privilege this particular cadre of migrants. Kapia (2015) notes, "conclusions" by the Hong Kong Government, which deem racial discrimination as "not a serious problem in Hong Kong" are reflective of "why so many ethnic minorities appear to be not faring well across many aspects of life" (Status of Ethnic Minorities in Hong Kong 1997-2014 Report, p. 1). Unlike their ethnic minority counterparts, the majority of the White labor force, largely constituted of British and Americans, work as managers and administrators (40.5%) and 'Professionals/associate professionals' (46.3%) (HKCSD, 2011, p. 4) which is likely reflective of the migration policies friendly to highly-skilled migrants and their countries of origin. Additionally, when analyzed by ethnicity and sex, Hong Kong's White ethnic minorities have the "highest medians of the monthly income from main employment for both males and females" (HKCSD, 2011, p. 84). In a territory where "productivist welfare capitalism" subordinates other policies (e.g., social, cultural, environmental) to economic policy (Holliday, 2000), the economic integration of White highly-skilled ethnic minorities as financial assets to Hong Kong, whilst perceiving lower earning ethnic minorities/migrants as a liability may reflect a financial hierarchy to earning one's belonging. This may underrate the contribution of other migrants such as domestic workers, service industry workers, and construction workers with countries of origin/ethnicities largely represented by the Global South. These migrants also play a pivotal role in global city growth and prosperity. Devaluing their contributions may impede the spirit of pluralism and inclusiveness, putting into question Hong Kong's 'Asia's World City' venture beyond the branding rhetoric and emphasis on global economic connectivity (Chui and Lui, 2009). Despite a seemingly positive positioning of White highly-skilled migrants, their integration within wider Hong Kong society remains to be fully realized as much of their day-to-day lives occur within an "expatriate bubble" (Knowles and Harper, 2009). In terms of highly-skilled migrants, the values and attributes of plurality and inclusiveness (Brand Hong Kong, 2015) highlighted in Hong Kong's 'Asia's World City' branding materials appears mismatched to a fragmented and socially incohesive status quo.

Towards Talent: Key Immigration Policies

Hong Kong has developed a number of immigration policy schemes for attracting and retaining highly-skilled labor in the territory. Key policies include the General Employment Policy, Immigration Arrangement for Non-local Graduates, the Admission Scheme for Mainland Talents and Professionals, the Quality Migrant Admission Scheme, the Capital Investment Entrant Scheme, and the Admission Scheme for the Second Generation of Chinese Hong Kong Permanent Residents. (ImmD, 2012). Under the General Employment Policy, applicants are required to have a confirmed employment offer to qualify and in 2014, a total of 31,676 professionals from overseas were admitted via this policy (Hong Kong Factsheet, 2015). The Employment of Mainland Graduates with Hong Kong Degrees came into effect in August of 2001 and in 2006, a mere 405 Mainland students gained approval to work in Hong Kong through this scheme (Hong Kong Yearbook, 2006). In May of 2008, this scheme expanded into what is now called the Immigration Arrangements for Non-local Graduates, which allows non-local students who have obtained a degree or higher qualification in a locally-accredited program in Hong Kong to remain and work (or leave and be able to return) for 12 months' stay. Under this arrangement, 41,194 non-local graduates were accepted in 2014 (Hong Kong Factsheet, 2015), most from Mainland China. In 2003, the Admission for Mainland Talents and Professionals was instituted to "meet local manpower needs and enhance Hong Kong's competitiveness in the globalised market." At the end of 2014, a total of 74,465 Mainland talents and professionals gained the right to work in Hong Kong through this scheme (Hong Kong Factsheet, 2015). With no sectoral restrictions, senior professionals are allowed intra-company transfers reflecting the immigration figures associated with this scheme. The Capital Entrant Investment Scheme was implemented in 2003 and allows entrants residency in Hong Kong through their investment in permitted investment assets of at least 10,000,000 Hong Kong Dollars without having to join or establish a business. In 2014, 27,997 applicants received approval through this scheme (Hong Kong Factsheet, 2015). As the Admission Scheme for the Second Generation of Chinese Hong Kong Permanent Residents is in its nascent stage, comprehensive data is not yet available for this category of highly-skilled migrants. Hong Kong's policy expansion towards talent sends a clear message that Hong Kong is ready for economic integration of the educated, skilled and financially secure.

In order to increase prospects for talented migrants, Hong Kong's Quality Migrant Admission Scheme introduced in June of 2006 with the "objective to attract talented individuals from Mainland and Overseas to Hong Kong" was implemented with an initial quota of one thousand application allowances (which has now been expanded) through two point-based tests, the General Points Test and the Achievement-Based Points Test (Hong Kong Yearbook, 2006). In 2014, quotas were allocated to 3,097 applicants (Hong Kong Factsheet, 2015). These points-tests signal a utilitarian and selective approach to migrant entry, focusing primarily on the economic contributions of newcomers. Despite formal immigration policy schemes, some highly-skilled migrants may experience precarity from issues of legal status to difficulties with translating professional qualifications (Nohl et. al, 2014). For example, British and American nationals are granted visa-free entry into Hong Kong as tourists. British nationals are permitted six months of stay as tourists, whilst Americans are granted three months of stay in Hong Kong as tourists. Their legal status becomes precarious should these migrants work during this time. To circumvent the duration of stay and status conundrum may find highly-skilled migrants taking a ferry ride to Macau or a short flight to a nearby country, signaling departure from the territory. This, in turn, renews the aforementioned time periods of visa-free stay upon re-entry providing a (precarious) buffer zone until a working visa is obtained. This precarity may go undetected with perceptions of highly-skilled (particularly White) migrants as unproblematic (Piper, 2013) allowing them to blend into Hong Kong's 'expatriate' landscape until status situations are resolved. With increasing opportunities for entry and work through favorable immigration policies towards 'talent' in global cities in Asia, the notion that highly-skilled migrants are "welcome" (Piper, 2013) in a broader sense, remains complex. Immigration policies to attract highly-skilled labor may be moving quicker than societal preparedness for integrating these newcomers.

Trends in Asia-Pacific Global Cities

The trend in Hong Kong towards managing migration through policies that favor the highly-skilled is mirrored across other major cities in the Asia-Pacific. According to Munck, Schierup and Wise (2011), migration provides a "ready-made" labor force with a "flexible" nature in that rights may be restricted and "mobility enhanced." Hong Kong's top-down approach to Asia's World City status in its locale illustrates a crafting of migration policy, which capitalizes on highly-skilled migrants — through access to their labor, authority to determine their conditions of stay, and claims to being a pluralistic city through their cultural capital. The branding of Hong Kong as a world city was advertised through its first chief executive, Tung Chee-hwa's 1999 policy address, stating that "Hong Kong should not only be a major Chinese city, but could become the most cosmopolitan city in Asia, enjoying a status comparable to that of New York in North America and London in Europe" (Hong Kong Government, 1999). In the same year that Tung Chee-hwa advocated for cosmopolitanism in Hong Kong, then Prime Minister of Singapore, GohChok Tong, "spoke of turning Singapore into 'a cosmopolis — an attractive, efficient and vibrant city exuding confidence and charm, and a magnetic hub of people, minds, talents, ideas, and knowledge' at the World Conference on Model Cities" (Ong and Yeoh, 2013, p. 86). Despite clear guidelines as to what constitutes a global city (Cai and Sit, 2003), aiming to become one is à la mode where strategies of self-presentation as 'global, cosmopolitan, multicultural, international, and pluralistic' are employed to attract and gain talent market share.

Singapore. Migration policies in locales of world city-identity construction favorable to the highly-skilled promote this cadre of migrants as productive for their cities/territories. In Singapore, low local birth rates, an ageing population and a shrinking workforce (National Population and Talent Division Government of Singapore [GOS], 2012-2015) echo some of the key issues faced by Hong Kong. Where Hong Kong differs is that Mainland Chinese talent is deemed as more of the immediate competition to local Hong Kong Chinese for jobs when compared to its foreign highly-skilled migrants. For Singapore 12% of the non-resident population falls into this category termed the "higher-skilled" talent. These migrants are presented as "complementing" Singapore's workforce by providing skills/expertise, which Singapore does not possess, in addition to facilitating Singaporean company expansion into regional and international markets (National Population and Talent Division GOS, 2012-2015). In its 2012 issues paper, *Building a good future for Singaporeans*, the Government recognized mounting concerns as its cultural fabric expands with newcomers to the city-state, claiming tighter controls to curb the intake of foreigners into Singapore (National Population and Talent Division GOS, 2012-2015). According to Yeoh and Lin (2012), Singapore's selective immigration policy liberalization facilitates the entrance of highly-skilled migrants whilst "tightening others related to low-skill labor." This demonstrates a particularistic approach to immigration privileging highly-skilled migrants, as seen in Hong Kong.

Government leaders became advocators of cosmopolitanism as a positive by-product of highly-skilled migration. The 1997 and 1999 National Rally Speeches of former Prime Minister Goh called to, "...welcome the infusion of knowledge which foreign talent will bring" signaling that "When Singapore becomes a first-world economy, it will be more international and more cosmopolitan...It will be less Asian. There will be many more people of different nationalities, races, and lifestyles in Singapore. This place will feel and look like any other Cosmopolitan city in the world" (as cited in Wee, Goh and Lim, 2013, p. 78). Contrary to Goh's vision, its traditional highly-skilled migrant group numbers such as that of the British and Americans are being surpassed, in addition to Malaysians, by highly-skilled nationals of China and India (Yeoh and Lin, 2012). Similar to Hong Kong, "a state-engineered 'cosmopolitanization' has been central to [Singapore's] aspirations of top-tier global city status" (Ong and Yeoh, 2013, p. 84).The political astuteness in Singapore's' migration management and its desire to develop as a global city whilst positioning its migrants as innocuous to its traditional ethnic groups (Chinese, Malays, Indians) may continue to be tested as the Government may see itself mitigating social tensions balanced with promoting itself as a talent-receiving hub and welcoming global city(-state). The local-newcomer tensions, reactions to new forms of diversity, are perhaps side effects of labor inflow that governments have been mal-prepared to handle.

Tokyo. Tokyo has been characterized as a global city, which is increasingly experiencing a "withdrawn" role from the state towards one where the state acts as more of a "cheerleader with exhortatory statements about the need for international competitiveness" (Waley, 2007, p. 1485). The adage of Tokyo as a global city was re-introduced by former Governor Ishihara (Yagahi, 2002) during his governance. With declining birthrates and an aging population (Governer Ishihara Policy Speech, 2005), Japan is ramping up its immigration policies in the race for talent as its "peacetime demographic changes of unprecedented scale" have led to labor shortages in both its unskilled and skilled sector (Akaha, 2010, p. 58). In May 2012, the Immigration Bureau of Japan introduced a points-based system providing preferential immigration treatment to highly-skilled foreign professionals. Three years later in April of 2015, this policy was updated with two levels to the Highly-Skilled Professional (HSP1 and HSP2, with the latter providing more perks) status to facilitate the entry of highly-skilled labor through easier procedures. In its 'Concept of Highly-skilled foreign Professionals,' the Report of the Council for the Promotion of Acceptance of Highly-skilled Professionals of 2009 is referenced, stating: "The quality, unsubstitutable human resources who have a complementary relationship with domestic capital and labor," and "the human resources who are expected to bring innovation to the Japanese industries, to promote development of specialized/technical labor markets through friendly competition with Japanese people and to increase efficiency of the Japanese labor markets." The language of complementing the existing domestic labor force reoccurs in the global city talent attraction marketing approach. The Immigration Bureau of Japan (2015) 'Details of Preferential Immigration Treatment' section on its website, explicitly highlights the preferential benefits for highly-skilled migrants. However, despite the positive welcoming of highly-skilled migrants in immigration processing, the social realities provide an alternative view. Tokyo has not been spared the local vs. foreigner conundrum. According to Nagy (2013a, p. 59), with the rise in foreign resident numbers in Tokyo, the perception by some of the emergence of a disruption to its homogeneity is "often articulated as *Gaikokujin Mondai* or 'foreigner problem.'" Nagy (2013b) finds however, that local governments at the city-level of Tokyo, are making strides towards multicultural coexistence more assiduously than national efforts. These strides appear more proactive compared to Hong Kong, which lacks a comprehensive strategy/policy to integrate migrants once they arrive to the territory.

Whilst the intricacies of local (i.e., cultural majority) reactions to demographic changes within its societies may be nuanced across these three global city locales in Asia, the notion of 'foreigner' seems to pervade all three. The motivation to attract talent and address labor shortages appears ripe in these global cities, however the development of comprehensive measures for migrant integration, at the least migrant incorporation, seem to lag behind. Strategies in these global cities, as well as emerging global cities across the region, to address the issue of integration/incorporation may be the next imperative juncture in migrant retention.

On Sense of Place: Lived Experiences of British and American Young Transmigrant Professionals in Hong Kong

Highly-skilled migrants are the actors of highly-skilled migration. To focus solely on the "global political economy" overlooks the notion that these migrants have agency in their life decisions (Ley, 2004). Thus, this draws on material from a pilot study conducted in 2014 with five British and American young transmigrant professionals exploring the notion of sense of place in the global city of Hong Kong. Sense of place "develops from every aspect of an individuals' life experience and that sense of place pervades everyday life and experience" (Rose, 1995, p. 88). Additionally, addressing multiple young transmigrant professional sites of residence, workplace and leisure is deemed important as "…migrants' lives are experienced not just at the level of the city, but also within specific urban sites — in its workplaces, homes, and a range of buildings, streets, and neighborhoods…" (Brickell and Datta, 2011, p. 17). It is not only about the sites of residence, workplace, and leisure places, but also what can be learnt *through* using these sites for enquiry. Thus, a qualitative purview into the lived experiences of young transmigrant professionals can present a more nuanced understanding of highly-skilled migration where macro-level insights may be gleaned through the exploration of the micro-layers of the everyday lives of these migrants (Lai, Collins, and Yeoh, 2013). We define young transmigrant professionals as highly-skilled working professionals between the ages of 18-40. British and Americans constitute the largest numbers of highly-skilled migrants by population (HK Census 2011, Table A105). We have selected this subgroup of highly-skilled migrants, particularly focusing on young transmigrant professionals, for two key reasons. Firstly, in terms of demographic representation, British and Americans are the largest highly-skilled migrant group represented in Hong Kong. Second, young transmigrant professionals specifically are a highly mobile segment in labor migration, arguably because of the earlier phase of career development and lifecourse stage before marriage and childbearing (Kley, 2011). Convenience sampling was employed with informants contacted via transmigrant network correspondence. Informants were screened to fit inclusion criteria, having to respond 'yes' to the following statements in order to partake in the study: "I was born outside of Hong Kong; I am a working professional in Hong Kong between the ages of 21-40; I maintain ties to my home country; I am British or American; I do not intend to permanently reside in Hong Kong; I do not identify as Asian; I do not have any children; I do not have dual citizenship."

A phenomenological approach to enquiry was used in the pilot study, aiming to "guard against…the taken-for-granted prejudices of common sense in everyday life" (Manen, 2014, p. 61). Phenomenological research is not merely interested in the collection of information from informants, rather the "aim is to collect examples of possible human experiences in order to reflect on the meaning that they may inhere in them" (Manen, 2014, p. 313). Everyday life young transmigrant professionals' sites of residence, workplace, and leisure places are used to capture broader possibilities of meaning. Pseudonyms (Mary, Shelly, Brenda, David and Greg) in lieu of informant names are used to bring their stories to life whilst protecting their identities. This pilot study provides insights on opportunities and challenges of being highly-skilled in Hong Kong through the accounts of these five lived experiences.

Lived Experience

Snapshots of everyday life offer a window into the temporary situatedness of young transmigrant professionals in their migration trajectories. The ways in which these young transmigrant professionals share their accounts of living, working and leisure time in Hong Kong helps to reveal social and environmental dimensions of a sense of place. The young transmigrant professionals have lived in Hong Kong for varying periods of time ranging from approximately one year to five years. This next section is divided into experiences of residence, experiences of workplace, and experiences of leisure places to further explore sense of place of young transmigrant professionals in Hong Kong providing insights for state considerations regarding migration policy and migrant incorporation.

Experiences of Residence. Mary has been living in Hong Kong for almost one year. She is of British nationality and works as a producer for a multinational news corporation. She lives together with her British boyfriend in Hong Kong. In terms of her residential choice, Mary states, "*I think we're the only White people in the building, it's quite [a] local place, which we like because it feels more like you're living in Hong Kong I guess*." In terms of sense of place and her residence, M47ary shares:

> "It's a really nice space to live in. I think when we bought furniture, when we furnished it, that's when it started feeling like home because we started buying bits and pieces for a while, so it took a while to get it all together, but once it was like fully furnished, we were like "oh right, we can relax now" kind of thing, that's when it started feeling…"

The notion of furnishing residential space and identifying a sense of place is an intersubjective feature (i.e., intersubjective verification, Seamon, 1979, p. 21) through many of the migrant accounts in this study. Shelly depicts herself as a "*typical English girl*" and has been living in Hong Kong for 18 months. Shelly works in the financial sector and has not lived anywhere apart from England (albeit taking a short backpacking trip through Australia) and finds the expatriate community/spaces as integral to her sense of belonging. In terms of sense of place regarding her residence, she states:

> "I would say it was once I went to Ikea and furnished it with frames and photographs, and rugs; the soft furnishings that make a place feel like home. The photographs, the making it clean, the rug, the bedspread, the textiles, the finishing touches for me is what makes it homey. It takes some time, it took a time for me because I was quite shocked from going from my own lovely house that I've just bought and done up to then coming here and stuff being old and not working and yet it's being so expensive and I want to save money but also want to live somewhere nice so I would say ya it took me a while, but once I got it furnished looking nice with lamps and rugs that's when."

Shelly's residential choices appear interconnected with her neighborhood choices. The Mid-levels is considered a high density highly-skilled transmigrant (expatriate) district.

> "So I am …I've just moved a week ago. But since I've arrived, I've stayed in the same area. It's within 1 minute of each other, my new flat. I've moved to, I live in the Mid-Levels. (um) I know that I pay a premium, but I want to live with all the other Expats, (um) I want to be close to all the nightlife, and all the coffee shops, the restaurants and I wouldn't live anywhere else because it's so local in other places… at least in the Mid-Levels… people there are professionals and they want to live in nice surroundings so you want to live around other people who want to live around in nice surroundings…"

In terms of residential situatedness within a neighborhood, Brenda also shares this sentiment as she remarks of the importance of living in Sheung Wan. Brenda is a human resources manager in her late 30's who lives together with her British boyfriend. The area of Sheung Wan can also be said to be a high-density young transmigrant professional enclave with increasing gentrification in the area. Brenda expresses that she is partial to her residential neighborhood in lieu of the residence itself. She states, "*…I'm a firm believer in, live in the neighborhood you want to live in, don't ever move close to your job. If I wouldn't have followed that I would have been living in Mong Kok and I would have no hope for a happy life in Mong Kok. (Um) and also in the past, I've made the mistake of moving somewhere (um) for work, and then they move the office location.*" Mong Kok has a high density of Chinese residents and Brenda mentions the challenge of forming a social life because of a lack of proficient English users in the area. For Brenda, the residence and neighborhood have been a pivotal piece to her sense of place in Hong Kong. Brenda states:

> "I was going to leave [Hong Kong] after a year, and I was traveling a ton for work and while Hong Kong is a really friendly place, it's really difficult to create relationships when you're there for a week and gone for three. (Like) you know (like) people only call you back so many times when you are never available to do anything. So after the first year I had a friend who kinda just told me kinda get your own flat and just do it, it'll make a big difference. So year two, I got my own flat. At like two and a half [years] I decided to put some

> pictures up and it's just been something that's happen gradually. So (you know) now, after three and a half years, I feel like (you know) I've got my yoga studio, I've got my gym, I've got my laundry place, as silly as it sounds…"

Brenda appears to have embedded herself within her neighborhood. She has established a routine and the personalization of her flat, a common thread shared by Mary and Shelly has lent to her sense of place. For Shelly and Brenda, the social dimensions surrounding their choices of residential habitation are highlighted in their descriptions of not only the residence itself, but also the expatriate community that surrounds them. For Mary as well as David, Mary's British boyfriend who has been living in Hong Kong for approximately one year, the feeling of 'home' emerged when they furnished their home together. David finds that over the time that he has lived in his flat with Mary, they have started to recognize other residents in the building, which is in a more ethnically Chinese neighborhood. David states,

> "You kind of get mixed reception from people — quite a few. So some people who speak really good English, you've obviously go on with and they're all really friendly and like to talk to you, some people who don't speak English are always smiling and happy, like two people talking in two different languages but smiling and laughing and then a few grumpy people. I don't know if they don't like the fact that foreigners are living in the building (um) but people generally on the whole seem quite nice there, so…"

David's awareness of foreigner reflects and environment where designations between local and other are distinct. Although he has chosen to settle in less of an expatriate area and feels at home through furnishing his flat with Mary, the notion that he is residing within a 'local' area raises questions of integration and belonging to Hong Kong.

Like David and Mary, Greg lives in more of an area with local Hong Kong Chinese residents. Greg is in his 20's and has lived in Hong Kong for approximately five years. He works in the environmental consulting sector and is the only informant with a Hong Kong Chinese partner (girlfriend in his case). He initially lived with a flatmate who was also a young transmigrant professional in the area of Wanchai. However, both he and his flatmate ended up partnering with girlfriends and decided to live separately. Greg lives in Tai Kok Chui and he describes the decision-making process as, "*we looked around and we're quite close to her parents now. So just along the railway, just a walk (um) and it's a similar setting so we do have security guards now. We're on top of shopping mall, there's a swimming pool. It looks pleasant (um) a podium area.*" In terms of his sense of place, Greg states, "*I guess part of it was emotional in that it's a big step.*" Living together with his girlfriend and taking the next step in the relationship grounded Greg and he now feels "*settled into a bit of a routine (you know) so I have the gym and I'm trying to do this and we still socialize a lot, there's a lot to see and do but you do feel there is a regularity to your life and it's a bit normal now and I couldn't pin point when I felt that that happened, but…*"

Despite the temporary nature of being in Hong Kong, the notion of feeling settled in one's residence/neighborhood of habitation is key in the lives of these transmigrants. Some find themselves more drawn to majority expatriate enclaves, whilst others situate their lives within more 'local' residencies and neighborhoods. The distinction between local and expatriate places of habitation is recurrent within these migrants accounts counter to the cosmopolitan orientations that Hong Kong as a global city markets. What remains prominent across these migrants' lived accounts, however, is the intersubjective personalization of their spaces as constituent in crafting their sense of place.

Experiences of Workplace. Young transmigrant professionals within these five accounts work in varied sectors. The composition of their workplace colleagues and workplace districts also vary. For Mary, her workplace serves as a social support network, where she sees her life as a normative experience shared by young transmigrant professionals in Hong Kong. In terms of her workplace environment, Mary finds, "*Everyone's really friendly, it's close knit (um) everyone socializes together at the weekend (um) in Hong Kong, everyone's, well most people, are kind of in the same sort situation, I guess, everyone's an expat, well not everyone, but most people (um) ya so the people are very open to doing things together and socializing.*" Mary describes her office as an "*English speaking office, but there are locals*" continuing "*There's definitely more expats, then you've got, I would say, 80% of the expats are of Asian heritage, so ABCs [American-born Chinese], CBCs [Canadian-born Chinese], BBCs [British-born Chinese] or like Korean, Indian heritage (you know) just a real mix, but I'd say and there's also quite a lot of people, I'd say 10 people who grew up in Hong Kong, born here and raised, but have expat parents, so they look Western, but they're Hong Kong, there's a mix...*" The terminology distinguishing highly-skilled migrants and overseas Chinese working in Hong Kong from the local population appears across the five accounts within this sample. Shelly finds the social environment of her workplace challenging, stating:

> "I don't feel a sense of belonging in the Hong Kong office, purely because of the people, the culture, the teaming. There's a huge team, well I think, people in Hong Kong — locals because it is quite local heavy. I think they team differently to how I'm used to teaming. In London, we would go out and drink in a bar together or we'd throw together a little lunch or we would do something where you are frequently bonding with the people and teaming with them. You talk about your personal lives a lot at work. Here, I don't know if they're speaking about their personal lives in another language so I can't understand, but they're not, their culture isn't very (um). They don't drink. They don't really go and go [um] sort of into bars or (like) pubs, or the areas I go so we haven't got much in common..."

Unlike Mary, Shelly mainly works with Hong Kong Cantonese locals at her position-level, noting, "*...at the more senior level, it is all expats.*" There is an undertone of frustration as she discusses perceived cultural differences which she finds make it challenging to form collegial bonds. Shelly does not speak/understand Cantonese, thus part of her feelings of exclusion may be linked with the challenge of working in an office where the majority of her direct work colleagues engage with one another in their native language, despite working in an English-language medium company. For Brenda, the cultural environment at work has also been challenging to navigate. Brenda finds, "*...Hong Kong for example, I mean (you know) working in Mong Kok is not the normal place that most expats go to work and (um) it's a smaller office. It's about thirty people and there's only four of us that are native English speakers, so I think for me the Hong Kong experience has been the most different just because of the language issues and the cultural issues.*" Brenda continues, "*You know the difference when you work in an international environment versus a local Hong Kong environment and so that was very different and so I think the combination of not everyone was excited that I was there. I was never invited to lunch. When I first moved, I didn't have, I needed to hire and build a team so I didn't have anyone on my team that spoke Mandarin or Cantonese so I was dealing with a ton of issues in China so there were just a lot of challenges and things to get* *through.*" In both Shelly and Brenda's experiences of the workplace, difficulty navigating cultural factors appears to evoke challenges to their sense of place, where linguistic and cultural value orientations affect experiences of their workplaces. Brenda finds a distinction between an international office vs. a local Hong Kong office. The lived realities of Brenda and Shelly appear to demonstrate cross-cultural challenges to Hong Kong's cosmopolitanism.

Greg and David find their workplace offices as welcoming environments. Greg is unique in that he works in a shared office space with multiple businesses operating in lieu of a single company, which he describes as an "incubator" and "Google-y" type of place where there are concerted efforts in making the atmosphere welcoming with music in the background, bean bags and a shared pantry to encourage interaction. It is important to note that despite the precarity of Greg's visa status (he is on a 6-month tourist visa, which he renews), he has been able to rent the shared office space and work there without issue. Greg states, "*Everyone's quite open and interested in doing interesting things so, even the staff are always friendly and chat to me, come in and when you're having lunch or whatever. It's just easy to talk to random people and see what they're doing with their business and what they're working on (um) it's a fun environment (you know) but, still not too crazy and you can get on with your work. So ya, I feel very comfortable going there now, definitely.*" The linguistic environment in Greg's workplace is favorable to him, as he describes most of his colleagues as bilingual where the office is comprised of " *...a bit more expats as well. There's quite a lot of people who are, (like) their parents are from Hong Kong, but they've maybe grown up in the US or whatever. So there's quite a few US accents, but so maybe I suppose, they can technically be expats. I don't know what you class them as if they have citizenship or they haven't really. I don't know. So there's quite a really bunch of those. But still, I would say, at least 50% locals, but ya- virtually everyone speaks good English. It's useful for me.*" Along with Greg, David finds a sense of place in the workplace, a multinational environmental consulting corporation, stating:

> "I guess I have my assigned seat (you know). I think not all firms do you know, some have these hot desking things where different people are in and out, but I have my seat and I know where it is and I think I'm lucky enough to have a window seat so I look out at the lion rock, but also I'm just on auto-pilot and go there every day. Sit there for too many hours, 8-9 hours 10 hours maybe. That's a significant portion of my Hong Kong life is actually spent within these confines."

David has had the experience working with both 'Western' and 'local' teams at his workplace. He depicts his experience of working in both contexts, stating:

> "I've just relatively recently moved to a new team, just internal training type thing and a bit of different skill development and I've moved from a team with a lot more Westerners in it to; I now sit in a team where I'm, I was the only Westerner until recently so definitely the sort of social dynamic has changed. (You know) we don't, we don't share the same interests I would have said, but it doesn't stop me socializing with them. They're still nice chatty people, we just have a different perspective on things, I think."

David has been living and working for the longest period in Hong Kong and also has a Hong Kong Chinese local girlfriend, which may contribute to his ability to adjust to teaming with non-Westerners. Although David appears open to the change in teaming, he still distinguishes himself as Westerner in the work context. The binaries of local vs. expat(riate); local vs. Westerner; and overseas Chinese vs. local Chinese are vivid through these young transmigrant professionals' accounts.

Experiences of Leisure. Leisure activities provide us a snapshot into young transmigrant professionals' lives. Where they recreate and spend their leisure time can help provide insights into their sense of place. Although Hong Kong is generally perceived as an urban cityscape, Mary finds:

> "There was another side to it [Hong Kong]. There was the beach, the mountains, the sport and all that stuff has actually become more and more [a] selling point for me of Hong Kong than any of the other stuff."

Mary enjoys outdoor activities and Hong Kong's natural landscape allows her to do so, however she also finds camaraderie through her leisure activities in high expatriate density areas, stating, "*Soho to Wanchai to LKF, yes…the beach. I appreciate having that…bars and stuff, I feel like there's definitely an aspect of that making me feel like I belong because yes, they're generally full of expats.*" Having others surrounding her sharing in belonging to the category of expatriate brings Mary a sense of place. In experiencing more natural landscapes of Hong Kong, Mary finds, "*Even Tai Long Wan, when you go, you see it's 50% expats, which is not reflecting the demographic make-up of Hong Kong…*" Although Mary lives in a more 'local' residential area, her leisure activities largely occur in expatriate environments.

Shelly also shares the sentiment of spending time within areas where there are "*like-minded people.*" When asked where she goes to spend her leisure, Shelly states:

> "I'm terrible. I rarely venture out of the Mid-Levels. I'm a terrible Expat in that when I first came, I wanted to experience the culture, see all the places. On weekends, I will often go to Tai Long Wan. I'm a real beach girl because I'm not from a hot climate, I love when it's hot here. I go on junk boats. We go to Sai…Sai Kung (is it?), Tai Long Wan, and Lantau hiking. I very much love going out to those places when I'm free, but on a night when I come home from work or whatever, I love to stay very close to where I live and going to the bars and restaurants because I pay a premium to live around there, I want to enjoy it on my time off..."

Shelly finds comfort and a sense of belonging within the expatriate community. She is willing to pay a higher price for rent in order to be close to the Soho area, which caters largely to the expatriate community with Western pubs, and international cuisine from Mediterranean fine dining to British pub fare, this area has a large concentration of young transmigrant professionals as patrons. When asked, "Do your places of leisure make you feel a sense of place in Hong Kong?" Shelly replies:

> "Um ya, that's exactly it. It wasn't at work. It wasn't at home. Those are the two places I didn't feel belonging because they were just the opposite of what I'm used to, but I liked, what made me feel a sense of belonging in Hong Kong is the going into bars and the drinking, and the socializing and the dining reminded me of being back home. That's what I would do back home. That's something that is similar, whereas where I live isn't what it's like back home. Where I work isn't similar to back home, but the going out, the drinking and the restaurants are quite similar to back home. The atmosphere is similar to back home; the

people, the food, the wine. It's all similar and then the weather is so much nicer so you can actually enjoy the things."

For Shelly, through her leisure activities, she is able to find her sense of place in Hong Kong. She points to her cultural normative practices to gauge her sense of place by either being similar or opposite to what she is accustomed to. Brenda shares the practices of spending her leisure in the Soho area as well, although she notes trying to challenge herself, stating:

"Ya, unfortunately. My New Year's resolution was that I wasn't going to eat or drink in Soho for the whole year and I think that lasted like a week. (Um) you know last night I went out and met a girlfriend I hadn't seen in a while and we met at La Piola – you know which is all the way down on Wellington. Ya, you do. I think you tend to stay closer to home just because it's convenient."

Brenda self-attests to spending most of her leisure in expatriate-oriented places. When asked if she feels a sense of place in Hong Kong through her leisure activities, Brenda replies:

"…so you know for me when you think about home, a big part of the culture — you know a lot of it is to do with sports and I think a lot of sports. I can't speak for everyone, but as an American it's difficult. You lose everything….I just missed out (um) and so you go to places or social events and you don't even know the rules of the sports you're watching and you've already seen the scores of the basketball games so (you know) what I mean, I think that impacts it a lot. It's weird, it's not necessarily so much as you've arrived, you're settled, you're at home, but at least people are speaking a version of English around you, at least there's foods that you can recognize."

The familiarity of 'home' is challenging to attain for Brenda. However, in engaging in Western actives, there is a degree of culturally relevant belonging. When asked about where he socializes, David replies:

"…I prefer Soho and Central which is close to the bars, but actually nicer and you can talk to people, it's more fun in my opinion. Or Wanchai, it's similar but a little bit of a mix. It's lots of live music as well and fun. Soho is very regimented and nice, but Wanchai's got a lot of weird stuff going on. I quite like it there (um) but then again it's all the same restaurant-bar-restaurant-bar, all clustered together. Everything under one roof almost."

Like David, Greg also frequents mostly Westernized areas, stating:

"Um, starting with the sporting venue, I play rugby as an optional choice, you know. So it's not really the physical venue although it has to be of a certain quality I guess, but it's more where the game is, you have to go there right, I think. (Um) In terms of all my other options, they are food and alcohol related, I think they are more in the Westernized part of town, I think. I don't think I'm limited to those."

However, for Greg, he finds that his frequenting of more Westernized parts of town are also attributed to the preferences of his peers. His peer circle affects his choices for leisure.

Greg states, "*...I think probably more often than not we end up in, well not more often than not, but 60-70% of the time in a more Westernized place and that's not necessarily my choice, it's more a function of the other people I socialize with, which is work, rugby, everything.*" Greg's primary leisure activity is playing rugby with a team comprised of mostly expatriates. When referencing spending some of his leisure in more 'local areas,' Greg states, "*...Ya, I think, I'm also happy in the really local bars where I live, where I may perhaps be the only White person among the Chinese people so...*" Greg's accounts provide for a more open attitude to engage in local and expatriate places, although through his social circles he finds himself in the more Westernized areas. In terms of his sense of place through his leisure activities, Greg points to being able to have exposure to a Western lifestyle within Asia whilst also being able to access more local (Cantonese) culture. Greg states,

> "I think if I was going to live in Asia, Hong Kong and Singapore would probably be the easiest places to come because there is a Western influence and it's almost like a home away from home? You can slip back into, you could almost be in Britain if you're in Soho. But then the more local places, and sports and stuff, that is still very Hong Kong. So I think, it's just you get to choose, which is nice, you know. You don't have to live full-Asian if you don't want to you can go to one of these bars or one of these restaurants and you can get a steak and kidney pie or Sunday Roast or whatever you want or you're favorite type of beer, I think you can find in anywhere now."

The choice to oscillate between cultures is the value-add that Greg finds of living in Hong Kong; he also cites Singapore as an alternative place to live within Asia because of its Western influence. These five young transmigrant professionals' accounts of their experiences of leisure largely are found within the expatriate community and places of Western influence. Familiarity and their cultural practices can be retained within Hong Kong through the 'expatriate' or 'Westernized' places which are culturally relevant to their lives whilst also having the option to engage in more 'local' places. This segmentation is not only visible in Hong Kong's landscape, but it is also apparent through these migrants' lexicon as they largely align their experiences more with an expatriate/Western proclivity.

Insights from Within: Opportunities and Challenges for Young Transmigrant Professionals

These five accounts across sites of residence, workplace, and leisure places have provided a glimpse into the everyday life of young transmigrant professionals and the sense of place created in everyday life in Hong Kong. These highly-skilled migrants identify professional and personal opportunities of living and working in Hong Kong. Being part of a wider young transmigrant professional, or expatriate, community and culturally relevant places (enclaves) allows these migrants to exercise familiar norms and practices in the city from eating, engaging in pub/bar culture, to partaking in group leisure activities, and fostering friendships with other young transmigrant professionals. Working in Hong Kong, in the words of Mary, can be "*a good kind of CV tick*" for Asia experience adding to their portfolios. Hong Kong also provides a gateway for travel to nearby countries, extending the professional opportunities for personal travel to fill one's bucket list.

Nonetheless, young transmigrant professionals are also met with a culturally unfamiliar landscape interspersed with enclaves of familiarity in which to situate their residential, workplace, and leisure activities where they are "*so far from home, sacrificing relationships with family and friends back home so there's got to be a reason for it.*" Although they may be able to exercise more autonomy over residential and leisure choices, the workplace may be less predictable. Those who work with more expatriate/international colleagues may find a working culture customary to their own norms. However, intercultural and linguistic differences attributed to demographic segmentation "foreigner/expatriate/overseas (Westernized) Chinese" vs. local Hong Kong Chinese may pose challenges for some to find bridges of commonality working in more local office environments. Further, English is a key linguistic factor to sense of place as migrants within this sample do not speak/understand Cantonese. Although, some migrants within this study shared being able to oscillate between local and expatriate environments, the term "expatriate" was key in the interview process and in the positioning of understanding sense of place.

Conclusion

Global cities within Asia are increasingly becoming centers of highly-skilled migrant attraction. The young transmigrant professionals' accounts within this study illustrate how these migrants create a sense of place, albeit transitory. Departure from Hong Kong as an inevitable event in the future echoes through their accounts. Whilst many highlight the professional and personal growth opportunities afforded by their sojourn and the ease of immigration procedures (afforded by favorable migration policies), there is also a notion that there are opportunity costs of migration, whether it is friends, family, familiarity of cultural norms or geographic orientation. These five accounts provide a glimpse into the spectrum of possibilities in experiencing sense of place within Hong Kong. The thread that binds these accounts is an awareness of the temporariness of their situations with prospects of unknown next stops on their mobility trajectories as Hong Kong is not forever and departure is in the horizon. These micro-level intentions of leaving seem counter to the macro-level strategies of global cities, such as Hong Kong, Singapore, and Tokyo where talent attraction and *retention* to fill labor gaps for addressing part of their demographic malaise primarily focus on highly-skilled migrants situating their lives within their borders. The accounts within this study bring to international highly-skilled migration the very complex human dimension — personal and professional goals, dreams and desires, which may transcend the boundary-ed aspirations of global cities such as Hong Kong to territorially retain highly-skilled migrants.

These young transmigrant professionals' accounts also depict how they situate their lives in Hong Kong amongst its existing majority population. As with other Asian global cities, although English may be useful as a language in which to navigate the city, there is an understanding of being an other, most notably an "expatriate" in colloquial terms, which is segmented from the local or resident population whether it be through residential enclaves of expatriate habitation or spatial delineations of highly-skilled migrant density in workplaces and leisure places, there is an incohesive element represented through the varying levels (social, economic, cultural) of fragmentation. Issues of local vs. foreigner are not new to global cities. However, with the rising numbers of highly-skilled migrants and the relative prosperity, which this cadre of migrants enjoys in relation to the local population of global cities, immigration policies alone may not be enough. These policies are geared towards attracting talent to their shores, yet further efforts may need to be employed for understanding growing mobilities and diversities in global cities.

There appears to be a gap between policies to attract talent versus policies to incorporate and retain talent. Young transmigrant professionals within the study were clear to express that Hong Kong was a temporary place for them to work and live, ruling out settlement within the territory. Hong Kong and other highly-skilled migrant attracting cities may have to take a deeper look into this matter. Is revolving door highly-skilled migration sustainable for Hong Kong and neighboring global cities? With Hong Kong lacking a formal multicultural policy, it has turned to its immigration policies for economic integration of migrants (Nagy, 2013b). However, solely relying on economic integration may not be enough as young transmigrant professionals arrive with cultural and linguistic practices differing from those of mainstream Hong Kong society. Further, for those who are outside of the ethnic majority, this may contribute to a further degree of separation in the absence of polices to prepare societies, particularly those which are more homogeneous, for growing diversity.

With global cities in Asia increasingly being challenged to address their growing diversities, laissez-faire approaches may fall short of sustaining social harmony within their societies. The zeal in which Asian global cities, such as Hong Kong, have approached highly-skilled migrant attraction may now have to be invested in policies towards incorporation and retention. Young transmigrants professionals could be viewed as more than labor supply to meet Hong Kong's workforce shortages. Changing demography comes with critical questions on how these Asian global cities envisage their future societies, which may require more holistic policy approaches to address their evolving social realities.

REFERENCES

Akaha, T. (2010). International migration and multicultural coexistence in Japan: Resistance and accommodation to change. *The Journal of Asiatic Studies*, *53*(2), 57-101.

A. T. Kearney. (2015). *Global cities index*. Retrieved from https://www.atkearney.com/research-studies/global-cities-index/2015.

Brand Hong Kong. (2015). Retrieved from http://www.brandhk.gov.hk/en/#/.

Brickell, K. and Datta, A. (2011) Introduction: Translocal geographies. In Brickell, K. and Datta, A. (ed.), *Translocal geographies spaces, places, connections (pp.* 3-20). Farnham: Ashgate.

Brooks, A. and Wee, L. (2015). *Consumption, Cities and States: Comparing Singapore with Asian and Western Cities*. Anthem Press.

Cai, J. and Sit, V. F. (2003). Measuring world city formation–The case of Shanghai. *The Annals of Regional Science*, *37*(3), 435-446.

Chiu, S. and Lui, T. L. (2009). *Hong Kong: becoming a Chinese global city*. Routledge.

Chu, S. (2010). Brand Hong Kong: Asia's world city as method? *Visual Anthropology, 24*(1-2), 46-58.

Ewers, M. C. (2007). Migrants, markets and multinationals: competition among world cities for the highly skilled. *GeoJournal*, *68*(2-3), 119-130.

Findlay, A. (1995). Skilled transients: The invisible phenomenon? In Cohen, R. (ed.),*The Cambridge Survey of World Migration* (pp. 515-522), Cambridge: Cambridge University Press.

Holliday, I. (2000). Productivist welfare capitalism: Social policy in East Asia. *Political studies*, *48*(4), 706-723.

Hong Kong Census and Statistics Department (2009). *Thematic household survey report: 39 on racial acceptance in Hong Kong.*Retrieved from http://www.statistics.gov.hk/pub/B11302392009XXXXB0100.pdf.

Hong Kong: Census and Statistics Department (2011). *Thematic report: Ethnic minorities.*

Hong Kong Census and Statistics Department (2011). Population by ethnicity, 2001, 2006 and 2011 (A104).Retrieved from http://www.census2011. gov.hk/en/main-table/A104.html.

Hong Kong Census and Statistics Department (2011). Population by nationality, 2001, 2006 and 2011 (A105).Retrieved from http://www. census2011.gov.hk/en/main-table/A105.html.

Hong Kong Census and Statistics Department (2013). *The fertility trend in Hong Kong, 1981 to 2012.*Retrieved from http://www.statistics.gov.hk/pub/B71312FA2013XXXXB0100.pdf.

Hong Kong Factsheet (2015). Retrieved from http://www.gov.hk/en/about/abouthk/factsheets/docs/immigration.pdf.

Hong Kong Immigration Department (2012). *Admission scheme for the second generation of Chinese Hong Kong permanent residents.*Retrieved from http://www.immd.gov.hk/eng/services/visas/secondgenerationhkpr.html.

Hong Kong Immigration Department (2015). *Enhancement measures on admission schemes for talent, professionals and entrepreneurs.*Retrieved from http://www.immd.gov.hk/eng/faq/enhancement-measures-on-admission-schemes.html#Admission.

Hong Kong Yearbook (2006). *Population and immigration.*Retrieved from http://www.yearbook.gov.hk/2006/en/20_01.htm.

Hong Kong Yearbook (2014). *Population and immigration.*Retrieved from http://www.yearbook.gov.hk/2014/en/pdf/E17.pdf.

HSBC (2015).*Expat explorer: Balancing life abroad.* Retrieved from https://expatexplorer.hsbc.com/survey/files/pdfs/overallreports/2015/HSBC_Expat_Explorer_2015_report.pdf.

Immigration Bureau of Japan (2015). Retrieved from http://www.immi-moj.go.jp/newimmiact_3/en/system/index.html.

Ishihara, S. (2005). *Policy speech by the governor of Tokyo, Shintaro Ishihara,* the First Regular Session of the Tokyo Metropolitan Assembly, February 23, 2005. Retrieved from http://unpan1.un.org/intradoc/groups/public/documents/apcity/unpan021946.pdf.

Kapai, P. (2015). *Status of ethnic minorities in Hong Kong 1997 -2014.* Hong Kong: Faculty of Law, The University of Hong Kong.

Knowles, C. and Harper, D. (2009). *Hong Kong: migrant lives, landscapes, and journeys.* University of Chicago Press.

Kley, S., (2011). Explaining the stages of migration within a life-course framework. *European Sociological Review,27(*4), 469–486.

Law, K. Y. and Lee, K. M. (2012). The myth of multiculturalism in 'Asia's world city': incomprehensive policies for ethnic minorities in Hong Kong. *Journal of Asian Public Policy*, *5*(1), 117-134.

Lee K. M and Law K. Y. (2013). Social exclusion in the "pluralistic and tolerant" society: Ethnic minorities in Hong Kong. In Law K. Y and Cheng Y. S. (eds.), *On the chessboard: Donald Tsang's legacy for C Y Leung (pp.* 333-358), Hong Kong: City University of Hong Kong Press.

Ley, D. (2004). Transnational spaces and everyday lives. *Transactions of the Institute of British Geographers*, *29*(2), 151-164.

Manpower Group. (2015). *Talent shortage survey.*Retrieved from http://www.manpowergroup.com.

Matthewman, J. (2011). *The rise of the global nomad how to manage the new professional in order to gain recovery and maximize future growth.* London: Kogan.

Munck, R., UlrikSchierup, C. and Delgado Wise, R. (2011). Migration, work, and citizenship in the new world order. *Globalizations*, *8*(3), 249-260.

Nagy, S. R. (2013a). *Local government migrant policies in Tokyo, Japan: National exclusion, local inclusion*. Edwin Mellen Press.

Nagy, S. R. (2013b). Politics of multiculturalism in East Asia: Reinterpreting multiculturalism. *Ethnicities*, *14*(1), 160-176.

National Population and Talent Division Government of Singapore (2012-2015). Retrieved from http://population.sg/introduction/#.Vl23tWQrJdh.

Nohl, A. M., Schittenhelm, K., Schmidtke, O. and Weiss, A. (2014). *Work in transition: Cultural capital and highly-skilled migrants' passages into the labour market*. University of Toronto Press.

Ong, F. and Yeoh, B. (2013). The place of migrant workers in Singapore between state multiracialism and everyday (un)cosmopolitanisms. In Lai, A. E., Collins, F. L. and Yeoh, B. S. (eds.) *Migration and diversity in Asian contexts (*pp. 83-106).Institute of Southeast Asian Studies.

Piper, N. (2013). *New perspectives on gender and migration: Livelihood, rights and entitlements*. Routledge.

Rose, G. (1995). Place Identity: A sense of place. In Massey, J., Jess, P. and Massey, D. (eds.*), A place in the World? Places, cultures, and globalization (*pp.88-132). Oxford: The Open University.

Sassen, S. (1995). On concentration and centrality in the global city. In P. Knox and P. Taylor (eds.), *World cities in a world system* (pp. 63–78). Cambridge: Cambridge University Press.

Sassen, S. (2001). *The global city: New York, London, Tokyo*. Princeton University Press.

Seamon, D. (1979). *A Geography of the Lifeworld: Movement, Rest, and Encounter.* London: Croom Helm.

Shachar, A. (2011, March). Highly-skilled immigration: The new frontier of international labor migration. *Proceedings of the 105th Annual Meeting* (Vol. 105, pp. 415-419).American Society for International Law.

Shen, S. (2010). Re-branding without re-developing: Constraints of Hong Kong's 'Asia's World City' brand (1997–2007).*The Pacific Review,* 203-224.

Van Manen, M. (2014).*Phenomenology of practice: Meaning-giving methods in phenomenological research and writing*. Left Coast Press.

Wah, T. C (1999). *1999 policy address by Chief Executive.*Retrieved from http://www.info.gov.hk/gia/general/199910/06/address1.htm.

Waley, P. (2007). Tokyo-as-world-city: Reassessing the role of capital and the state in urban restructuring. *Urban Studies*, *44*(8), 1465-1490.

Yagahi, H. (2002). Tokyo no risutorachuringu to sekaitoshi no yumefutabi [Tokyo's restructuring and the dream of world city again]. In T. Kodama (ed.) *DaitoshikenhenoKoso* [Perspectives on the Restructuring of Metropolitan Areas] (135-164), Tokyo: Tokyo University Press.

Yeoh, B. and Lin, W. Q. (2012). *Rapid growth in Singapore's immigrant population brings policy challenge*s. Migration Policy Institute. Retrieved from http://www.migrationpolicy.org/article/rapid-growth-singapores-immigrant-population-brings-policy-challenges.

EPILOGUE: THE WAY FORWARD

Lucy Jordan[*] *and Qingwen Xu*[†]

This volume has drawn primarily on empirical research conducted with diverse (im)migrant populations across the globe to address issues of social identity, occupational challenges and health practices. These three topics cut across the significant diversity of global sending and receiving locations, both within and between, national borders and are significant issues for migrants and their families regardless of many characteristics including demographic characteristics, socioeconomic background, and occupational niche. In the introductory chapter we argue that the social and economic outcomes of migration on the lives of migrants and their families, as well as their communities where they live, are the results of incoherent and incomplete global governance institutions and mechanisms that fail to adequately regulate and facilitate the social protection of welfare of migrants. The chapters in this volume have covered a wide range of migrant workers, and offered examples of their personal, family, occupational and institutional experiences to illuminate the challenges they face in achieving well-being even as they remain committed to bettering the lives of their families and communities, in origin countries and new host countries and communities.

The edited volume is divided into three parts focusing on (1) precarious jobs, low-skill workers and health and mental health; (2) internal migration; and (3) mobility and social identity. While these sections bring together common themes, an overview of the volume highlights the challenges all migrants and 'people on the move' face — challenges to financial security, social integration, life satisfaction, health and well-being. Almost unanimously the authors highlight a need for governments both national and local and transnational organizations to take a lead in promoting and supporting the development of policies and service strategies to help alleviate persistent social exclusionary impacts of migration. The authors draw on data from individual people, both migrants and their families in the case of Samson and Acejo (Chapter 9), to illustrate the critical contributions migrants

[*] Department of Social Work and Social Administration, University of Hong Kong.
[†] School of Social Work, Tulane University.
Editor of the Book: Lucy P. Jordan, Department of Social Work and Social Administration, University of Hong Kong, Pokfulam Road, Hong Kong. Email: jordanlp@hku.hk.
Editor of the Book: Qingwen Xu, School of Social Work, Tulane University, 127 Elk Place, New Orleans, LA 70112, USA. Email: qxu2@tulane.edu.

make to the contemporary global economy, while uncovering amongst sub-populations of immigrants tenacious disadvantage, and perhaps, surprisingly challenges facing "more successful" migrants — young professionals in high-skill occupations (Kerelian and Jordan) and voluntary return migrants (Segal). The recurrent themes of challenge and exclusion are accompanied by the hope and diligence which migrants, their families, and communities cultivate and practice as they seek to better their lives in what is truly an "age of migration" (Castles 2013).

In addition to highlighting the challenges through the experiences of migrants and their families, the chapters in this volume offer a number of policy and practice solutions which are grounded in empirical work. These solutions can be roughly categorized into:

1. Legal and regulatory frameworks that are enforceable and address the realities of diverse migrants;
2. Partnerships between sending and receiving governments, as well as non-governmental organization, to facilitate the pre- and post- migration experiences;
3. Culturally responsive interventions to address individual, familial and community stress associated with separation and integration; and
4. Community interventions to prepare receiving/host societies to partner in social integration of diverse groups of migrants.

In this final brief Epilogue, we seek to synthesize the intersectionality among the individual chapters, highlight the broader implications for evidence-based practice and policy in migration studies, and present a preliminary roadmap for 'a way forward'.

Government Responsibility

Governments and civil society organizations have an important role to play in establishing and regulating occupation and industrial standards. Large section of the world's migrant labor is in low-skill, low-end occupational sectors, and the existence of legally binding contracts does not necessarily ensure protection. On the one hand, a fixed term contract offers relative stability for migrant laborers vis-à-vis legally binding contracts for set duration of employment, and stipulating minimum standards thus addressing some of the occupational challenges migrant workers face. Throughout the Asian region, fixed term migration is well documented as the region consists of sending countries and many critical receiving destinations of female migrant domestic workers, as well as male seafarers and semi-skilled manufacturing and construction workers. On the other, while contract labor does afford some protections, for example, legal employment agreements, as discussed by Matthew and Sugrue (Chapter 2) and Jaffe and Weng (Chapter 10), the presence of a legal contract does not ensure that migrants are truly protected from violations to their human rights and contractual agreements. These two chapters illustrate the linkages between the occupational conditions — and vulnerabilities — experienced by two highly gendered migration streams, female domestic and care workers and male seafarers within the globalized circuits of migration, where unequal partners contribute to vulnerable occupational conditions. For female migrant women, the domestic care they provide is often operated outside or in the shadows of state regulation, meaning that enforcement of rights violations can be difficult given power differentials and the private domestic sphere of employment (Kontos and Bonifacio, 2015). For male seafarers, multiple sovereign nations, which should be active players in one shipping vessel, in fact result in the lack of any singular legal framework to protect the interests of migrant workers who often travel outside any sovereign nation's international waters, further compounding the 'who is responsible' question.

There is a compelling need for advocacy and intervention to educate and facilitate the attainment of appropriate legislations and international collaborative mechanisms for the exercise of rights. While the shipping industry is an excellent example of how sovereign regulation fails to address the migrant seafarers' vulnerability, the regulatory frameworks for migrant domestic workers are more bound to national sovereign legalistic frameworks as most domestic labor occurs within one national jurisdiction. The failure to protect here is better represented by divergent rights given to the workers across sovereign nations as well as low accountability and lack of enforcement within jurisdictions. For example, Hong Kong offers relatively liberal protective legislation (Constable, 2014) ensuring minimum pay, statutory holidays and weekly rest days, and mandatory two week maternity coverage compared to Singapore — although recent changes have occurred in favor of migrant rights — where minimum pay is relatively lower, paid leave is less generous, and pregnancy is forbidden with mandatory testing and positive pregnancy is grounds for break of contract and deportation to origin country (Huang and Yeoh, 2007). Given such differences, Filipino and Indonesian domestic workers either endure such rights-deprivation situation in Singapore, or face unpredicted contract termination during economic downturns in Hong Kong; neither governments lack the motivation to enforce migrant domestic workers' rights to decent work (Hickey, Narendra, and Rainwater, 2013).

The lack of attention to lifecycle and the 'humanness' of migrants is not confined only to the low-skill and low-wage end of migrant workers, as reflected in Kerelian and Jordan (Chapter 12) where the topic is on an often-neglected population, young professional migrants in relatively high-status occupations in Hong Kong. Skilled migrant workers are generally considered comparative privileged, thus perhaps not as prone to the risks associated with more economically precarious low-skilled migrants. The analysis young professional migrants in Hong Kong highlights how regional strategies may encourage competition among different migrant receiving destinations, which could translate into improved occupational conditions as governments vie for talent, possibly supporting positive health and well-being outcomes amongst this migrant group at a minimum. The analysis, however, illuminates how even in an era of competition for global talent, national policy approaches may be falling short of optimal design in retaining the pool of talent migration, thus failing to address the longer term lifecycle of this sought after migrant workers.

Nonetheless, in migrant receiving cities and countries, policies and practices do demonstrate clear divergent strategies towards different types of migrants, which highlights an inequitable policy approach. For example, in the case of Hong Kong and almost all other countries, talent migrants do have a pathway to permanent settlement; but foreign domestic workers are explicitly excluded from such a right of permanent settlement (Constable, 2014) as represented in legal proceedings in 2013 which explicitly denied permanent residency status to foreign domestic workers (Vallejos and Domingo v. Commissioner of Registration). The different classification of migrants all provides important, and indeed essential functions to host societies, and equality in access to social and citizenship rights should not be a privilege afforded only to a few.

This issue of equal accessibility to social and economic rights also concerns internal migrants as is clearly articulated by Ma and Wu (Chapter 8) in their case study of contemporary China, and the mismatch between the historical and currently necessitated welfare boundary. Their argument demonstrates the relevance of considering how the local boundaries within large and dynamically growing countries and/or emerging economies such as China, India, and Vietnam reflect similar conflicts with international boundaries globally; in both instances migrants often face restricted access to basic services and opportunities which are afforded to local residents even as the migrants make substantial contributions to the social and economic development of host societies and communities. This theme of exclusion and marginality is re-emphasized by Le, Nguyun and Nguyun, (Chapter 6) as well as Borhade and Zhang (Chapter 7) in their exploration of rural-to-urban migration in Vietnam and India.

SOCIAL EXCLUSION AND INTEGRATION

As an echo perhaps to the challenges more temporary migrants face, Hilado and Lundy and Li, Ramos and Do (Chapters 3 and 5) reveal the longer term outcomes of ethnic and occupational segmentation in host societies, suggesting that a pathway to citizenship alone may not be a singular panacea to well-being and social integration. Li and colleagues (Chapter 3) evidence how, despite arriving to the mainland U.S. as citizens, Puerto Rican women are no different from Mexican female immigrants who lack similar citizenship rights. This chapter highlights the profound impact of gender, race and culture related struggles, prejudice and discrimination in the United States, but the findings should serve as a warning to other countries and locations as well, where diverse populations with differing claims to citizenship struggle against similar socially exclusionary conditions. This point has particular relevance for the current global crises of refugees and social conflicts, most notably occurring in the European Union. Extensive global migration flows are not a new phenomenon; however, the current era appears to be one increasingly marked by social conflicts and unpredictability in many traditional destinations of immigration as national governments struggle to incorporate diverse populations and address inequalities — social, ethnic, and economic — at a time when the global economic growth continues to remain uncertain. Some scholars (e.g., de Haas, 2010) argue that a climate of steady economic growth would facilitate the integration of diverse sub-populations into host societies; however this argument is neither valid as economic risks continue to rotate toward various markets, nor bode well for the integration of migrants in the current era.

The focus on the critical commitment needed from government and other institutional bodies is not to say that community and grassroots organizations do not have a role to play in facilitating positive outcomes for migrants and their families. Le, Nguyen and Nguyen (Chapter 6) highlight how the absence of support is strongly indicated in day-to-day struggles on informal and precarious rural-to-urban migrants in Vietnam. It is not surprising that these migrants predominantly working in unregulated and informal employment reveal a very vulnerable portrait of the precarious nature of migration, which does not benefit from government protections that albeit partially inadequate exist in regulated flows of migration within other countries of high internal migration like China as well as international migration such as foreign domestic workers and seafarers. Hidalgo and colleagues (Chapter 3) underscore the importance of informal social support networks in facilitating the acculturation process, on emotional and practical (economic) levels, sketching the positive impact social support can make in comparison to Le, Nguyen and Nguyen. Their analysis of Mexican women in Chicago demonstrates how social support networks help migrants to achieve financial stability while also offering social-emotional and cultural benefit beyond the economic benefits. Thus, an important question to ask is, beyond the intention to regulate migration, how can governments and host societies facilitate the development and sustainability of such supporting social networks? The feasibility of the promotion of strong civil society networks within host societies is fragile in many contexts. For example, in China and Vietnam, the operational space for grassroots organizations is constricted by government laws of suppression (Spires, 2011; Spires and Chan, 2014; Stern and O'Brien, 2012; Xiao and Lin, 2015), while there is also increasingly hostile environment to some grassroots movements in traditional immigrant receiving countries such as the US and within Europe fueled by concerns about terrorism and links with immigrant populations (Gould and Klor, 2015). This presents somewhat of a challenge to institutional bodies, specifically, how to promote what is considered desirable grassroots social support while maintaining social cohesion.

Government contracting of services is one potential mechanism which can be utilized to encourage the development of specific types of organizations and services, as many grassroots organizations lack adequate financial support. There is a well-established body of literature that examines the complex interplay between governments and civil society organizations (CSO) demonstrating how these aspects of conditionality operate in the relationship between CSOs and governments (e.g., Smith and Lipsky, 1993; Pekkanen, Smith and Tsujinaka, 2014). There remains open debate about how the balance of creative synergy of civil society and government regulation can best be obtained, as too tight government regulation may suppress grassroots solutions or cause them to operate outside of government regulation. Thus the exploration of this area merits further attention. Unfortunately, in the current climate rational debates about the balance of government and grassroots-community based approaches is, on the one hand in countries like China overshadowed by the suppression of many CSOs, and on the other in countries like the U.S. overshadowed by deeply divisive and partisan politics which detracts from reasonable exploration of more rational policy approaches.

The importance of more localized community-based responses is also highlighted by Sen and Aguilar (Chapter 4) who examine the linkages between HIV/AIDS and migration in Sub-Saharan Africa. They argue that the prevention and interventions with HIV/AIDS in the context of migration needs to focus on mitigating the social disruption that so often accompanies migration events, and specifically call for interventions to target generating community social capital in addition to current prevention and intervention efforts that more narrowly focus on behavior modification. This approach reflects a respect for indigenous knowledge and cultural practices that draw on resources within local communities, which is particularly relevant in regions like Sub-Saharan Africa where the importation of ideologies and practices from foreign destinations can result in the continued dominance of non-indigenous knowledge building, replicating centuries of colonial and post-colonial practices.

Promoting the support and maintenance of more informal and grassroots solutions to address challenges amongst migrants is not meant to offer a free-pass to government, nor to the private sector either, as both government and private sector institutions benefit significantly from the current global migration regime. The partnership between governments and the private sector is a significant driver of global migration with economic growth and profit maximization as primary goals, and in democratic countries, everyday citizens also play a key role in supporting the global world order that includes gross social and economic inequalities. This is illustrated by how the lack of authentic legal and regulatory frameworks between flag nations (government) and vessel owners contributes to precarity in the occupational and personal lives of seafarer migrants presented by Jaffee and Weng (Chapter 10). In this instance it is the failure of adequate legally binding and enforceable regulations that result in an ambiguously defined but powerful partnership outside formal structures between government and the private sector, a partnership with dire consequences for the individual migrants who have little recourse to stand against powerful state and business interests.

Segal's Chapter 11 on return migration offers an alternative perspective of how partnerships amongst multiple stakeholders can be mutually beneficial. A coordinated policy approach to return migration that involves the migrant, native origin government and country of immigration provides an important example of best practices involving sending and receiving locations as well as individual migrants. Similar to established best practice knowledge about preparation for out-migration (implication here is that best practice *knowledge* does not necessarily translate into best practice *implementation*), preparation for migrants to successfully reintegrate would help all stakeholders. The involved government parties need to recognize the fluid and changing nature of global migration trajectories, which could serve as a generative opportunity to capitalize on changing global economic and social conditions in countries of origin and destination. One-way immigrant trajectories may not reflect the 21st century reality of a connected and globalized world as well as they did during eras of less sophisticated transport and communication networks. Although in reference to return migration, Segal's closing statement — *Nations may need to join hands in facilitating the process of return and reintegration so that benefits of networks, acquired knowledge and skills, and life changing experiences can be maximized for the country of origin, the sending nation, and the global community* — is call to action to address the broader context of global migration and labor mobility.

In conclusion we offer a broad call to action to all stakeholders, government, civil society, private sector as well as ordinary people both migrants and natives to recognize the reality of the 21st century interconnected and globalized world. The world has been becoming a single place due to such increasing and diversifying migration, although such one place is not reflected in current classifications of the world's nations and the perpetuation of political divisions between people. It should be fully aware that the freedom of movement of people remains significantly more tightly restricted than the freedom of movement of capital, and this imbalance continues to contribute to significant gains, especially for private sector industries, but also for governments and individuals who benefit from the generated profits. It is unlikely that the current system of sovereign nation states will be replaced by some form of world government but a renewed commitment to migrants' rights as human rights is needed. At the policy level, international organizations have not been able to restrain superpower and member states' interests impede international efforts to enforce unified standards. At the practice level, protecting migrant workers' and their families' rights should be restructured by improving coordination and efficient service provision within an effective system of cross-national governance. Thus, the progress needed should be augmented by a renewed commitment to strengthening international collaboration, promoting migrants' rights and wellbeing and renewing a commitment to end inequality.

The reality of multicultural and diverse societies is evident globally, including in such traditionally homogenous cultures as Korea and Japan, suggesting the inevitable need to address issues of social conflict and division which are prevalent in nations where generations of diverse migration have occurred (Kim, 2015; Watson, 2010). The value of equality is perhaps the most pertinent to both international immigrants and internal migrant workers; notions of social economic rights and social justice would inform a range of policy themes and practices designed to promote social inclusion and enhance wellbeing. Despite the difficulties of transcending differences, non-government and informal social fabrics would help shape a human community for migrants and their families without subjecting to some remote and powerful global political authorities. A common commitment to diversity, equality and human rights ideals, as recommended by all authors in this collection, has helped to achieve a lot, and represents the possibility of much more progress towards greater equality to come.

References

Castles, S. (2013). *The age of migration : International population movements in the modern world.* New York : Palgrave Macmillan.

Constable, N. (2014). Born out of place : Migrant mothers and the politics of international labor. Oakland: University of California Press.

De Haas, H. (2010). Migration and development: A theoretical perspective 1. *International Migration Review,* 44(1), 227-264.

Gould, E. D. and Klor, E. F. (2015). The long-run effect of 9/11: Terrorism, backlash, and the assimilation of Muslim immigrants in the West. *The Economic Journal.* First online July 16, 2015.

Hickey, M., Narendra, P. and Rainwater, K. (2013). A Review of Internal and Regional Migration Policy in Southeast Asia. Migrating Out of Poverty Working Paper, NO. 8. Retrieved from http://www.solutionexchange-un-gen-gym.net/wp-content/uploads/2015/11/Review-of-internal-and-regional-migration-policy-in-SEA.pdf.

Huang, S. and Yeoh, B. S. A.(2007). Emotional labour and transnational domestic work: The moving geographies of 'maid abuse' in Singapore. *Mobilities,* 2(2), 195-217.

Kim, N. H. J. (2015). The retreat of multiculturalism? Explaining the South Korean exception. *American Behavioral Scientist,* 59(6), 727-746.

Kontos. M. and Bonifacio, G.T. (2015). *Migrant domestic workers and family life: International perspectives.* Basingstoke: Palgrave Macmillan.

Pekkanen, R. J., Smith, S.R. and Tsujinaka, Y. (2014). *Nonprofits and advocacy engaging community and government in an era of retrenchment.* Baltimore: Johns Hopkins University Press.

Stern, R.E. and O'Brien, K. J. (2012). Politics at the boundary: Mixed signals and the Chinese state. *Modern China,* 38(2), 175-198.

Smith, S. R. and Lipsky, M.(1993). *Nonprofits for hire: The welfare state in the age of contracting. Cambridge*, MA: Harvard University Press.

Spires, A. J., Tao, L. and Chan, K. M. (2014). Societal support for China's grass-roots NGOs: Evdience from Yunnan, Guangdong and Beijing. *The China Journal,* 71(1), 65-90.

Spires, A. J. (2011). Contingent symbiosis and civil society in an authoritarian state: Understanding the survival of China's grassroots NGOs. *American Journal of Sociology,* 117(1), 1-45.

Vallejos Evangeline Banao v. Commissioner of Registration and Another, HCAL 124/2010 (Hong Kong Court of Final Appeal, 2013).

Watson, I. (2010). Multiculturalism in South Korea: A Critical Assessment. *Journal of Contemporary Asia,* 40(2), 337-346.

Xiao, M. L. and Lin, H. Z. (2015). Carrots and sticks: A case study of government-caused Danwei tradition in Chinese NGOs. *International Journal of Voluntary and Nonprofit Organizations,* first online, June 17, 2015.

INDEX

#

A

D

E

F

G

H

I

M

N

Q

R

S

T

U

X

Y

Z